STUDENT WORKBOOK Capstone Curriculum

Module 10

Theology and Ethics

God *the* Son

Jesus, the Messiah and Lord of All:

HE CAME

. . . .

Jesus, the Messiah and Lord of All:

HE LIVED

. . . .

Jesus, the Messiah and Lord of All:

HE DIED

. . . .

Jesus, the Messiah and Lord of All:

HE ROSE AND WILL RETURN

This curriculum is the result of thousands of hours of work by The Urban Ministry Institute (TUMI) and should not be reproduced without their express permission. TUMI supports all who wish to use these materials for the advance of God's Kingdom, and affordable licensing to reproduce them is available. Please confirm with your instructor that this book is properly licensed. For more information on TUMI and our licensing program, visit *www.tumi.org* and *www.tumi.org/license*.

Capstone Module 10: God the Son Student Workbook

ISBN: 978-1-62932-010-6

© 2005, 2011, 2013, 2015. The Urban Ministry Institute. All Rights Reserved.
First edition 2005, Second edition 2011, Third edition 2013, Fourth edition 2015.

Copying, redistribution and/or sale of these materials, or any unauthorized transmission, except as may be expressly permitted by the 1976 Copyright Act or in writing from the publisher is prohibited. Requests for permission should be addressed in writing to: The Urban Ministry Institute, 3701 E. 13th Street, Wichita, KS 67208.

The Urban Ministry Institute is a ministry of World Impact, Inc.

All Scripture quotations, unless otherwise noted, are from The Holy Bible, English Standard Version, copyright © 2001 by Crossway Bible, a division of Good News Publishers. Used by permission. All Rights Reserved.

Contents

Course Overview
3   About the Instructor
5   Introduction to the Module
7   Course Requirements

13   **Lesson 1**
Jesus, the Messiah and Lord of All: He Came

45   **Lesson 2**
Jesus, the Messiah and Lord of All: He Lived

83   **Lesson 3**
Jesus, the Messiah and Lord of All: He Died

123   **Lesson 4**
Jesus, the Messiah and Lord of All: He Rose and Will Return

157   Appendices

About the Instructor

Rev. Dr. Don L. Davis is the Executive Director of The Urban Ministry Institute and a Senior Vice President of World Impact. He attended Wheaton College and Wheaton Graduate School, and graduated summa cum laude in both his B.A. (1988) and M.A. (1989) degrees, in Biblical Studies and Systematic Theology, respectively. He earned his Ph.D. in Religion (Theology and Ethics) from the University of Iowa School of Religion.

As the Institute's Executive Director and World Impact's Senior Vice President, he oversees the training of urban missionaries, church planters, and city pastors, and facilitates training opportunities for urban Christian workers in evangelism, church growth, and pioneer missions. He also leads the Institute's extensive distance learning programs and facilitates leadership development efforts for organizations and denominations like Prison Fellowship, the Evangelical Free Church of America, and the Church of God in Christ.

A recipient of numerous teaching and academic awards, Dr. Davis has served as professor and faculty at a number of fine academic institutions, having lectured and taught courses in religion, theology, philosophy, and biblical studies at schools such as Wheaton College, St. Ambrose University, the Houston Graduate School of Theology, the University of Iowa School of Religion, the Robert E. Webber Institute of Worship Studies. He has authored a number of books, curricula, and study materials to equip urban leaders, including *The Capstone Curriculum*, TUMI's premiere sixteen-module distance education seminary instruction, *Sacred Roots: A Primer on Retrieving the Great Tradition*, which focuses on how urban churches can be renewed through a rediscovery of the historic orthodox faith, and *Black and Human: Rediscovering King as a Resource for Black Theology and Ethics*. Dr. Davis has participated in academic lectureships such as the Staley Lecture series, renewal conferences like the Promise Keepers rallies, and theological consortiums like the University of Virginia Lived Theology Project Series. He received the Distinguished Alumni Fellow Award from the University of Iowa College of Liberal Arts and Sciences in 2009. Dr. Davis is also a member of the Society of Biblical Literature, and the American Academy of Religion.

Introduction to the Module

Greetings, in the strong name of Jesus Christ!

The identity of the person and work of Jesus of Nazareth is arguably the most critical subject in all Christian reflection and ministry. Indeed, it is impossible to minister in the name of the Lord Jesus Christ if that ministry is based upon false and ignoble views of who he was (and is), what his life signified, and what we are to make of him today. Everything is at stake in our right conception of his life, death, resurrection, ascension, and return. This module highlights his majestic person and deeds, and mastering the biblical material on him is the task of all responsible discipleship and ministry.

In the first lesson, *Jesus, the Messiah and Lord of All: He Came*, we consider the significance of the Nicene Creed for Christological studies. We will look specifically at how the Nicene Creed helps frame our thinking as urban ministers about a study of the biblical materials on Jesus, especially in the sense of helping us view Christ's work as two movements: his humiliation (i.e., his becoming human and dying on the cross for our sakes) and his exaltation (his resurrection, ascension, and the hope of his return in power). We will also discover the biblical teaching on Jesus's nature before he came to earth, as preexistent Word or Logos. We will consider his divinity as well as two historical heresies regarding Christ's divinity, and close our discussion by commenting on the significance of Jesus' divinity for our faith and discipleship.

Next, our second lesson, *Jesus, the Messiah and Lord of All: He Lived*, explores the humanity of Christ. We will focus on his dual reasons for coming to earth: to reveal to us the Father's glory and redeem us from sin and Satan's power. We will also look at the creedal language regarding Jesus' humanity, his conception by the Holy Spirit and birth to the Virgin Mary, and investigate some of the historical errors connected with denying either Jesus' divinity or humanity. We close this lesson by considering three important aspects of Jesus' life and ministry on earth. These include his identity as the Baptized One who identifies with sinners, the Proclaimer of the Kingdom of God, reasserting God's right to rule over creation, and as the Suffering Servant of Yahweh who would give his soul as a ransom for many.

In our third lesson, *Jesus, the Messiah and Lord of All: He Died*, we will explore the theological implications of Jesus' humiliation and death, his descent in his divine person on our behalf. We will consider Jesus' humiliation in the Incarnation, his life and ministry, as well as his death. In considering his sacrifice on Calvary, we will explore some of the historical models for understanding his work on the cross. These include the perspective of his death as a ransom for us, as a propitiation (divine satisfaction) for our sins, as a substitutionary sacrifice in our place, as a victory over the devil and death itself, and as a reconciliation between God and humankind. We will also explore some of the historical alternative views of Jesus' death. These include his death as 1) a moral example, 2) a demonstration of God's love, 3) a demonstration of God's justice, 4) a victory over the forces of evil and sin, and 5) a satisfaction of God's honor.

Finally, in our fourth lesson, *Jesus, the Messiah and Lord of All: He Rose and Will Return*, we begin with a consideration of the various aspects and implications of two events which mark the exaltation of Christ. The *resurrection* serves as a vindication of Jesus' Messiahship and sonship, and his *ascension* grants to our Savior a position of dignity and authority that allows him to fill all things with his glory. We explore these in light of the biblical teaching of the Creedal language, enabling us to understand God's intent to exalt Jesus of Nazareth to supreme heir of all things as a result of his death on the cross. We will close our study by looking at the last three statements regarding Christ's person in the Nicene Creed. We will consider his coming in glory, his judgment of the nations, and discuss briefly the nature of his coming reign of the Kingdom of God.

Perhaps no study of doctrine can compare with the thrill of understanding from a biblical and creedal way the richness, wonder, and mystery of God's Son, Jesus of Nazareth. His humiliation and ascension is the heart of the Gospel, and the center of our devotion, worship, and service. May God use this study of his glorious person to enable you to better love and serve him who alone has been given the preeminence by the Father. To him be the glory!

- *Rev. Dr. Don L. Davis*

Course Requirements

Required Books and Materials

- Bible (for the purposes of this course, your Bible should be a translation [ex. NIV, NASB, RSV, KJV, NKJV, etc.], and not a paraphrase [ex. The Living Bible, The Message]).

- Each Capstone module has assigned textbooks which are read and discussed throughout the course. We encourage you to read, reflect upon, and respond to these with your professors, mentors, and fellow learners. Because of the fluid availability of the texts (e.g., books going out of print), we maintain our *official* Capstone Required Textbook list on our website. Please visit *www.tumi.org/books* to obtain the current listing of this module's texts.

- Paper and pen for taking notes and completing in-class assignments.

Suggested Readings

- Kelly, J. N. D. *Early Christian Doctrines*. 5th ed. San Francisco: HarperCollins, 1978.

- ------. *Early Christian Creeds*. 3rd ed. London: Longman, 1972.

- Kereszty, Roch and A. J. Stephen Maddux. *Jesus Christ: Fundamentals of Christology*. Staten Island, NY: Alba House, 2002.

- Witherington, Ben. *The Jesus Quest: The Third Search for the Jew of Nazareth*. 2nd ed. Downers Grove: InterVarsity, 1997.

- Wright, N. T. *Who Was Jesus?* Grand Rapids: Eerdmans, 1992.

- Yoder, John Howard. *Preface to Theology; Christology and Theological Method*. Grand Rapids: Brazos Press, 2002.

Course Requirements

Summary of Grade Categories and Weights

Attendance & Class Participation	30%	90 pts
Quizzes	10%	30 pts
Memory Verses	15%	45 pts
Exegetical Project	15%	45 pts
Ministry Project	10%	30 pts
Readings and Homework Assignments	10%	30 pts
Final Exam	10%	30 pts
Total:	100%	300 pts

Grade Requirements

Attendance at each class session is a course requirement. Absences will affect your grade. If an absence cannot be avoided, please let the Mentor know in advance. If you miss a class it is your responsibility to find out the assignments you missed, and to talk with the Mentor about turning in late work. Much of the learning associated with this course takes place through discussion. Therefore, your active involvement will be sought and expected in every class session.

Attendance and Class Participation

Every class will begin with a short quiz over the basic ideas from the last lesson. The best way to prepare for the quiz is to review the Student Workbook material and class notes taken during the last lesson.

Quizzes

The memorized Word is a central priority for your life and ministry as a believer and leader in the Church of Jesus Christ. There are relatively few verses, but they are significant in their content. Each class session you will be expected to recite (orally or in writing) the assigned verses to your Mentor.

Memory Verses

The Scriptures are God's potent instrument to equip the man or woman of God for every work of ministry he calls them to (2 Tim. 3.16-17). In order to complete the requirements for this course you must select a passage and do an inductive Bible study (i.e., an exegetical study) upon it. The study will have to be five pages in length (double-spaced, typed or neatly hand written) and deal with one of the aspects of the person and work of Jesus of Nazareth highlighted in this course. Our desire and hope is that you will be deeply convinced of Scripture's ability to change and practically affect your life, and the lives of those to whom you minister. As you go

Exegetical Project

through the course, be open to finding an extended passage (roughly 4-9 verses) on a subject you would like to study more intensely. The details of the project are covered on pages 10-11, and will be discussed in the introductory session of this course.

Ministry Project

Our expectation is that all students will apply their learning practically in their lives and in their ministry responsibilities. The student will be responsible for developing a ministry project that combines principles learned with practical ministry. The details of this project are covered on page 12, and will be discussed in the introductory session of the course.

Class and Homework Assignments

Classwork and homework of various types may be given during class by your Mentor or be written in your Student Workbook. If you have any question about what is required by these or when they are due, please ask your Mentor.

Readings

It is important that the student read the assigned readings from the text and from the Scriptures in order to be prepared for class discussion. Please turn in the "Reading Completion Sheet" from your Student Workbook on a weekly basis. There will be an option to receive extra credit for extended readings.

Take-Home Final Exam

At the end of the course, your Mentor will give you a final exam (closed book) to be completed at home. You will be asked a question that helps you reflect on what you have learned in the course and how it affects the way you think about or practice ministry. Your Mentor will give you due dates and other information when the Final Exam is handed out.

Grading

The following grades will be given in this class at the end of the session, and placed on each student's record:

A - Superior work	D - Passing work
B - Excellent work	F - Unsatisfactory work
C - Satisfactory work	I - Incomplete

Letter grades with appropriate pluses and minuses will be given for each final grade, and grade points for your grade will be factored into your overall grade point average. Unexcused late work or failure to turn in assignments will affect your grade, so please plan ahead, and communicate conflicts with your instructor.

Exegetical Project

As a part of your participation in the Capstone *God the Son* module of study, you will be required to do an exegesis (inductive study) on one of the following Scripture passages:

- ☐ John 1.14-18
- ☐ Titus 2.11-14
- ☐ Hebrews 1.5-14
- ☐ Hebrews 2.14-17
- ☐ Colossians 1.13-20
- ☐ 1 Timothy 3.16
- ☐ Philippians 2.5-11

Purpose

The purpose of this exegetical project is to give you an opportunity to do a detailed study of a major passage that speaks to the nature of the person and work of Jesus Christ, the Son of God. Christian leadership essentially is anchored on the truth regarding the person of Jesus. It is neither possible nor credible to become an effective urban minister while retaining false, low, and ignoble views about Jesus. In one sense, error in this doctrine is detrimental not only in the area of faith, but also crippling in the area of discipleship, service, and ministry. In Colossians, Paul asserts that it is Jesus Christ who is the heart of all ministry; "Him we proclaim, warning everyone and teaching everyone with all wisdom, that we may present everyone mature in Christ" (Col. 1.28). Christian ministry rises and falls with a biblical, life-honoring response of the Scriptures regarding the divinity and humanity of Jesus, God's Son.

Therefore, this project will allow you to use one of the above texts as a base to explore your understanding of its relevance to the person of Christ. As you study one of the above texts (or a text which you and your Mentor agree upon which may not be on the list), our hope is that your analysis of the text will make more clear to you the glorious nature of the person for whom we have sacrificed our entire lives to serve and embody. Truly, to be a Christian leader is to become like Christ himself (1 Cor. 11.1; Phil. 2.5; Rom. 8.29). Our desire is that the Holy Spirit will give you insight into the person of Christ in order that you may love him more in spirit and truth, obey him heartily in your own personal walk of discipleship, and serve him gladly as a servant leader in the role God has given you in your church and ministry.

This is a Bible study project, and, in order to do *exegesis*, you must be committed to understand the meaning of the passage in its own setting. Once you know what it meant, you can then draw out principles that apply to all of us, and then relate those principles to life. A simple three step process can guide you in your personal study of the Bible passage:

Outline and Composition

1. What was *God saying to the people in the text's original situation*?
2. What principle(s) does *the text teach that is true for all people everywhere*, including today?
3. What is *the Holy Spirit asking me to do with this principle here, today*, in my life and ministry?

Once you have answered these questions in your personal study, you are then ready to write out your insights for your *paper assignment*.

Here is a *sample outline* for your paper:

1. List out what you believe is *the main theme or idea* of the text you selected.
2. *Summarize the meaning* of the passage (you may do this in two or three paragraphs, or, if you prefer, by writing a short verse-by-verse commentary on the passage).
3. *Outline one to three key principles or insights* this text provides on the person and work of Jesus Christ.
4. Tell how one, some, or all of the principles may relate to *one or more* of the following:
   a. Your personal spirituality and walk with Christ
   b. Your life and ministry in your local church
   c. Situations or challenges in your community and general society

As an aid or guide, please feel free to read the course texts and/or commentaries, and integrate insights from them into your work. Make sure that you give credit to whom credit is due if you borrow or build upon someone else's insights. Use in-the-text references, footnotes, or endnotes. Any way you choose to cite your references will be acceptable, as long as you 1) use only one way consistently throughout your paper, and 2) indicate where you are using someone else's ideas, and are giving them credit for it. (For more information, see *Documenting Your Work: A Guide to Help You Give Credit Where Credit Is Due* in the Appendix.)

Make certain that your exegetical project, when turned in meets the following standards:

- It is legibly written or typed.
- It is a study of one of the passages above.
- It is turned in on time (not late).
- It is 5 pages in length.
- It follows the outline given above, clearly laid out for the reader to follow.
- It shows how the passage relates to life and ministry today.

Do not let these instructions intimidate you; this is a Bible study project! All you need to show in this paper is that you *studied* the passage, *summarized* its meaning, *drew out* a few key principles from it, and *related* them to your own life and ministry.

Grading

The exegetical project is worth 45 points, and represents 15% of your overall grade, so make certain that you make your project an excellent and informative study of the Word.

Ministry Project

Purpose

The Word of God is living and active, and penetrates to the very heart of our lives and innermost thoughts (Heb. 4.12). James the Apostle emphasizes the need to be doers of the Word of God, not hearers only, deceiving ourselves. We are exhorted to apply the Word, to obey it. Neglecting this discipline, he suggests, is analogous to a person viewing our natural face in a mirror and then forgetting who we are, and are meant to be. In every case, the doer of the Word of God will be blessed in what he or she does (James 1.22-25).

Our sincere desire is that you will apply your learning practically, correlating your learning with real experiences and needs in your personal life, and in your ministry in and through your church. Therefore, a key part of completing this module will be for you to design a ministry project to help you share some of the insights you have learned from this course with others.

Planning and Summary

There are many ways that you can fulfill this requirement of your study. You may choose to conduct a brief study of your insights with an individual, or a Sunday School class, youth or adult group or Bible study, or even at some ministry opportunity. What you must do is discuss some of the insights you have learned from class with your audience. (Of course, you may choose to share insights from your Exegetical Project in this module with them.)

Feel free to be flexible in your project. Make it creative and open-ended. At the beginning of the course, you should decide on a context in which you will share your insights, and share that with your instructor. Plan ahead and avoid the last minute rush in selecting and carrying out your project.

After you have carried out your plan, write and turn in to your Mentor a one-page summary or evaluation of your time of sharing. A sample outline of your Ministry Project summary is as follows:

1. Your name
2. The place where you shared, and the audience with whom you shared
3. A brief summary of how your time went, how you felt, and how they responded
4. What you learned from the time

Grading

The Ministry Project is worth 30 points and represents 10% of your overall grade, so make certain to share your insights with confidence and make your summary clear.

Jesus, the Messiah and Lord of All
He Came

Lesson Objectives

Welcome in the strong name of Jesus Christ! After your reading, study, discussion, and application of the materials in this lesson, you will be able to:

- Articulate the significance of the Nicene Creed for Christological studies.

- Define carefully the topic of Christology and speak of its general importance in our training as leaders in the Church.

- Show precisely how the Nicene Creed helps frame our thinking about a study of the biblical materials on Jesus, especially in the sense of helping us view Christ's work as two movements, his humiliation (i.e., his becoming human and dying on the cross for our sakes) and his exaltation (his resurrection, ascension, and the hope of his return in power).

- Outline the ways in which a study of Christology can be of very special help today for those like us who work in urban communities, seeing how a new understanding of Christ can enable us to better communicate God's love to humankind, and his glorious kingdom promise.

- Detail precisely the key elements of the nature of Jesus before he came to earth, as preexistent Word or *Logos*, using the Nicene Creed as a key to understanding Jesus' deity.

- Lay out the three different ways in which Jesus' preexistence is seen in the Scriptures, first as God the Son, a divine person equal with God, as the Expected One in OT Messianic prophecy, and then as the Incarnate, the Word of God made flesh, God in human form.

- Provide details and refute two of the central historical heresies regarding Christ's divinity, and comment on the significance of Jesus' divinity for our faith and discipleship.

Devotion

My Lord and My God

John 20.19-29 - On the evening of that day, the first day of the week, the doors being locked where the disciples were for fear of the Jews, Jesus came and stood among them and said to them, "Peace be with you." [20] When he had said this, he showed them his hands and his side. Then the disciples were glad when they saw the Lord. [21] Jesus said to them again, "Peace be with you. As the Father has sent me, even so I am sending you." [22] And when he had said this, he breathed on them and said to them, "Receive the Holy Spirit. [23] If you forgive the sins of anyone, they are forgiven; if you withhold forgiveness from anyone, it is withheld." [24] Now Thomas, one of the Twelve, called the Twin, was not with them when Jesus came. [25] So the other disciples told him, "We have seen the Lord." But he said to them, "Unless I see in his hands the mark of the nails, and place my finger into the mark of the nails, and place my hand into his side, I will never believe." [26] Eight days later, his disciples were inside again, and Thomas was with them. Although the doors were locked, Jesus came and stood among them and said, "Peace be with you." [27] Then he said to Thomas, "Put your finger here, and see my hands; and put out your hand, and place it in my side. Do not disbelieve, but believe." [28] Thomas answered him, "My Lord and my God!" [29] Jesus said to him, "Have you believed because you have seen me? Blessed are those who have not seen and yet have believed."

Before we as leaders and workers for Christ serve our Lord by serving others, we are first and foremost people of worship. Loving the Lord our God is the first and greatest commandment (cf. Matt. 22.30 ff.), and those who truly love the Lord unconditionally will make an impact on their family and friends, co-workers and associates, neighbors, and even their enemies. What is the key to this kind of impact?

Thomas the Twin, one of Jesus' disciples, reveals in this episode the power of a true vision of Jesus Christ in making an impact. Filled with doubt and skepticism because of his absence at the appearance of Christ after his resurrection, Thomas firmly states that he will not believe without solid empirical, firsthand evidence of the Lord's resurrection. Slow to embrace the testimony of his fellow disciples, he laid out a clear criterion of evidence that would compel his faith. "Unless I see in his hands the mark of the nails, and place my finger into the mark of the nails, and place my hand into his side, I will never believe." A high standard, indeed, for the young headstrong disciple!

Jesus does appear again in the presence of the disciples, this time with Thomas being present. Jesus clearly meets the standard set out by Thomas: "Put your finger here, and see my hands; and put out your hand, and place it in my side. Do not *disbelieve*, but *believe*." Thomas' answer reveals how his doubt about the reality of Jesus' resurrection melted away in a single moment of recognition, love, and passion. His answer, in my mind, shouts out the purpose and intention of all true study of Christ from a theological perspective: "My Lord and my God!" What began in Thomas as a kind of stubborn intellectual quest for physical evidence of Jesus' resurrection was transformed into the white-hot passion of a disciple whose exclamation shows the real meaning of Christological investigation. "My Lord and my God!" This will be the true, honest, and spontaneous confession of every person who seriously looks at the truth regarding Jesus of Nazareth and, from the inner soul, comes to see him as he really is. Only the Spirit of God can enable any man or woman or child to *really* see the Lord Jesus; but, if he does and they yield their hearts to that revelation, they will join Thomas' affirmation in a personal confession that will lead to similar works, sacrifices, and courage as they recognize that this humble yet exalted Savior is in fact *their Lord* and *their God*.

May God so illumine our hearts and minds through the Scriptures to see Jesus of Nazareth as he really is so we can exclaim with Thomas with similar joyful and reverent voice to the object of our worship and the Leader of our ministries: "My Lord and my God!"

Nicene Creed and Prayer

After reciting and/or singing the Nicene Creed (located in the Appendix), pray the following prayer:

> *God of grace, your eternal Word took flesh among us when Mary placed her life at the service of your will. Prepare our hearts for his coming again; keep us steadfast in hope and faithful in service, that we may receive the coming of his kingdom, for the sake of Jesus Christ the ruler of all, who lives and reigns with you and the Holy Spirit, one God, now and forever. Amen.*
>
> ~ Presbyterian Church (U.S.A.) and Cumberland Presbyterian Church. The Theology and Worship Ministry Unit. **Book of Common Worship**. Louisville, KY: Westminster/John Knox Press, 1993. p. 177.

Quiz

No quiz this lesson

Scripture Memorization Review

No Scripture memorization this lesson

Assignments Due

No assignments due this lesson

You Need to Be More Balanced

In reaction to a more Christ-centered approach to Christian worship and ministry, some have suggested a "more balanced approach." Such a view suggests that although a solid study of Jesus of Nazareth is critical for Christian discipleship, it is not helpful to overemphasize this (or any other doctrine) to the exclusion of others. The notion of *Christomonism* is the idea that one might so emphasize the person of Jesus that you blow your study out of proportion, that you actually lose sight of other, equally important subjects of Scripture, and even become involved in both error and misinterpretation of Scripture and the tradition. The study of Jesus must be kept in its proper balanced place in the overall set of Christian doctrine. What would you say is *the proper position* of the study and knowledge of Christ in a "balanced" approach to the understanding of Christian doctrine?

"That's Mean-Spirited Fundamentalism!"

In a lecture at a major university, a rabbi in conversation about Christian-Jewish dialogue, gave his comment on the claim that Jesus of Nazareth is the *only way* to relationship with God. After detailing Christianity's deep dependence upon Judaism's history, faith, and Scripture, the rabbi eloquently and passionately accused those of the evangelical Christian community of being close-minded, elitist, and even some of being hate mongers. "How is it possible that they would suggest that they are the *only true religion* in a world that has been tortured and torn because of religious bigotry and violence. This kind of claim to exclusive rights to God creates division and conflict between people of God. How dare they say that Jesus of Nazareth is the *only way* to God! That is nothing but mean-spirited fundamentalism!" What do you make of the current "scandal of particularity" in the academic study of religion, that is, the "scandal" of the Christian confession that faith in the person of Jesus *is the only way to God*?

It's Time to Move On

Many in our Christian churches believe today that the era of Christian doctrine is done. By this they don't mean that the study of Christian doctrine is altogether unimportant nor that informed Christians are not to be desired. Rather, they insist that the world is tired of hearing about ancient controversies about what they perceive to be unimportant conflicts over doctrinal minutiae. Instead of focusing on dry and boring discussions about theological conflicts in the past, we need to be relevant and on point regarding the key issues of our place and time. Their argument is simple and hard hitting. Since, most people don't really care about ancient battles that obscure people of long ago had over Christ's nature and being, we probably shouldn't spend much time in our pulpits and presentations on it. We need to be on point, contemporary, and relevant. Others, taking an opposite position, believe that the study of Christian doctrine undergirds all our worship, fellowship, and ministry. Without the truth regarding who Christ really was, is, and will be, we cannot properly evangelize nor serve a world without God. In your opinion, whose argument makes most sense?

CONTENT

Jesus, the Messiah and Lord of All: He Came

Segment 1: Prolegomena for the Study of Christ

Rev. Dr. Don L. Davis

Summary of Segment 1

The Nicene Creed provides a clear and concise summary for our understanding of the person and work of Jesus Christ. The doctrine of Christ, or "Christology," involves a detailed investigation of the biblical materials on Jesus, especially in the sense of helping us view Christ's work as two movements, his humiliation (i.e., his becoming human and dying on the cross for our sakes) and his exaltation (his resurrection, ascension, and the hope of his return in power).

Jesus Christ is the foundation of the Christian faith (1 Cor. 3.11). Christianity rests upon the uniqueness, indeed the deity, of Jesus of Nazareth. Accept this basic doctrine of Scripture and the entire Christian scheme of incarnation, miracles, atonement, and resurrection makes supremely good sense. Abandon this central fact and the faith collapses into confusion. Christians may differ on the mode of baptism, on the role of women in the church, or on the fine points of prophecy. But true Christians, whatever their denomination, agree that everything turns on the deity of Christ.

~ Bruce Demarest, **Jesus Christ: The God-Man**.
Eugene, OR: Wipf and Stock Publishers, 1978. p. 28.

Our objective for this segment, *Prolegomena for the Study of Christ*, is to enable you to see that:

- The Nicene Creed has great significance for us as we investigate what the Scriptures teach regarding Christ, formally called "Christology."

- The doctrine of Christology has great importance in our training as leaders in the Church, especially in the way it serves to ground our entire understanding of the Christian story and faith.

- The Nicene Creed frames our thinking about the person and work of Jesus, especially in its shaping of our view of Christ's work as *two interrelated movements*: his *humiliation* (i.e., his becoming human and dying on the cross for our sakes) and his *exaltation* (his resurrection, ascension, and the hope of his return in power).

- A fresh new study of Christology can empower urban Christian workers and ministers to better communicate God's love to humankind, and give a more compelling witness to his glorious kingdom promise.

I. Significance of the Nicene Creed for Christological Study

Video Segment 1 Outline

A. Definition of Christology

1. *Christos* = Messiah, Christ, anointed One; *logos* = study of, knowledge of

2. The person of Christ is central to the Christian faith in a manner unique from that of other religions.

   The close kinship of Christ with Christianity is one of the distinctive features of the Christian religion. If you take away the name of Buddha from Buddhism and remove the personal revealer entirely from his system; if you take away the personality of Muhammad from Islam, or the personality of Zoraster from the religion of the Parsees, the entire doctrine of these religions would still be left intact. Their practical value, such as it is, would not be imperiled or lessened. But take away from Christianity the name and person of Jesus Christ and what have you left? Nothing! The whole substance and strength of the Christian faith centers in Jesus Christ. Without him there is absolutely nothing.

~ Sinclair Patterson in William Evans. **The Doctrines of the Bible**. Chicago: Moody Press, 1974. p. 53.

3. The study of the person and work of Christ are central to every dimension of Christian faith and practice.

   a. Eternal life is knowing the Father and Jesus Christ, John 17.3.

   b. The understanding of God and his plan for redemption is exclusively centered in the person of Jesus Christ, 1 John 5.20.

His true significance can be understood only when his relationship to the people in whose midst he was born is understood. In the events that are set in motion in his earthly career, God's purpose and covenant with Israel is fulfilled. He is the One who comes to do what neither the people of the OT nor their anointed representatives, the prophets, priests, and kings, could do. But they had been promised that One who would rise up in their own midst would yet make good what all of them had utterly failed to make good. In this sense Jesus of Nazareth is the One anointed with the Spirit and power (Acts 10.38) to be the true Messiah or Christ (John 1.41; Rom. 9.5) of his people. He is the true prophet (Mark 9.7; Luke 13.33; John 1.21; 6.14), priest (John 17; Hebrews), and king (Matt. 2.2; 21.5; 27.11), as, e.g., his baptism (Matt. 3.13ff.) and his use of Isaiah 61 (Luke 4.16-22) indicate. In receiving this anointing and fulfilling this messianic purpose, he receives from his contemporaries the titles Christ (Mark 8.29) and Son of David (Matt. 9.27; 12.23; 15.22; cf. Luke 1.32; Rom. 1.3; Rev. 5.5).

~ R. S. Wallace. "Christology." **Elwell's Theological Dictionary**. Electronic ed. **Bible Library**. Ellis Enterprises, 1998-2001.

4. "*The scandal of particularity*:" the phrase given for Christianity's belief that knowledge of God and salvation from sin is found only in the person of Jesus of Nazareth, the Messiah of the Hebrews.

   a. John 4.22

   b. Rom. 9.4-5

   c. Gen. 49.10

   d. Isa. 2.3

5. What you think of Jesus Christ will determine your eternal fate and destiny, John 8.21-24.

B. Importance of the Creed for Christology

   1. The Creed provides us with an *accurate representation of the Apostolic Tradition*: "Apostolicity."

   2. The Creed provides us with a *concise summary of the Bible's teaching*.

   3. The Creed provides us with *a credible standard for evangelical credential of its leaders*.

God himself was manifested in human form for the renewal of eternal life.
~ Ignatius, (c. 105, E) 1.58. David W. Bercot, ed. *A Dictionary of Early Christian Beliefs*. Peabody: Hendrickson Publishers, 1998. p. 93.

II. The Two Movements of Christ's Revelation: the Humiliation and Exaltation of God the Son (Phil. 2.5-11 as Model for Christology)

> The Christians trace the beginning of their religion to Jesus the Messiah. He is called the Son of the Most High God. It is said that God came down from heaven. He assumed flesh and clothed Himself with it from a Hebrew virgin. And the Son lived in a daughter of man.
> ~ Aristides. (c. 125, E) 9. 265. Ibid. pp. 93-94.

A. First movement: the humiliation of Christ (*his descent to earth and death*), Phil. 2.6-8

1. The eternal God of heaven in the person of God the Son humbled (emptied) himself of his divine characteristics to come to earth.

2. He did not count his equality with God something to hold onto.

3. He made himself nothing, taking on the form of a servant in the *likeness of men*.

4. Then, *as one in human form*, he humbled himself becoming obedient to the point of death, even on the Roman stake of misery and torture.

> O the great God! O the perfect child! The Son in the Father and the Father in the Son. . . . . God the Word, who became man for our sakes.
> ~ Clement of Alexandria (c. 195, E) 2.215. Ibid. p. 95.

B. Second movement: the exaltation of Christ (*his ascent to heaven and lordship*), Phil. 2.9-11

1. The humbled and crucified Son of God has been raised from the dead and exalted by the Father to the position of eternal glory, honor, and authority to reign as Lord over all creation.

2. *God has highly exalted him*, bestowing on him the highest name in the universe.

3. At Jesus' name every knee will bow in submission and allegiance.

4. Every tongue shall willingly or unwillingly confess that Jesus is Lord.

5. The exaltation (the bowing, confessing, and acknowledging of all creation to Jesus' lordship) will bring glory and honor to God the Father who exalted the Son for his sacrifice and obedience.

III. Making the Case for a Study of Christ in Urban Ministry and Mission

A. The onslaught of religious falsehood and error: *the need exists for those who can identify the religious lies of the enemy today and refute them with the clear message of salvation by faith in Jesus Christ.*

1. 1 Tim. 4.1-3

2. A study of Christ can arm us against the surge of demonic deception in our time, John 8.31-32.

B. The confusion of spiritual darkness: *the need exists for those who can demonstrate how Jesus of Nazareth has reasserted God's authority and right to rule in the world, and how he can bring deliverance and victory to all who believe in him.*

1. 2 Tim. 4.1-5

2. A study of Christ can overthrow the strongholds of the enemy and bring every thought captive to the obedience of Christ, 2 Cor. 10.3-5.

Christ's name is extending everywhere, believed everywhere, worshiped by all the above-enumerated nations, reigning everywhere.
~ Tertullian (c. 197, W) 3.158. Ibid. p. 93.

C. The need for equipped urban shepherds: *the need exists for a new generation of urban pastors who can represent the interests of Christ with conviction and power.*

1. Jer. 23.1-2, 4

2. A study of Christ can equip urban pastors to ground urban disciples in the truth of God and his kingdom promise, Col. 2.6-10.

D. The advance of the Gospel in the city: *the need exists for those who can teach and proclaim Christ with power and clarity in unreached urban neighborhoods.*

1. Acts 1.8

2. A study of Christ can ignite a new movement of evangelism, discipleship, and church planting in communities where Christ is not yet known!

    a. John 8.28

    b. 1 Pet. 3.18

    c. John 12.32

Conclusion

» Christology is the study of the doctrine of Jesus Christ, his person and work.

» The Nicene Creed frames our understanding of the Bible's teaching about Jesus, his descent from his position of glory to earth in the Incarnation (his *humiliation*), and his ascent after his death and resurrection to the exalted position of Lord and Ruler of all (his *exaltation*).

» Jesus is the Word of God made flesh, the Messiah who was prophesied in the OT and revealed in his Incarnation as the Word made flesh.

Segue 1

Student Questions and Response

Please take as much time as you have available to answer these and other questions that the video brought out. The study of the doctrine of Christ is integral to every phase of our lives and ministries as disciples of Christ. The more clearly and biblically we comprehend his person and work, the better we can properly worship and serve in his name. The questions below are designed to help you summarize the key facts covered in our first segment. Be precise in your answers, and support your ideas and responses with Scripture.

1. What is the meaning of "*Christos*" and "Christology?" Why is the study of Christology so significant to every dimension of Christian faith and practice?

2. What is the "scandal of particularity." How ought we as believers in Christ understand Jesus' exclusive claim to be Lord and Savior of the world?

3. Is it possible that God has communicated himself also through other religions and saviors as well as through the person and work of Jesus? In what sense can we say that Jesus of Nazareth is the final and only way to a relationship with God? What does this mean for sharing the Gospel in a multi-cultural and diverse society such as ours?

4. What place does the Nicene Creed play in helping us understand the nature of Christ's person and work? How does the Creed help us understand the biblical materials, i.e., those claims of the Bible upon which the Creed is based?

5. Why is it important to allow Scripture to be the most authoritative source for all knowledge about Jesus Christ? What ought we to do if we encounter

differences between what Scripture teaches about the Lord Jesus and other sources claiming to be authoritative about Jesus?

6. Explain the two movements of Christ's work embodied in the concept of "humiliation" and "exaltation." Be specific and use Scripture.

7. Give several reasons why the study of Christ's person and work are especially important for urban ministers and churches.

Jesus, the Messiah and Lord of All: He Came

Segment 2: Christ as the Preexistent Logos

Rev. Dr. Don L. Davis

Summary of Segment 2

Jesus of Nazareth is the Son of God, and before he came to earth for the purposes of revealing God's glory and redeeming creation he existed as the preexistent Word or *Logos*. His preexistence is explicitly taught in the Scriptures, including his position as God the Son, a divine person equal with God, as the Expected One in OT Messianic prophecy, and then as the Incarnate, Word of God made flesh, God in human form.

Our objective for this segment, *Christ as the Preexistent Logos*, is to enable you to see that:

- The Holy Scriptures teach explicitly that Jesus of Nazareth, before he came to earth, existed as a member of the Godhead, the preexistent Word or *Logos*. This biblical teaching is heartily affirmed in the Nicene Creed, a central, early ecumenical (universal) creed that confesses the preexistence and deity of Jesus Christ.

- Jesus' preexistence and personhood is laid out in three interrelated and important ways in Scripture, first as God the Son, a divine person equal with God, as the Expected One in OT Messianic prophecy, as well as the Incarnate, Word of God made flesh, God in human form.

- When either Jesus' divine or human natures are denied or falsely understood, the resulting teaching is heresy. Two of the central historical heresies regarding Christ's divinity are Ebionism and Arianism, both of which distort the biblical teaching of Jesus as God's Son.

- Understanding, affirming, and celebrating the divinity of Jesus is central to our ongoing worship and discipleship. Confessing the truth of Jesus as God's Son continues to be significant for every aspect of our faith and witness to the world.

I. The Preexistent Word (*Logos*) in the Nicene Creed and Scripture

Video Segment 2 Outline

A. Importance of the Creed for Christology

Prior to Jesus' ministry, we can speak only of a diverse Jewish hope of a new age often involving one or more intermediary or redeemer figures—messiah, prophet, exalted hero, archangel, even God himself. A century later all these categories and more were either superseded or focused in one man, Jesus Christ. Ignatius spoke of Jesus in straightforward terms as "our God, Jesus (the) Christ" (Eph. 18.2[1]; Rom. 3.3[2]), and showed how Christology was well on the way toward the classical creedal statements of the ecumenical councils. "There is one physician, who is both flesh and spirit, born and yet not born, who is God in man, true life in death, both of Mary and of God, first passible and then impassible, Jesus Christ our Lord" (Eph. 7.2[1]). In the course of that hundred years, the claims of Christianity appeared and began to take definitive shape.

~ James G. G. Dunn. "Christology." **The Anchor Bible Dictionary**. D. N. Freedman, ed. (Electronic ed.). Doubleday: New York, 1996.

[1] Ignatius' letter to the Ephesians.

[2] Ignatius' letter to the Romans.

B. Creedal language on Jesus' preexistence

1. "We believe in One Lord Jesus Christ": *The Creed confesses unqualified allegiance in Jesus of Nazareth as Lord and Messiah.*

    a. Jesus is the anchor of our faith, Heb. 12.1-2.

b. In him alone do we have eternal life, 1 John 5.11-13.

c. No access to God is possible without a relationship with God through him, John 14.6.

2. "The Only Begotten Son of God": *The Creed confesses the unique relationship and sonship Jesus possessed with God the Father.*

   a. Jesus has a unique relationship to the Father.

      (1) Ps. 2.7

      (2) Heb. 1.5

   b. Jesus is one with the Father.

      (1) John 10.30

      (2) John 1.1

      (3) John 17.21

   c. Jesus is Messiah, Son of the Blessed.

      (1) Mark 14.61-62

      (2) Luke 22.70

3. "God from God, Light from Light, True God from True God": *The Creed confesses that Jesus of Nazareth was begotten of God in the sense that he shared the same essence and substance as the Father.*

   a. Titus 2.13

Search, then, and see if the divinity of Christ is true.
~ Tertullian (c. 197, W) 3.36. David W. Bercot, ed. *A Dictionary of Early Christian Beliefs*. Peabody, MA: Hendrickson Publishers, 1998. p. 96.

b. Rom. 9.5

c. 1 John 5.20

4. "Begotten not created": *The Creed confesses that Jesus was begotten by God but not made by him; the relationship with the Father and Son is unique.*

   a. All things were made through Christ, he himself was in the very form of God, Phil. 2.6

   b. Jesus as the begotten Son of God does not diminish his equality with God, John 5.18-19

5. "Of the same essence of the Father": *The Creed confesses that Jesus shared the same essence with the Father, that is, they shared the same nature and substance in his preexistent state.*

   a. Jesus shared in the Father's glory before his descent into the world, John 17.1-5

   b. Jesus has life in himself even as the Father has life in himself, John 5.26-27

6. "Through whom all things were made": *The Creed confesses that Jesus was the One through whom God made the heavens and the earth.*

   a. John 1.1-5

The Son is the cause of all good things, by the will of the Almighty Father.
~ Clement of Alexandria (c. 195, E) 2.524. Ibid. p. 95.

b. Col. 1.15-17

II. Christ as the Preexistent Word (*Logos*)

For Christ is King, Priest, God, Lord, Angel, and Man.
~ Justin Martyr (c. 160, E) 1.211. Ibid. p. 94.

A. The Preexistent Logos: God was manifested in the flesh.

1 Tim. 3.16 - Great indeed, we confess, is the mystery of godliness: he was manifested in the flesh, vindicated by the Spirit, seen by angels, proclaimed among the nations, believed on in the world, taken up in glory.

Isa. 7.14 - Therefore the Lord himself will give you a sign. Behold, the virgin shall conceive and bear a son, and shall call his name Immanuel.

1. He is called God.

    a. Heb. 1.8

    b. John 1.14

    c. John 1.18

    d. John 20.28

2. Divine names are ascribed to Jesus.

    a. Lord

        (1) Acts 2.20-21 and Rom. 10.13 with Joel 2.31-32

        (2) 1 Pet. 3.15 with Isa. 8.13

b. First and Last, Rev. 1.17 with Isa. 41.4; 44.6

c. Alpha and Omega, Rev. 22.13 with Rev. 1.8

d. I Am, Exod. 3.14 with John 8.58

e. His title as Son is linked to the Father.

(1) The baptismal instruction of the Great Commission, Matt. 28.19

(2) Paul's benediction to the Corinthians, 2 Cor. 13.14

3. Jesus possesses the attributes of God.

a. Preexistence, John 1.1; Phil. 2.6

b. Self-existent life, John 5.21, 26; John 1.4; Heb. 7.16

c. The fullness of the Godhead in bodily form, Col. 2.9

d. Creator of all things, John 1.3; Heb. 1.10; Col. 1.17-18

e. Upholder and sustainer of all creation, Col. 1.17; Heb. 1.3

f. Authority to forgive sins, Mark 2.5-10; Luke 7.48

g. Raising the dead back to life, John 6.39-40; 11.25

h. Judge of all men, John 5.22; 2 Tim. 4.1; Acts 17.31; Matt. 25.31-46

B. The Expected One: OT Messianic Prophecy

1. Jesus is the seed of the woman who would crush the serpent's head, Gen. 3.15.

2. Jesus is the seed of Abraham, the One through whom all the families of the earth would be blessed, Gen. 12.1-3 (see also Gen. 15.5-6; 17.4-8).

3. Jesus is the High Priest after the eternal priesthood of Melchizedek, Gen. 14.18-20 with Heb. 6.20-7.22.

4. Jesus is the Royal King in David's line appointed to reign forever as Lord, Isa. 9.6-7.

5. Jesus as Servant of Yahweh, anointed One of God, Isa. 61.1ff. with Luke 4.18-19

C. The Incarnate One: the Word Made Flesh

1. The Word became flesh and dwelt among us, John 1.14-18.

2. The One who shared in God's form (*morphe*) took on the form of a human being, Phil. 2.5-11.

3. The Son is the image of the invisible God through whom all things were made, hold together, and owe their purpose to, Col. 1.15-20.

D. Errors associated with misreading the deity of Jesus Christ

1. Ebionism: Christ is not God.

    a. A party of Jewish Christians who said Jesus was an ordinary man upon whom the power of God came at his baptism

    b. Christ came upon Jesus at the baptism, but left him later in life.

    c. Jesus was not God; an ordinary man whom God came upon at a particular time of his life

    d. *Ebionism ignores the plain teaching of the Scriptures.*

2. Arianism: Christ is not fully God.

    a. Arius was a *presbyter* (church leader) in Alexandria in the early Church who denied Jesus' divinity.

    b. His views were condemned at the Council of Nicea (the same Council that gave us the Nicene Creed).

I have shown from the Scriptures that none of the sons of Adam are, absolutely and as to everything, called God, or named Lord. But Jesus is Himself in His own right, beyond all men who ever lived, God, Lord, King Eternal, and the Incarnate Word. . . . He is the Holy Lord, the Wonderful, the Counselor, the Beautiful in appearance, and the Mighty God.
~ Irenaeus (c. 180, E/W) 1.449. Ibid. p. 95.

c. Basic view: Arians believed in the absolute transcendence of God.

   (1) Only God is eternal; all other things, (including the Word) is created.

   (2) The Word is the first and highest of God's creation, but is not God nor self-existing.

d. Jehovah's Witnesses are modern Arians.

e. *Arians mishandle the biblical testimony regarding the divinity of the Word made flesh.*

E. Modern response to argument for Christ's deity: Functional Christology

   1. Places emphasis in Christology on what Jesus *did* and not on who Jesus is and was

   2. Under-emphasizes the Bible's testimony of the *person* of Jesus as well as his *work*

III. Implications of the Deity of Jesus Christ for Our Faith and Discipleship

A. Jesus reveals to us the person of God, John 1.18; 14.9.

B. God has visited planet earth for the purpose of revelation and redemption, Phil. 2.5-11.

> *He who has the Almighty God, the Word, is in want of nothing.*
> ~ Clement of Alexandria (c. 195, E), 2.493. Ibid. p. 95.

C. Human being and Divine being have been forever united in the One Lord Jesus Christ, John 1.14.

D. Jesus deserves all praise, glory, and adoration as Lord and God, cf. John 20.28 with Phil. 2.9-11.

Conclusion

» Before our Lord Jesus came to earth, he dwelt as a member of the Godhead (Trinity) as the preexistent Word or *Logos*.

» The language of the Nicene Creed, as it explains and illumines the meaning of Scripture, helps us understand Jesus' divine nature. It agrees with the Bible's testimony concerning Jesus' co-equality with God in his attributes and titles.

» Jesus is seen as God's divine Son, the fulfillment of the OT Messianic prophecy, and as the Incarnate, Word of God made flesh, God in human form.

The following questions were designed to help you review the material in the second video segment. A proper understanding of the divinity of Jesus Christ is key to our confidence and assurance in our worship of him as our King and Savior, our confidence in him as Lord of the harvest, and our service to him as our King. Despite the common trend to ignore this central doctrine in our teaching and preaching, we must be resolute to carefully consider the meaning of this teaching for our worship and discipleship today. Concentrate on being as careful as possible as you give your answers to the following questions, and support your arguments with Scripture.

1. What is the meaning of the term *Logos* as applied to Jesus Christ? How does this teaching about Jesus as the preexistent One relate to the Creed's affirmation of the divinity of Christ?

2. Explain the nature of Jesus' relationship to God the Father as the "only begotten Son of God?" How is this concept different from Jesus as the "first created" Son of God?

Segue 2

Student Questions and Response

3. What do you understand the Nicene Creed to mean when it affirms that Jesus is "of the same essence of the Father?" How does this concept help us understand Jesus' *equality* with God in both nature and substance?

4. How does the Creed affirm the biblical teaching of Jesus' role in creation? What are the implications of this for the way in which God is *sustaining the universe today*?

5. List some of the titles and attributes that the Scriptures teach that Jesus shares with God. How does this help us understand the divinity of Christ?

6. Explain the ways in which Jesus of Nazareth fulfills the OT prophecy concerning the coming of the Messiah. Why is this important evidence to further support Jesus' preexistence as the *Logos*?

7. How does John's testimony of Jesus' Incarnation help us understand the relationship of the "*Word made flesh*?" How are we to best understand and explain the mystery of the divine coming in the form of a human being in the person of Jesus Christ?

8. List out carefully the false teachings of the two historical heresies covered in our last segment, Ebionism and Arianism. How has *Functional Christology* sought to explain the relationship of the divine and human in Jesus?

9. Give several reasons why is it so important for us to properly understand and affirm the divinity of Christ in our urban churches. Why is it important for your personal discipleship?

*The hymnic/confessional fragment preserved in Hebrews 1.1–4 describes Jesus as the "radiance of his glory" **(apaugasma tes doxes)** and the "exact representation of his very being" **(charakter tes hypostaseos**, Heb. 1.3). The juxtaposition of **doxa** with **hypostasis** in the ontological characterization of Jesus clearly articulates Jesus' status. Jesus is God's glory, God's very being. This hymn/confession formed part of the author's strategy to distinguish between Jesus and angels, as the catena of OT texts and the sustained midrash on these texts proves (see Heb. 1.5 – 2.18). The binatarian shape and content of the hymn/confession—its focus upon Jesus and God and Jesus as God—alleviates potential confusion between Jesus and powerful angelic figures. Jesus is* *ontologically superior to any and all angelic agents; Jesus is equal with God; Jesus is God. The performative force of singing this hymn (or reciting, if a confession) was to strengthen community identity. No less powerful than the Lord's Supper or baptism, the ritual of confessing "Jesus as the glory of Yahweh" created and reinforced the boundary lines between Christianity and Judaism.*

~ R. P. Martin and P. H. Davids.
Dictionary of the Later New Testament and Its Developments. (electronic ed.).
Downers Grove, IL: InterVarsity Press, 2000.

Summary of Key Concepts

This lesson focuses upon the person of Jesus, the Messiah and Lord of all, in terms of the validity and necessity of studying the person and work of Christ as Savior, and, specifically in this lesson, his preexistence as the Word of God. That Jesus, the second member of the Trinity, God the Son, came to earth for the sake of revealing God's glory and redeeming humankind is one of the most profound revelations of Scripture. The study of Christ is not merely for our intellectual curiosity or our mild religious study; it is the heart and soul of what it means to be a follower of Christ, to affirm in our lives that we cannot know God except through the mediator of his own choosing, the Lord Jesus Christ. "He Came" is the foundational affirmation of the Christian community. The same Lord who dwelt in eternal splendor and glory with the Father was revealed to us in the flesh through the Incarnation. As we meditate upon this lofty truth, we are led not only to wonder at its depth, but to worship and revere the One who with such great humility came to earth in order to redeem us from the tyranny of sin. Below are some of the central theological truths covered in this lesson.

- The Nicene Creed has great significance for us as we investigate what the Scriptures teach regarding Christ, formerly called "Christology."

- The doctrine of Christology has great importance in our training as leaders in the Church, especially in the way it serves to ground our entire understanding of the Christian story and faith.

- The Nicene Creed frames our thinking about the person and work of Jesus, especially in its shaping of our view of Christ's work as *two interrelated movements*: his *humiliation* (i.e., his becoming human and dying on the cross for our sakes) and his *exaltation* (his resurrection, ascension, and the hope of his return in power).

- A fresh new study of Christology can empower urban Christian workers and ministers to better communicate God's love to humankind, and give more compelling witness to his glorious kingdom promise.

- The Holy Scriptures teach explicitly that Jesus of Nazareth, before he came to earth, existed as a member of the Godhead, the preexistent Word or *Logos*. This biblical teaching is heartily affirmed in the Nicene Creed, a central, early ecumenical (universal) creed that confesses the preexistence and deity of Jesus Christ.

- Jesus' preexistence and personhood is laid out in three interrelated and important ways in Scripture, first as God the Son, a divine person equal with God, as the Expected One in OT Messianic prophecy, as well as the Incarnate, the Word of God made flesh, God in human form.

- When either Jesus' divine and human natures are denied or falsely understood, the resulting teaching is heresy. Two of the central historical heresies regarding Christ's divinity are Ebionism and Arianism, both of which distort the biblical teaching of Jesus as God's Son.

- Understanding, affirming, and celebrating the divinity of Jesus is central to our ongoing worship and discipleship. Confessing the truth of Jesus as God's Son continues to be significant for every aspect of our faith and witness to the world.

Student Application and Implications

Now is the time for you to discuss with your fellow students your questions about the study of Christ and the concept of the preexistent Son of God coming to earth in the Incarnation. While we cannot possibly plumb the depths of this important teaching on the divinity and preexistence of Jesus Christ, it is highly important as leaders that we seek to do so. As both worshipers of God and witness bearers of the Gospel, we must strive constantly to meditate upon and master the truths regarding Jesus as God's Son and the Messiah. No truths you will encounter as a Christian leader will strengthen, empower, and direct you more than those that relate to your Lord and Savior Jesus Christ. In light of this, it is critical for us to understand the dimensions of Christ's divinity, and apply that knowledge to our own discipleship in him. What particular questions do you have in light of the material you have just studied? Maybe some of the questions below might help you form your own, more specific and critical questions.

* As a Christian leader, why would the study of the doctrine of Christ be so important to your ongoing equipping for ministry? Explain.

* In what ways are current trends in preaching and teaching moving away from or heading toward a more doctrinally focused diet on the Word? Why is teaching the doctrine of Christ so important for our urban churches, especially?

* What difference does it make for urban ministry if we fail to emphasize or affirm the divinity of Christ? Explain your answer.

* What do we mean when we say that Jesus is "fully human, fully divine" being fully God and fully human?

* What is the relationship between a solid understanding of the divinity of Christ and our worship and praise of him as Lord? Explain.

* In light of so many current New Age religions and the onslaught of Islamic faith, how ought we to prepare our congregations and students with a biblical knowledge of Christ?

* In your opinion, do you believe that we better prepare others in the truth of the doctrine of Christ by studying the *biblical truths* concerning him, or carefully identifying and refuting the *errors and heresies* associated with his person today? Defend your answer.

* What is the best venue to train and teach others the doctrine of Christ–from the pulpit, in seminars, Sunday School, or some other venue? Who is responsible to teach the body the truths concerning the doctrine of Christ?

* What concept, if any, is still troubling for you to understand and explain in regard to the person and work of Christ in the Incarnation? What must you do in order to gain a better grasp of that area in connection to Christ?

If you had understood what has been written by the prophets, you would not have denied that He was God, Son of the Only, Unbegotten, Unutterable God.
~ Justin Martyr (c. 160, E) 1.262. David W. Bercot, ed. *A Dictionary of Early Christian Beliefs*. Peabody, MA: Hendrickson Publishers, 1998. p. 96.

He's the Angel Michael

In an exchange with some local Jehovah's Witnesses regarding the person of Christ, one of the Witness ministers explains that they do not believe that Jesus was preexistent but the first created being of God. Developing his argument further, he explains that Jesus of Nazareth was actually the angel Michael before his earthly appearance and ministry in Israel. This view that Jesus was actually the firstborn of

God's creation in the sense as *God's first created being* is an old, well-worn idea. What would you say to the Witnesses regarding their unique view of God's Son?

The Christ Came Upon Him

How would you respond if someone in arguing their view of the person of Jesus, made a distinction between Jesus and the Christ. In other words, they argue that the *Christ* spirit, the power of God's anointing, came upon the human being Jesus *at the baptism*; Jesus was simply a holy man whom God chose to place his spirit upon, and was therefore not *preexistent* with the Father before his human existence. How would you explain the relationship of the human being Jesus with the identity of the *Christ, the anointed One of God*.

Doctrine Is Key, but Not on Sunday Morning

Many congregations today are de-emphasizing the teaching and preaching of doctrine in the pulpits and classrooms of the Church. With such an emphasis on being seeker friendly, on lifestyle evangelism, on a strategic focus on being less doctrinaire in our services, many churches have opted to keep doctrine in less public forums and reserve the pulpit and public teaching for more "contemporary and comprehensible subjects." If you were the senior pastor of a growing church, what would your philosophy be regarding the role of teaching something like the doctrine of Christ in the prime-time Sunday morning hourly slot? Would you teach this material, and if so, how?

Jesus Only

In hearing of one church's mission statement of understanding themselves as a community that anchors its devotion on the person and work of Jesus Christ, a number of churches in the denomination have begun to confront it about that statement. Accusing the congregation of being a "Jesus only" focused church (called *Christomonistic*), the other pastors are suggesting that focusing too exclusively upon the person of Christ can lead to a denial of the Trinity and to the exclusion of other important theological themes. The church under investigation has countered that they, of course, are Trinitarian, and that they know that there are other themes of doctrine. However, error in regards to the person of Christ spills into every other area of confession, doctrine, and faith. In other words, if you go wrong with the doctrine of Christ, you cannot go right with anything else. Whose position appears to be most consistent with the teaching of Scripture?

The Nicene Creed provides a clear and concise summary for our understanding of the person and work of Jesus Christ. The doctrine of Christ, or "Christology" involves a detailed investigation of the biblical materials on Jesus, especially in the sense of helping us view Christ's work as two movements, his humiliation (i.e., his becoming human and dying on the cross for our sakes) and his exaltation (his resurrection, ascension, and the hope of his return in power). Jesus of Nazareth is the Son of God, and before he came to earth for the purposes of revealing God's glory and redeeming creation he existed as the preexistent Word or *Logos*. His preexistence is explicitly taught in the Scriptures, including his position as God the Son, a divine person equal with God, as the Expected One in OT Messianic prophecy, and then as the Incarnate, the Word of God made flesh, God in human form.

Restatement of the Lesson's Thesis

If you are interested in pursuing some of the ideas of *Jesus, The Messiah and Lord of All: He Came*, you might want to give these books a try:

Dodd, C. H. *The Founder of Christianity*. New York: Macmillan, 1970.

Fredriksen, Paula. *From Jesus to Christ: The Origin of the New Testament Images of Jesus*. New York: Oxford University press, 1988.

Brown, Raymond. *Jesus, God and Man: Modern Biblical Reflections*. New York, Paulist Press, 1980.

Resources and Bibliographies

Now is the time to try to nail down this high theology to a real practical ministry connection, one which you will think about and pray for throughout this next week. What in particular is the Holy Spirit suggesting to you in regards to your own devotion to Christ as the Son of God, the divine Lord, worthy of your own personal worship and obedience? How would you describe your own appreciation and comprehension of Jesus as the preexistent *Logos*? In what ways has your knowledge of the divinity of Jesus actually influenced the ministry that you are currently doing in the city? What particular situation comes to mind when you think about how the

Ministry Connections

biblical teaching about Christ's exalted preexistent status ought to impact your attitudes, perspectives, and conduct as you worship and serve the Lord Jesus in the city? In what relationship or issue can this teaching make an immediate impact on the way in which you comprehend your responsibility as a witness of Christ in your family, neighborhood, job, and ministry. Ask God the Holy Spirit to deepen your understanding of these truths as they relate to your particular ministry and relationships in your life today.

Counseling and Prayer

An important element in your understanding and application of biblical truth is the role of prayer and supplication. As you investigate these truths regarding the nature of Christ's person and work, you will need to consistently and fervently ask the Lord for wisdom to understand his truth, and for courage to obey its implications in every area of your life. Furthermore, it will be important for you also to pray that God the Holy Spirit provide you with specific opportunity to teach and relate these truths to those to whom you minister, enabling them to practically benefit from the insights that they contain. Please be encouraged to share with your mentor or instructor, as well as your fellow students specific requests related to your own personal life and ministry. Ask God to enable you and them to apply these truths concerning Christ's exalted person and status where he leads, and be ready to lift up others to the Lord with these same key requests in mind.

Scripture Memory

John 1.14-18

Reading Assignment

To prepare for class, please visit *www.tumi.org/books* to find next week's reading assignment, or ask your mentor.

Other Assignments

Your ability to benefit from the classroom sessions you have with your fellow students is directly tied to the level of disciplined, focused study you engage in between classes. Therefore, please make certain that you set aside ample time to read all the assignments, do any homework, and memorize any Scripture associated with the assignments at the end of each lesson in this module. This is especially important seeing as how *you will be quizzed on the content (the video content) of this lesson next week*.

In light of this, please make sure that you spend time covering your notes of this weeks lesson and discussion, and focus especially on the main ideas of the lesson. Read the assigned reading, and summarize each reading with no more than a paragraph or two for each. In this summary please give your best understanding of what you think was the main point in each of the readings. Do not be overly concerned about giving detail; simply write out what you consider to be the main point discussed in that section of the book. Please bring these summaries to class next week. (Please see the "Reading Completion Sheet" at the end of this lesson.)

Looking Forward to the Next Lesson

In today's lesson we saw how the Nicene Creed provides a clear and concise summary for our understanding of the person and work of Jesus Christ, defined in two movements, his humiliation (i.e., his becoming human and dying on the cross for our sakes) and his exaltation (his resurrection, ascension, and the hope of his return in power). Coming to earth to reveal God's glory and redeem creation, Jesus' preexistence is seen in his position as God the Son, a divine person equal with God, as the Expected One in OT Messianic prophecy, and then as the Incarnate, the Word of God made flesh, God in human form. In our next lesson we will explore with greater intensity the general purpose for Jesus' coming to earth: to reveal to us the Father's glory and redeem us from sin and Satan's power. With a focus on Jesus' humanity, we will discuss the unity of Jesus' divine and human nature, look at Jesus as the Baptized One who identified with the plight and peril of the sinners he came to save, the Proclaimer of the Kingdom of God, and the Suffering Servant of Yahweh.

Capstone Curriculum

Module 10: God the Son
Reading Completion Sheet

Name _____

Date _____

For each assigned reading, write a brief summary (one or two paragraphs) of the author's main point. (For additional readings, use the back of this sheet.)

Reading 1

Title and Author: _____ Pages _____

Reading 2

Title and Author: _____ Pages _____

Jesus, the Messiah and Lord of All
He Lived

Lesson Objectives

Welcome in the strong name of Jesus Christ! After your reading, study, discussion, and application of the materials in this lesson, you will be able to:

- Articulate the general purpose for Jesus' coming to earth: to reveal to us the Father's glory and redeem us from sin and Satan's power.

- Outline the creedal language regarding Jesus' humanity, his conception by the Holy Spirit and birth to the Virgin Mary.

- Summarize two of the prominent historical errors that have arisen from contesting Jesus' becoming a human being: Nestorianism—*that Christ was two distinct persons*, and Eutychianism—*that Christ has one blended nature*. The Councils of Nicea (325) and Chalcedon (381) settled these questions, affirming that Jesus was *fully God and fully human*.

- Evaluate and refute errors associated with misreading Jesus' humanity: *Docetism* which asserted that *Jesus was not human* and *Apollinarianism* which asserted that *Jesus was not fully human*.

- Restate the practical implications of the unity of Jesus' divine and human nature, and the significance of Jesus' humanity for us: Jesus, our high priest, can empathize with our needs and represent us before God. As our Second Adam, we will be conformed to his image in our future glorification with him.

- Identify and biblically defend the concept of Jesus as the Baptized One who identified with the plight and peril of the sinners he came to save, as well as the concept of Jesus as the Proclaimer of the Kingdom of God–Jesus reasserting God's right to rule over creation, showing through his person, miracles, healings, and exorcisms the signs of the Kingdom present in his own person on earth.

- To analyze and unpack the idea of Jesus as the Suffering Servant of Yahweh, sketching his Messianic mission from the public announcement of his ministry, and the way in which Jesus revealed himself as the expected Servant of Yahweh through his proclamation of good news to the poor, his demonstration of justice among God's people, and his vicarious sacrifice on behalf of God's people as a "ransom for many."

Today this Scripture Has Been Fulfilled in Your Hearing

Luke 4.14-21 - And Jesus returned in the power of the Spirit to Galilee, and a report about him went out through all the surrounding country. [15] And he taught in their synagogues, being glorified by all. [16] And he came to Nazareth, where he had been brought up. And as was his custom, he went to the synagogue on the Sabbath day, and he stood up to read. [17] And the scroll of the prophet Isaiah was given to him. He unrolled the scroll and found the place where it was written, [18] "The Spirit of the Lord is upon me, because he has anointed me to proclaim good news to the poor. He has sent me to proclaim liberty to the captives and recovering of sight to the blind, to set at liberty those who are oppressed, [19] to proclaim the year of the Lord's favor."[20] And he rolled up the scroll and gave it back to the attendant and sat down. And the eyes of all in the synagogue were fixed on him. [21] And he began to say to them, "Today this Scripture has been fulfilled in your hearing."

Will the real Jesus please stand up? Like the old game show where contestants sought to fool a celebrity panel on what they really were in real life, at the time of Jesus many were playing a guessing game on the true identity of Jesus Christ. Undoubtedly, the fervor of anticipation was at a high level during this moment in Jesus' earlier ministry. Some would come to view Jesus as an itinerant rabbi whose teaching threatened the well-being of the nation. Others would go so far to suggest that he was mentally challenged, self-deluded, even controlled by the powers of the evil one. Surely the tension of these questions had begun to simmer that early Sabbath morning in his hometown of Nazareth, as Luke tells us, "where he had been brought up." Going to the synagogue, which was his spiritual discipline, he was the reader for the service. Luke tells us that he took the scroll of Isaiah and read from the 61st chapter: "The Spirit of the Lord is upon me, because he has anointed me to proclaim good news to the poor. He has sent me to proclaim liberty to the captives and recovering of sight to the blind, to set at liberty those who are oppressed, to proclaim the year of the Lord's favor." On this reading he handed the scroll back to the attendant, and sat down.

The statement he made next was the most anticipated statement of that town, their time, and all human history. Jesus replied, "*Today*, this Scripture has been fulfilled in your hearing." By this answer, Jesus here identifies himself as the long awaited Servant of Yahweh, the Messiah king who would come to reign and rule over God's Kingdom.

Here are a sampling of a number of important texts which provide an overall context to understand Jesus' momentous announcement of himself as the Servant-King (i.e., the Messiah [anointed One] of God):

> Isa. 9.6-7 - For to us a child is born, to us a son is given; and the government shall be upon his shoulder, and his name shall be called Wonderful Counselor, Mighty God, Everlasting Father, Prince of Peace. [7] Of the increase of his government and of peace there will be no end, on the throne of David and over his kingdom, to establish it and to uphold it with justice and with righteousness from this time forth and forevermore. The zeal of the Lord of hosts will do this.

> Isa. 11.2-5 - And the Spirit of the Lord shall rest upon him, the Spirit of wisdom and understanding, the Spirit of counsel and might, the Spirit of knowledge and the fear of the Lord. [3] And his delight shall be in the fear of the Lord. He shall not judge by what his eyes see, or decide disputes by what his ears hear, [4] but with righteousness he shall judge the poor, and decide with equity for the meek of the earth; and he shall strike the earth with the rod of his mouth, and with the breath of his lips he shall kill the wicked. [5] Righteousness shall be the belt of his waist, and faithfulness the belt of his loins.

> Isa. 42.1-4 - Behold my servant, whom I uphold, my chosen, in whom my soul delights; I have put my Spirit upon him; he will bring forth justice to the nations. [2] He will not cry aloud or lift up his voice, or make it heard in the street; [3] a bruised reed he will not break, and a faintly burning wick he will not quench; he will faithfully bring forth justice. [4] He will not grow faint or be discouraged till he has established justice in the earth; and the coastlands wait for his law.

Jesus here announces in his hometown that without doubt or equivocation, he is the fulfillment of the ancient prophetic hope of the Servant King who would come and inaugurate afresh the reign of God over his people and his creation. For the rest of his ministry, he would give concrete, tangible evidence that he was the King of Israel, the Servant of Yahweh who would give his own soul as a ransom for the sins of many (Isa. 53.1ff.).

It can be said that our appropriation of the benefits and blessings of Messiah are directly connected to our understanding and convictions about him. In other words, the work of God in this era is to believe on the One whom God anointed and sent, Jesus of Nazareth (cf. John 6.35). Allegiance to him, love and worship of him, obedience and trust in him is the essence of citizenship in the Kingdom of God. Jesus is the *one true Messiah* [anointed One] of God, and without him, apart from him is no forgiveness, mercy, direction, or grace.

If you have found Jesus, you have found the One. You need look for none other. May God give us the wisdom to realize that the Scriptures of the Messiah and the Kingdom come *has been fulfilled in the person of Jesus of Nazareth.*

> Mark 1.14-15 - Now after John was arrested, Jesus came into Galilee, proclaiming the gospel of God, [15] and saying, "The time is fulfilled, and the kingdom of God is at hand; repent and believe in the gospel."

After reciting and/or singing the Nicene Creed (located in the Appendix), pray the following prayer: **Nicene Creed and Prayer**

> *Almighty God who wonderfully created us in your image and yet more wonderfully restored us through your Son, Jesus Christ: Grant us to share in his divine life as he shares our humanity; who is now alive, and reigns with you in the unity of the Holy Spirit one God, for ever and ever.*
>
> ~ The Church of the Province of South Africa.
> **Minister's Book for Use With the Holy Eucharist and Morning and Evening Prayer.**
> Braamfontein: Publishing Department of the Church of the Province of South Africa. p. 27.

Put away your notes, gather up your thoughts and reflections, and take the quiz for Lesson 1, *Jesus, the Messiah and Lord of All: He Came.*. **Quiz**

Review with a partner, write out and/or recite the text for last class session's assigned memory verses: John 1.14-18. **Scripture Memorization Review**

Turn in your summary of the reading assignment for last week, that is, your brief response and explanation of the main points that the authors were seeking to make in the assigned reading (Reading Completion Sheet). **Assignments Due**

Could Jesus Have Sinned?

In a discussion on the humanity of Jesus, it became clear in an adult Sunday School class that real confusion reigned concerning Jesus' ability or inability to commit sin as a human being. Those who said that it was possible argued that, in light of the numerous verses that suggest that Jesus was like us in every way *except without sinning*, he had to be *able to sin* (if he were *truly like us*). Others argued that, given his divine nature and holy nature, Jesus could not have sinned because he was *God in the flesh,* and since it was impossible for God to sin, *neither could Jesus* (being himself *God*). How would you have sought to settle their discussion on this critical theological question?

It Doesn't SEEM Like the Kingdom Is Present

In discussing Jesus' announcement of the Kingdom present in his person in Mark 1.14-15 and other texts, some students raised the question of whether or not this interpretation was defensible in light of the *actual problems and situations that the world was undergoing.* "If the Kingdom in some sense has already come in the person of Jesus, then why are things so bad, why are so many innocent people suffering in the world today, and why doesn't he stop all the mayhem and cruelty on earth?" If the Kingdom really was inaugurated in the announcement of Jesus at his sermon at Nazareth, then why don't we see more *signs of its presence in the midst of the earth today?* How would you answer these and similar questions about Jesus as the Inauguration and Proclaimer of the Kingdom of God in this age?

The Head and Not the Tail

Much of today's current teaching tends to practice a kind of selective hermeneutic regarding the meaning of Jesus' ministry for us as the Suffering Servant of Yahweh. With boldness and courage, many television evangelists and religious broadcasters have crafted a well-articulated scheme of "health and wealth" which tends to define Christianity as a means of receiving prosperity and blessing in light of the correct and ongoing applications of "laws" of prosperity. In many ways, the images of Jesus as Suffering Servant are replaced with ideas of "storehouses of blessing," of "confessing until the blessings come," and related phrases all focused on the individual coming into a knowledge of God's principles of blessings, and applying these laws so the attached and associated gifts of grace would manifest themselves.

This focus raises serious questions about the nature of Christ, of Christian discipleship, and the present and ongoing validity of some of the primary images and symbols of the Christian life: the cross, the altar, the blood, the Lamb. This focus on prosperity and blessing applies with great intensity certain select texts, all of which tend to emphasize the "triumphant crown wearing" side of Christian discipleship over against the "humble cross bearing" side. How would you suggest we begin to understand the differences in emphasis, and how does Jesus as our Suffering Servant help us understand what God's will might be for us in the Church today?

Jesus, the Messiah and Lord of All: He Lived

Segment 1: Christ's Human Nature

Rev. Dr. Don L. Davis

Jesus appeared on earth as a man to reveal to humankind the Father's glory and redeem us from sin and Satan's power. Jesus was fully human, conceived by the Holy Spirit and carried to birth by the Virgin Mary. Two ancient heresies contested Jesus' becoming a human being: Nestorianism—that *Christ was two distinct persons*, and Eutychianism—that *Christ has one blended nature*. The Councils of Nicea (325) and Chalcedon (381) settled these questions, and affirmed that Jesus was *fully God and fully human*. Additional errors misread the meaning of Jesus' humanity: *Docetism* which asserted that *Jesus was not human* and *Apollinarianism* which asserted that *Jesus was not fully human*. Jesus, however, is fully human and can represent us perfectly before God as our high priest, mediator, and new pattern for glorified humanity as our Second Adam.

Our objective for this segment, *Christ's Human Nature*, is to enable you to see that:

- The general purpose for Jesus' coming to earth was to reveal to us the glory of God the Father in his person, as well as to redeem humankind from the penalty and power of sin and Satan.

- The Scriptures teach the full and certain humanity of Jesus of Nazareth, who was conceived by the Holy Spirit and born to the woman, the Virgin Mary.

Summary of Segment 1

"... Christ perfectly fulfilled and united in His person the three main strands of Old Testament Messianic expectation. The Carpenter of Nazareth is first the Prophet who proclaims the Word of the Lord, then the Priest who abolishes sin by sacrifice and intercession, and finally the King who rules over the entire universe. This threefold scheme provides a picture of the mediatorial work which our Lord came to earth to accomplish."
~ Bruce Demarest, *Jesus Christ: The God-Man*. Eugene, OR: Wipf and Stock Publishers, 1978. p. 102.

- Two prominent historical errors that contested Jesus' humanity were put forth and refuted in the early Church councils. Nestorianism, the doctrine that *Christ was two distinct persons*, and Eutychianism, the doctrine that *Christ has one blended nature* were rejected as heresies because of their rejection of the full humanity of Jesus. The Councils of Nicea (325) and Chalcedon (381) settled these questions, affirming that Jesus was *fully God and fully human*.

- The early councils also refuted and rejected other key errors associated with misreading Jesus' humanity: *Docetism* which asserted that *Jesus was not human* and *Apollinarianism* which asserted that *Jesus was not fully human*.

- The doctrine of the humanity of Christ is filled with many and important practical implications of the unity of Jesus' divine and human nature. Being like us in every way *yet without sin*, Jesus as our high priest can empathize with our needs and represent us before God. As our Second Adam, we will be conformed to his glorious body in the time of glorification to come.

We who believe that God really lived on earth, and took upon Him the low estate of human form, for the purpose of man's salvation, are very far from thinking as those do who refuse to believe that God cares for anything. . . . Fortunately, however, it is a part of the creed of Christians even to believe that God did die, and yet that he is alive forevermore.

~ Tertullian (c. 207, W), 3.319.
David W. Bercot, ed. **A Dictionary of Early Christian Beliefs**.
Peabody, MA: Hendrickson Publishers, 1998. p. 96.

Video Segment 1 Outline

I. The Purpose of God the Son's Coming to Earth: Revelation and Redemption

A. For Revelation

1. Jesus revealed to us God's very *being and person*.

a. John 1.14-18

b. Matt. 11.27

c. John 14.8-11

2. Jesus revealed to us *God's exalted salvation purpose*, 2 Tim. 1.8-10.

3. Jesus revealed to us *God's mission program.*

a. 1 John 3.8

b. Gen. 3.15

c. Luke 24.44-48

B. For Redemption

1. As the Nicene Creed affirms, Jesus became human for our redemption (i.e., "Who for us men and for our salvation").

a. 1 Tim. 2.5-6

b. Luke 2.10-11

c. Heb. 2.9-10

2. To pay the penalty as a *sacrifice in our place*

   a. 1 Pet. 3.18

   b. Titus 2.14

   c. Heb. 9.28

3. To set us free from *the power of sin's dominion*, Rom. 6.6-11

4. To deliver us from the kingdom of Satan, Col. 1.13

5. To reassert God's right to rule in his universe, Mark 1.14-15

II. **Jesus of Nazareth, the God-man: the Unity of Jesus' Personhood**

   A. His Godhood: Christ was conceived of the Holy Spirit.

   1. The biblical evidence

      a. The visitation to Mary, Luke 1.31-35

      b. Matthew's account of Joseph's dilemma, Matt. 1.18-25

> *If Christ was only man, how did he say, "Before Abraham was, I am?" For no man can be before someone from whom he himself has descended. Nor can it be that anyone could have been prior to him of whom he himself has taken his origin. Yet, Christ, although he was born of Abraham, says that he is before Abraham. . . . . How can it be said that "I and the Father are one," if he is not both God and the Son?*
> ~ Novatian (c. 235, W), 5.624, 625. Ibid. p. 99.

2. Its theological significance

   a. The Holy Spirit's working and God's overshadowing power made Mary pregnant with Jesus: *she had no sexual intimacy with any man who served as the seed giver of Jesus' person.*

   b. The Holy Spirit was the active cause of Mary's conception: *no human male was involved in his unique conception.*

   c. Jesus shared human nature fully, and did not lack any human element that is found in all of us as human beings.

   d. Jesus was conceived in the womb of a woman, was nurtured through a human mother, and grew as other human beings in the context of human family and growth.

B. His Humanity: Christ was born of the Virgin Mary.

   1. The biblical evidence

      a. Messiah's birth in the Lukan account, Luke 2.4-7

      b. The prophetic promise of a virgin giving birth to Messiah, Isa. 7.14

      c. Mary's pregnancy and birth of Jesus in Matthew, Matt. 1.25,

As he was born of Mary in the last days, so did he also proceed from God as the First-Begotten of every creature.
~ Irenaeus (c. 180, E/W), 1.576.
Ibid. p. 101.

d. Jesus, a descendant of David's tribe and family, Rom. 1.3 (cf. 2 Sam. 7.12-16; Ps. 89.36-37; Isa. 9.6-7; Jer. 23.5-6; Jer. 33.15-17; etc.)

e. Paul's assertion of Jesus' human lineage, Gal. 4.4 (cf. the human genealogies of Matt. 1.1-17 and Luke 3.23-38).

2. Its theological significance

   a. Jesus was born to a woman as a fully human person.

      (1) Matt. 2.11

      (2) Matt. 12.47

      (3) Matt. 13.55

   b. He referred to himself as a man, John 8.40.

   c. Jesus' *physical nature* was in every way just like our own.

      (1) He grew in wisdom and stature, in favor with God and people, Luke 2.52.

      (2) He had the appearance of a man, with a human body, John 4.9; Luke 24.13; John 20.15; cf. Heb. 2.14.

      (3) His contemporaries recognized his human nature, 1 John 1.1-3.

      (4) He experienced hunger and thirst, and needed food and water for sustenance, Matt. 4.2; Mark 11.12; John 19.28.

      (5) He experienced fatigue, needed sleep and rest as we do, John 4.6; Matt. 8.24.

      (6) He suffered physically and died on the cross, Heb. 2.9.

d. Jesus' *psychological nature* was in every way like our own.

   (1) He loved his own till the end, and had compassion for the lost (John 13.1-3; Matt. 9.36; 14.14; 20.34).

   (2) He wept over Lazarus' passing, John 11.35.

   (3) He experienced sorrow, and could be troubled at various affairs and events, Matt. 26.37; John 12.27.

   (4) He felt the loneliness of isolation, Mark 15.34.

   (5) His knowledge was remarkable in its scope, but his understanding had genuine limits (cf. John 4.18 with Mark 9.21).

   (6) He mourned over Jerusalem's hard-heartedness, Matt. 23.37.

   (7) He longed for human companionship in the Garden, Matt. 26.36, 40.

   (8) He was tempted in all points as we are, Heb. 4.15.

C. Errors associated with misreading the unity of Christ's person

   These errors arose from individuals in early Church history wrestling with the question "What does it really mean that Jesus was fully God as well as fully human?" The Nicene Council (325) and the Council of Constantinople (381) settled the question that Jesus was fully God and fully human. These errors emerged from attempts to define precisely just what this means theologically.

   1. Nestorianism: *Christ was two distinct persons.*

      a. Nestorius, patriarch (*bishop*) of Constantinople (428 A.D.)

         (1) Poor language: denied that Mary could be referred to as the *theotokos* (God-bearer)

         (2) Argued that God could not have a mother (no being could give birth to a member of the Godhead)

The perfect Word born of the perfect Father was begotten in perfection.
~ Clement of Alexandria (c. 195, E), 2.215. Ibid. p. 101.

What did the Church confess about Christ back in the fifth century? Four things stand out: (1) His proper deity; (2) His authentic humanity; (3) the union of His divine and human natures in a single person–His person was fully integrated, not split or divided; and (4) the proper distinction of the two natures. In the union each nature retains its peculiar properties, as the creed put it, without "confusion," "change," "division," or "separation."
~ Bruce Demarest, *Jesus Christ: The God-Man*. Eugene, OR: Wipf and Stock Publishers, 1978. p. 64.

(3) Mary didn't bear God, but a man who was a means for God to reveal himself

b. His teachings seemed to suggest a split between two different beings in the person of Jesus

2. Eutychianism: *Christ has one blended nature.*

a. A leader of a monastery in Constantinople (ca. 375-454)

(1) He taught that after Jesus was born, he only possessed a single nature (not two natures in one person)

(2) Jesus' humanity blended with his deity and nearly obliterated it

(3) Unclear as to what this single, blended nature is: a confusing teaching

b. His teachings confuse the importance of the integrity of the two natures in one person in Jesus

3. The Council of Chalcedon, 451

a. Denounced ideas of Eutyches

b. Affirmed the two-nature declaration as orthodox

c. Mary was declared to be the "God-bearer" (*theotokos*) of God the Son, who became human.

d. Jesus was declared to be "consubstantial with the Father," through his deity and "consubstantial with us in manhood" in his humanity.

e. Concluded that Christ's divinity and humanity exists in two natures "without confusion, without change, without division, without separation."

D. Implications of the unity of Jesus' personhood

1. Both natures of Jesus have integrity and are united in his person.

2. The precise definition of Jesus' two natures cannot be fully explained.

3. Jesus is the perfect mediator between God and humankind, for he can represent both perfectly.

III. "And Became Human": Further Aspects Concerning Jesus' Humanity

A. Aspects of Jesus' human nature

1. His humanity had *integrity*: the Word was made flesh, John 1.14.

2. His humanity was *in every way like our own*: he shares our essential human nature.

a. Heb. 2.14

The Hypostatic Union of the Two Natures of Jesus

The hypostatic union may be defined as "the second person, the preincarnate Christ came and took to Himself a human nature and remains forever undiminished Deity and true humanity united in one person forever." When Christ came, a Person came, not just a nature; he took on an additional nature, a human nature—He did not simply dwell in a human person. The result of the union of the two natures is the theanthropic Person (the God-man).
~ P. P. Enns. *The Moody Handbook of Theology.* (Electronic ed.) Chicago: Moody Press, 1997.

b. Heb. 2.17-18

3. His humanity was *sinless*.

   a. Heb. 7.26

   b. Heb. 4.15

   c. Heb. 9.13-14

   d. 1 Pet. 1.19

   e. 1 Pet. 2.22

   f. 1 John 3.5

4. His humanity was *representative*: Jesus was the Second Adam (cf. Rom. 5.12-21; 1 Cor. 15.22-49).

   a. As second Adam, Jesus is the Head and Source of new life for redeemed humanity.

   b. As second Adam, Jesus is God's Pattern for providing salvation through his righteousness.

   c. As second Adam, Jesus is the true Image bearer for all humanity.

B. Errors associated with misreading Jesus' humanity:

1 John 4.2-3 - By this you know the Spirit of God: every spirit that confesses that Jesus Christ has come in the flesh is from God, [3] and every spirit that does not confess Jesus is not from God. This is the spirit of the antichrist, which you heard was coming and now is in the world already.

1 Tim. 3.16 - Great indeed, we confess, is the mystery of godliness: he was manifested in the flesh, vindicated by the Spirit, seen by angels, proclaimed among the nations, believed on in the world, taken up in glory.

1. *Docetism*: Jesus was not human (heresy in the early Church).

    a. *Dokeo* (Greek, meaning "to seem or appear")

    b. Jesus only appeared to be a human being.

    c. God could not unite with human flesh; Jesus' physical nature was not real, an illusion (like a spirit or ghost).

    d. Directly refuted by Jesus' own words, Luke 24.38-43

2. *Apollinarianism*: Jesus was not fully human.

    a. Bishop of Syria in 4th century

    b. Jesus could not have both human reason and divine reason.

    c. Jesus was a compound being, a combination of human and divine elements.

d. The Word took the body only; it took the place of the human soul. Jesus did not have a *human* soul but a *divine* soul.

e. Multiple problems: Jesus has no human will. Humanity is not affirmed (condemned as heretical at Council of Constantinople [381]).

C. The implications of Jesus' humanity: Jesus is *fully human*.

1. Empathy: as our high priest, he can empathize with our needs and concerns, Heb. 2.14-18.

2. Representation: as our second Adam, he represents us perfectly to the Father, Rom. 5.12ff.

3. Hope for immortality: as our image bearer, we know that our bodies will one day be conformed to his own glorious body.

    a. 1 Cor. 15.48-49

    b. Rom. 8.29

    c. Phil. 3.20-21

    d. 1 John 3.2

Conclusion

» In the hypostatic union of Christ, Jesus' divine and human natures are perfectly joined in one person: Jesus is fully human, in every way as we are, *yet without sin*.

» The Nicene Creed affirms the teaching of Holy Scripture of the full Godhood and humanity of Jesus Christ.

» Jesus on Nazareth was conceived by the Holy Spirit and born of the Virgin Mary. His divine and human natures are intact, perfectly united in his one person.

The *Kenosis* (Self-Emptying) of Christ: Of What Did He Empty himself?

The *kenosis* problem involves the interpretation of Philippians 2.7, "(He) emptied [Gk. *ekenosen*] Himself." The critical question is: Of what did Christ empty Himself? Liberal theologians suggest Christ emptied Himself of *His deity*, but it is evident from His life and ministry that He did not, for His deity was displayed on numerous occasions. Two main points may be made. (1) "Christ merely surrendered the independent exercise of some of his relative or transitive attributes. He did not surrender the absolute or immanent attributes in any sense; He was always perfectly holy, just, merciful, truthful, and faithful."30 This statement has merit and provides a solution to problem passages such as Matthew 24.36. The key word in this definition would be "independent" because Jesus did on many occasions reveal His relative attributes. (2) Christ took to Himself an additional nature. The context of Philippians 2.7 provides the best solution to the *kenosis* problem. The emptying was **not a subtraction but an addition**. The four following phrases (Phil. 2.7–8) explain the emptying: "(a) taking the form of a bond-servant, and (b) being made in the likeness of men. And (c) being found in appearance as a man, (d) He humbled Himself by becoming obedient to the point of death." The "emptying" of Christ was taking on an additional nature, a human nature with its limitations. His deity was never surrendered [emphasis mine].

~ P. P. Enns. **The Moody Handbook of Theology**. Chicago: Moody Press, 1997.

Segue 1

Student Questions and Response

Please take as much time as you have available to answer these and other questions that the video brought out. This lesson highlights the full humanity of the person of Jesus of Nazareth, and his ability to empathize, represent, and serve as a pattern for a new humanity in the Kingdom to come. Articulating the relationship between the divine and human natures of Christ has been one of the central theological discussions throughout the history of the Church. Our ability to understand Jesus' humanity greatly impacts our opportunity to counsel others who are enduring hardship and need to believe in a Savior who truly empathizes and understands their plight. Your ability to understand his human nature is therefore critical to your ability to persuade others of Jesus' empathy during times of crisis. Answer the following questions with these ideas in mind, and support your answers with Scripture.

1. Explain the purposes given in this lesson regarding the appearance of Jesus as a human being upon earth: revealing the Father's glory in the Incarnation and redeeming humankind from the power, penalty, and presence of sin and Satan.

2. What are the divine-human contributions in the conception and birth of Jesus Christ? How do these contributions help us understand the integrity and unity of the divine and human natures that he possesses?

3. What is the theological significance and certainty of the virgin birth of Jesus? In what way did Jesus share our human nature without sharing the sinful *Adam's sin nature*? Explain your answer.

4. What is *Nestorianism* and why was it condemned in the Councils of Nicea and Constantinople?

5. What is *Eutychianism* and why was it condemned in the Councils of Nicea and Constantinople?

6. What does it mean when we say that "the humanity of Jesus was sinless?" How, too, should we understand Jesus as the *Second Adam*, as the representative of a new humanity before God?

7. Explain the heresies of *Docetism* and *Apollinarianism*, and why were they rejected as alternative views for understanding the humanity of Jesus Christ.

8. What are the key ramifications of being able to assert that Jesus of Nazareth in every way is fully human even as we are, in terms of his ability to empathize with us, represent us before God, and serve as the pattern for our glorified humanity in the world to come?

Jesus, the Messiah and Lord of All: He Lived

Segment 2: The Messianic Mission of Jesus Christ

Rev. Dr. Don L. Davis

Three important aspects of Jesus' life help us to understand the meaning of his Messianic mission. Jesus is the Baptized One who identified with the plight and peril of the sinners he came to save. Furthermore, Jesus is the Inauguration and Proclaimer of the Kingdom of God, reasserting God's right to rule over creation, showing through his person, miracles, healings, and exorcisms the signs of the Kingdom present in his own person on earth. Jesus is also the expected Servant of Yahweh who proclaimed good news to the poor, demonstrated justice among God's people, and ultimately, gave up his life as a vicarious sacrifice and a ransom for many.

Our objective for this segment, *The Messianic Mission of Jesus Christ*, is to enable you to see that:

- Jesus of Nazareth entered the world as a member of Israel, as the Baptized One who identified with the plight and peril of the sinners he came to save.

- In the person of Jesus, the long-awaited Kingdom of God has been manifested. In his person, the Kingdom of God has come. Jesus is therefore the Proclaimer of the Kingdom of God, reasserting God's right to rule over creation, showing through his person, miracles, healings, and exorcisms the signs of the Kingdom present in his own person on earth.

- In fulfillment of the OT prophecy, Jesus is the Suffering Servant of Yahweh. From the public announcement of his public ministry and throughout his encounters in life, Jesus revealed himself as the expected Servant of Yahweh who would proclaim the Good News to the poor, do justice among God's people, and ultimately, give his life as a substitutionary sacrifice for the sins of the people.

Summary of Segment 2

Video Segment 2 Outline

We sing hymns to the Most High alone and to His Only-Begotten, who is the Word and God.
~ Origen (c. 248, E), 4.639. David W. Bercot, ed. *A Dictionary of Early Christian Beliefs.* Peabody, MA: Hendrickson Publishers, 1998. p. 99.

I. **Jesus Is the Baptized One Who Identified with Sinners.**

    A. The biblical portrait of Jesus as the Baptized One

        1. John the Baptizer (cf. Matt. 3.1-12; Mark 1.2-8; Luke 3.1-20; John 1.19-28)

        2. John as the forerunner of the Messiah in OT prophecy

            a. He is the messenger who clears the way before Messiah, Mal. 3.1.

            b. He is the voice crying in the wilderness, cf. Isa. 40.1-3 with Matt. 3.1-3.

            c. He would instruct the people in the ways of the Lord, Mal. 2.7.

            d. He would come in the spirit and power of Elijah.

                (1) Mal. 4.5-6

                (2) Matt. 11.13-14

            e. Prophecies were made regarding John's life and mission before Messiah would appear, cf. Luke 1.13-17.

        3. Jesus acknowledges John as the messenger before Messiah, Matt. 11.10-11.

4. Jesus is baptized by John, Matt. 3.13-15.

5. God confirms Jesus' identity and sonship at the baptism, Matt. 3.16-17.

B. The theological implications of Jesus as the Baptized One who identifies with sinners

1. Jesus is the fulfillment of the OT Messianic prophecy.

2. Jesus identifies completely with sinners in his baptism (he was baptized not because of a need to repent, but a desire to empathize with the people of God).

3. Jesus is well able to represent us in his priestly office because of his deep sympathy and love for those who are broken and despised.

a. Heb. 2.14-18

b. Heb. 4.15-5.2

II. Jesus Is the Proclaimer of the Kingdom of God.

A. The biblical portrait of Jesus as the Proclaimer of the Kingdom of God

1. The OT in numerous places asserts God as the King of the universe.

Christ performed all those miracles . . . by the inherent might of His authority. For this was the proper duty of true Divinity, as was consistent with His nature, as was worthy of Him.
~ Arnobius (c. 305, E), 6.425. Ibid. p. 100.

a. Ps. 145.11-13

b. 1 Chron. 29.11

c. Dan. 4.34-35

2. Because of the rebellion of Satan (i.e., Satan = *adversary*) and the first human pair, the world has been thrown into chaos and sin.

   a. The devil has rebelled against God, Isa. 14.12-17 cf. Ezek. 28.13-17.

   b. Humankind participated in the voluntary rebellion of Adam and Eve, Gen. 3.1-7 with Rom. 5.1-11.

3. God made a covenant with David that one descending from his royal line would come and rule in justice in God's Kingdom forever, cf. 2 Sam. 7.1-17 with Ps. 89.3-4.

4. The hope of the Kingdom is that God would reassert his kingly rule over creation, destroying Satan, delivering God's nation Israel, ending Gentile domination and oppression, and refreshing creation.

   a. In the day of the Lord the serpent would be destroyed.

   b. Israel would be regathered and restored.

c. The social order would be changed: Gentile oppression would cease.

d. All creation would be transformed.

5. Jesus proclaimed himself as the presence of the Kingdom of God in his person at his first appearing.

   a. He introduced himself as *the promised Messiah* of the Kingdom which had then come into being, Mark 1.14-15.

   b. His most often used title by which *he referred to himself was the "Son of Man,"* an allusion to Daniel's coming king, Dan. 7.13-14.

   c. He *exercised dominion over Satan and his minions* through his ministry of exorcism and deliverance.

      (1) Luke 11.17-23

      (2) Luke 10.17-20

      (3) Acts 10.36-38

   d. He gave *signs of the Kingdom's coming* and the visible end of the curse's power through his healings and miracles.

      (1) The feeding of the 5,000 (cf. Mark 6.30-44)

      (2) He opened the eyes of the blind, John 9.1-7.

      (3) He commanded the storm winds and waves, Matt. 8.23-27.

      (4) He healed the lame, paralyzed, and the sick, e.g., Mark 2.1-12.

      (5) He brought the dead back to life again, John 11.

e. His *teaching* outlined the reassertion of God's kingdom ethic in the here and now, e.g., the Sermon on the Mount, Matt. 5-7.

   (1) Love as the supreme commandment and fulfillment of the Law's ethical norms, Matt 22.34-40

   (2) He himself as the subject proper of Moses, the Psalms and the Prophets (i.e., the Old Testament in its entirety), John 5.39-40; Luke 24.27, 44-48

f. His *character* reveals the glory of the Father's own splendor as well as his kingdom righteousness, John 1.14; Matt. 5.17-18.

B. The theological implications of Jesus as the Proclaimer of the Kingdom of God

1. Jesus is the fulfillment of the OT prophecy regarding the coming Lord and Messiah, Acts 2.34-36.

2. In Jesus' first appearing, the Kingdom of God has appeared and been inaugurated. Although it will not be consummated until his Second Coming, Jesus has translated those who believe into the Kingdom of his Son, Col. 1.13; 1 John 3.8.

3. Jesus' mission on earth was the display and reassertion of God's rule in this domain, to defeat the devil and to restore his creation under God's rulership, 1 John 3.8.

III. Jesus is the Suffering Servant of Yahweh.

A. The biblical portrait of the Servant of Yahweh

He is called His Servant by the God of all things, and Israel, and Light of the Gentiles.
~ Origen (c. 228, E), 9.314. Ibid. p. 370.

1. Jesus inaugurated his public ministry in Nazareth by an appeal to an OT Messianic text regarding Yahweh's Suffering Servant, Isaiah 61.1 with Luke 4.18-19

2. Jesus thus identifies himself with the Servant of the Lord in the OT (e.g., the prophet Isaiah)

   a. He concentrated on meeting the needs of the broken and the beaten, suggesting that "only the sick need a physician," Mark 2.14-17

   b. He rebuked the religious leaders for their inability to be merciful and compassionate to the poor, Luke 18.9-14

   c. He made treatment of the poor the litmus test of the quality of one's relationship with God, Matt. 25.31-46

3. Jesus is acknowledged by the early Christian community to be the Servant of the Lord, John 1.41; Acts 4.27; Acts 10.38

4. Jesus fulfills the OT witness regarding the faithful Servant of the Lord who would judge and lead justly over God's people (cf. Matt. 12.16-20 with Isa. 42.1-4)

5. Jesus is Yahweh's Servant whose prophetic word brings sustenance and power to those who hear, (cf. Matt. 11.29-30 with Isa. 50.4)

6. Jesus in his death would be the dramatic Sacrificial Servant of Isaiah 53, the one whose life and experience of suffering would end in his substitutionary death for all humankind, Isa. 53.2-6

B. The theological implications of Jesus as the Servant of Yahweh

1. Jesus is the fulfillment of the OT Messianic prophecy regarding the Servant of Yahweh.

2. In all of his life and relationships, Jesus demonstrated that quality of lowliness and humiliation that allowed him be to both forgiving and compassionate to sinners and the sick throughout his earthly life.

3. Jesus not only fulfilled the prophecies of Yahweh's Servant regarding his humble life and cruel death, but he will fulfill all the prophecies regarding the reassertion and completion of God's Kingdom to come at his Second Coming, Isa. 11.1-4.

Conclusion

» Three key biblical motifs can be seen to comprise Jesus' life and Messianic ministry on earth.

» As the Baptized One, Jesus identified with the sinners he came to redeem.

» As the Proclaimer of the Kingdom of God, Jesus inaugurated the reign of God and reasserted God's right to rule over creation.

» As the Suffering Servant of Yahweh, Jesus fulfilled the OT prophecies of God's anointed servant, preaching the Good News to the poor, doing justice among the people, and giving his life as a ransom for many.

Segue 2

Student Questions and Response

The following questions were designed to help you review the material in the second video segment. In each of these three biblical motifs (images, themes), Jesus reveals himself to be the long awaited Messiah of Israel. In his baptism he identified with the sinners he came to redeem. In his kingdom proclamation he inaugurated the reign of God and reasserted God's right to rule over creation. In his fulfillment of OT prophecy, he expressed clearly the signs of the One anointed of God to give his life as a ransom for many. An understanding of these motifs are central for urban ministry, especially since the urban community is desperate for One who understands its pain, proclaims the good news of peace and reconciliation, and who can restore the relationships we have broken with God and one another. Answer the following questions with these key applications in mind as you try to clearly understand the facts supporting these great biblical themes.

1. What role does John the Baptist play in the narrative of Jesus of Nazareth and the announcement of the Messiah?

2. How are we to understand the meaning of the baptism of Jesus by John, especially since Jesus had never sinned–why would Jesus participate in a *baptism to repentance*? Explain your answer.

3. How might the baptism of Jesus related to his role for us as high priest, i.e., as one who must be able to empathize with the needs and weaknesses of the people (cf. Heb. 4.14-15 Since then we have a great high priest who has passed through the heavens, Jesus, the Son of God, let us hold fast our confession. [15] For we do not have a high priest who is unable to sympathize with our weaknesses, but one who in every respect has been tempted as we are, yet without sin)?

4. In the story of God, how did the Jews of Jesus' day understand the coming manifestation of the reign of God to come about? How did Jesus' teaching and ministry signal a new understanding of the timetable and manifestation of the Kingdom *in his own person*?

5. How did Jesus give evidence in miracles and healings that the long prophesied Kingdom of God had in fact come in his life and ministry? How did his teaching demonstrate the present reality of the Kingdom come in his life?

6. What is the relationship between Jesus' initial inauguration of the Kingdom and his Second Coming? Explain your answer.

7. How did Jesus announce his identity in his public announcement in his hometown Nazareth? With whom did he identify himself? Why is this significant for understanding Jesus' role as Messiah?

8. How does the OT (e.g., Isaiah 53) outline the ministry of the Servant of Yahweh as a *substitutionary sacrifice for the sins of the people*? How did the death of Jesus fulfill this important prophecy?

9. Why can we be confident that if Jesus is truly the Suffering Servant of Yahweh that he will return and finish the work that he began through his Incarnation, his death and resurrection?

The Importance of the Nicene Creed in Christological Controversy

The Nicene Creed, which is used in worship today, is dated from the Council of Constantinople in 381. All creeds that use the phrase "of the same substance (reality, being, essence) as the Father" were regarded as Nicene. The Council of Constantinople also eliminated the anathemas from the Creed of 325 and added a statement affirming the deity of the Holy Spirit as well as the one holy catholic Church, the forgiveness of sins, and the resurrection of the dead. The Council of Nicea, in affirming that Jesus Christ was truly God, raised the question of the humanity of Christ, and therefore of the doctrine of the person of Christ. The Church of the 5th century, in an amazingly catholic theological endeavor, defined its understanding of the person of Jesus Christ at the Council of Chalcedon (431) in which it affirmed that Jesus Christ is truly God and truly man in one person (one acting subject).

~ John H. Leith. "Creeds." **The Anchor Bible Dictionary**. D. N. Freedman, ed. (Vol. 1). (electronic ed.). New York: Doubleday Publishers, 1996. p. 1205.

CONNECTION

Summary of Key Concepts

This lesson focuses upon the important lessons of Christ's person in his humanity as well as the richness of his life and ministry as the promised Messiah demonstrated in his baptism, kingdom ministry, and identification with the image of the Suffering Servant of Yahweh. The critical concepts associated with this lesson are important for urban leaders to understand and apply as they not only follow the Lord in their own personal discipleship, but also as they lead others to maturity. Listed below are some of these critical ideas and truths.

- The general purpose for Jesus' coming to earth was to reveal to us the glory of God the Father in his person, as well as to redeem humankind from the penalty and power of sin and Satan.

- The Scriptures teach the full and certain humanity of Jesus of Nazareth, who was conceived by the Holy Spirit and born to the woman, the Virgin Mary.

- Two prominent historical errors that contested Jesus' humanity were put forth and refuted in the early Church councils. *Nestorianism*, the doctrine that *Christ was two distinct persons*, and *Eutychianism*, the doctrine that *Christ has one blended nature* were rejected as heresies because of their rejection of the full humanity of Jesus. The Councils of Nicea (325) and Chalcedon (381) settled these questions, affirming that Jesus was *fully God and fully human*.

- The early councils also refuted and rejected other key errors associated with misreading Jesus' humanity: *Docetism* which asserted that *Jesus was not human* and *Apollinarianism* which asserted that *Jesus was not fully human*.

- The doctrine of the humanity of Christ is filled with many important practical implications of the unity of Jesus' divine and human nature. Being like us in every way *yet without sin*, Jesus as our high priest can empathize with our needs and represent us before God. As our Second Adam, we will be conformed to his glorious body in the time of glorification to come.

- Jesus of Nazareth entered the world as a member of Israel, as the Baptized One who identified with the plight and peril of the sinners he came to save.

- In the person of Jesus, the long awaited Kingdom of God has been manifested. In his person, the Kingdom of God has come. Jesus is therefore the Proclaimer of the Kingdom of God, reasserting God's right to rule over creation, showing through his person, miracles, healings, and exorcisms the signs of the Kingdom present in his own person on earth.

- In fulfillment of the OT prophecy, Jesus is the Suffering Servant of Yahweh. From the public announcement of his public ministry and throughout his encounters in life, Jesus revealed himself as the expected Servant of Yahweh who would proclaim good news to the poor, do justice among God's people, and ultimately, give his life as a substituionary sacrifice for the sins of the people.

Student Application and Implications

Now explore with your fellow students your more personal questions about the person and work of Jesus as Messiah who lived among us. Your ability to make disciples of Jesus is directly connected to your understanding of who he was, what he did (and why), and how what he did (and is doing) applies to both your life and your ministry. As you have pondered some of the truths covered in this lesson, what kinds of issues and ideas have come to the surface that you personally want answers for? What issues have come to light through this study that affect your own personal discipleship and walk with the Lord? The questions below are designed to help you form your own, more specific and personal questions.

* How is it possible that God could become a human being for the purpose of revelation and redemption? Is it necessary for us to understand *how* this is possible, or should we simply concentrate on *that* it occurred? Explain your answer.

* To what extent are the theories about *how* Jesus' divine and human natures united ultimately an issue of mystery and faith, not reason and analysis. Explain your answer.

* Is it right to say that Jesus is *in every way* just like us except that he *never sinned*? In other words, was Jesus like us in his emotions, thoughts, human feelings and needs, in every way?

* In what ways do the errors concerning Jesus' humanity (i.e., those *ancient heresies*) find expression in the speculations about Jesus today? How do the ideas that people have of Jesus today parallel those which were refuted in the great Councils of the Church?

* Why is it extremely important to be able to say to others that Jesus feels our weakness and understands our vulnerabilities? How does the doctrine of his humanity help us explain and communicate this to those whom we serve in the city?

* How should we as urban ministers proclaim the Kingdom of God as *present* in the city today? In what senses must we in our preaching and teaching emphasize *both sides of the perspective* of Christ's inaugurating the Kingdom in his first coming, and consummating it in his Second Coming?

* The NT affirms that God's intent is that we as his people are conformed to his image, both in his death as well as in his resurrection, ascension, and return (cf. Rom. 8.29; Gal. 4.10ff.; Phil. 3.20-21; 2 Cor. 3.18; 1 John 3.1-2;

Rom. 6.1-11, etc.). How might the teaching of Jesus as the Suffering Servant of Yahweh help us understand God's purpose to conform us to his image, sharing in his suffering and death in order to share in his exaltation and glory (1 Pet. 2.21-25; Rom. 8.16-18).

CASE STUDIES

He's Been There Before

In counseling a bereaved family who recently lost a young child, you are called as pastor to give comforting words to them. Of all the thoughts that have caused them the greatest pain, the one lingering idea is their fear of death. They are Christians, they love the Lord and are faithful members of a solid, biblical, missions-minded church, but the absence of their daughter/sister has crushed the family. They want to believe that God understands and that he is taking care of little Sarah, but on their darkest days, they are nearly overwhelmed with grief and pain. How might the teaching of the humanity of Jesus help you help them cope with the loss of their little one? How might the knowledge that Jesus has experienced death help you comfort them with the loss of Sarah? How does Paul integrate his knowledge of Christ into his counsel to the Thessalonians on this same subject (i.e., 1 Thess. 4.13-17)?

Would He Have Come?

To do good theology we must be willing to use our imaginations as well as our reason to understand what God has given for us. In a discussion on the nature of God's purposes and the Incarnation, some advanced seminary students in a Christology class raised the question of the *necessity and inevitability* of the Incarnation. They asked, in what sense, if any, was the Incarnation an actual inevitability? In other words, would Jesus of Nazareth have been born if Adam had not sinned, and humankind had not needed a Savior? One student believes that all such thinking is of little or no value, since the secret things belong to God and the things which are revealed belong to us (Deut. 29.29). Another believes that such thinking is helpful, imitating the work of the angels with the prophets to understand the purposes and intentions of God recorded in Scripture (1 Pet. 1.10-12). What do you think?

Compromised Faith or Merely Identifying with Sinners?

▶3 The current "insiders movements" are an important and powerful phenomena of the Holy Spirit in missions today. Many countries are now inaccessible to foreign Christian workers, missionaries, or "tent makers"— Christians who go into "closed nations" to work in secular positions for the sake of sharing the Gospel. Many Buddhists and Muslims (among others) are coming to Christ, but, retaining their original cultural customs and contacts for the sake of "identifying with their fellow countrymen for the sake of the Gospel." For instance, some Buddhist "followers of Christ" have professed faith in Jesus, but refuse to go by the term "Christian," which in many cultural contexts is equal to saying "I'm a pro-Westerner and have turned my allegiance away from my people." There are reports of robust movements within Islamic communities of individuals who have come to Jesus by faith but still remain within the cultural boundaries of Islam and Islamic society. Arguing analogies with Judaism and early Christianity, these believers are convinced that there is no other way to reach these millions without true *identification with them, which means retaining a connection with them within their religious and cultural grids.* Is this compromising faith or simply like Jesus *identifying with sinners for the sake of salvation*?

Jesus of Nazareth or the Christ of Faith

▶4 In many of our churches today, the teaching concerning Jesus of Nazareth is in exile. The ethics, principles, and commands of the Lord Jesus are often overlooked for "principles and laws" of prosperity and blessing, and the hard sayings of Jesus are replaced by the golden statements of television evangelists who promise a faith that includes only riches, health, joy, and prosperity. Frankly, in extreme cases, those who suffer illness and poverty have only themselves to blame because of their inability to apply the truths of Scripture, which oftentimes are not integrated into the teaching of Christ. This teaching is so popular today that many assume it to be the heart and soul of Jesus' own teaching about the Kingdom. Positive thinking, prosperity and blessing, health and comfort–this has become the mantra that substitutes for Christ's humble demands to take up our crosses and follow him. In what ways are we to teach the *humanity of Christ* today; does his life offer us a *pattern to follow*, or did Christ suffer in the flesh in order that *we might have an abundance that excludes his kind of suffering and lack*?

Jesus appeared on earth as a man to reveal to humankind the Father's glory and redeem us from sin and Satan's power. Jesus was fully human, conceived by the Holy Spirit and carried to birth by the Virgin Mary. Two ancient heresies contested Jesus' becoming a human being: *Nestorianism*—that Christ *was two distinct persons*, and *Eutychianism*—that Christ *has one blended nature*. The Councils of Nicea (325) and Chalcedon (381) settled these questions, and affirmed that Jesus was *fully God and fully human*. Additional errors misread the meaning of Jesus' humanity: *Docetism* which asserted that *Jesus was not human* and *Apollinarianism* which asserted that *Jesus was not fully human*. Jesus, however, is fully human and can represent us perfectly before God as our high priest, mediator, and new pattern for glorified humanity as our Second Adam.

Three important aspects of Jesus' life help us to understand the meaning of his Messianic mission. Jesus is the Baptized One who identified with the plight and peril of the sinners he came to save. Furthermore, Jesus is the Inauguration and Proclaimer of the Kingdom of God, reasserting God's right to rule over creation, showing through his person, miracles, healings, and exorcisms the signs of the Kingdom present in his own person on earth. Jesus is also the expected Servant of Yahweh who proclaimed good news to the poor, demonstrated justice among God's people, and ultimately, gave up his life as a vicarious sacrifice and a ransom for many.

Restatement of the Lesson's Thesis

If you are interested in pursuing some of the ideas of *Jesus, the Messiah and Lord of All: He Lived*, you might want to give these books a try:

  Brown, Raymond E. *The Birth of the Messiah*. New York: Doubleday, 1979.

  Hoehner, Harold W. *Chronological Aspects of the Life of Christ*. Grand Rapids: Zondervan, 1977.

  Ladd, George Eldon. *Jesus and the Kingdom*. New York: Harper, 1964.

  Meier, John P. *A Marginal Jew: Rethinking the Historical Jesus*. New York: Doubleday, 1991.

Resources and Bibliographies

In covering so much theological ground in our lesson, we must take the time to pause and ponder what this high theology has to do with our lives in practical ministry connection. The humanity and life of our Lord touches upon dozens of practical issues in our lives which we need to address. What particular questions has

Ministry Connections

the Holy Spirit been suggesting to you regarding your understanding of the life of Jesus, and how you are living in conjunction with his life today? Is there a particular idea that the Lord has given to you regarding your own life and ministry that you need to apply this week in connection to the principles you have learned here? Is there a particular situation that comes to mind when you think about how God might want to form this teaching in your own walk with God, your relationships with others, or in your teaching and mentoring of other disciples. Lift these and your own questions up to God, asking for his wisdom and help as you explore the connections of these truths and your own life situation today.

Counseling and Prayer

As in every lesson, it is critical that we solicit the prayer of our brothers and sisters, and our leaders to help us both process and apply the truths of God. God's truth concerning the doctrine of Christ is for our *formation and transformation*, not merely for our *curiosity and consideration*. Prayer activates truth in a way that study cannot do alone. Ask your mentor and/or instructor to pray for you during the week–to apply the truth, to connect with others, and to teach and preach the truths in a new and fresh way in your church and ministry. Pray that the Holy Spirit will enable you to freshly comprehend and apply the life-giving power of the doctrine of Christ–his peerless life and genuine ministry–to others. Ask God to grant you wisdom as you seek to make this teaching come alive, in your own life as well as others. Be confident that he will grant wisdom to us if we only believe (James 1.5).

Scripture Memory

Hebrews 2.14-17

Reading Assignment

To prepare for class, please visit *www.tumi.org/books* to find next week's reading assignment, or ask your mentor.

Other Assignments

Please read carefully the assignments above, and as last week, write a brief summary for them and bring these summaries to class next week (please see the "Reading Completion Sheet" at the end of this lesson).

Now is the time for you to beginning planning your own ministry project, as well as determining what Scripture passage you will use for your exegetical project. It is important that you neither postpone nor procrastinate in selecting both your ministry and study projects. The sooner you determine what you want to do, the more time you will have to prepare, and the better (and hopefully, more informative and inspiring) your projects will be!

.....

Looking Forward to the Next Lesson

In this lesson we explored the integrity of Jesus' human nature, and the unity between Jesus' divine and human natures. Conceived by the Holy Spirit and the Virgin Mary, Jesus is he whose divine and human natures are intact, perfectly united in his one person. We also considered the three key biblical motifs that comprised Jesus' life and Messianic ministry on earth. As the Baptized One, Jesus identified with the sinners he came to redeem. As the Proclaimer of the Kingdom of God, Jesus inaugurated the reign of God and reasserted God's right to rule over creation. Finally, as the Suffering Servant of Yahweh, Jesus fulfilled the OT prophecies of God's anointed servant, preaching good news to the poor, doing justice among the people, and giving his life as a ransom for many.

In our next lesson entitled, *Jesus, the Messiah and Lord of All: He Died*, we will consider the significance of the humiliation of Jesus Christ, to use Oden's language, in both his lowliness in life and his sacrifice in death for the world.

This curriculum is the result of thousands of hours of work by The Urban Ministry Institute (TUMI) and should not be reproduced without their express permission. TUMI supports all who wish to use these materials for the advance of God's Kingdom, and affordable licensing to reproduce them is available. Please confirm with your instructor that this book is properly licensed. For more information on TUMI and our licensing program, visit *www.tumi.org* and *www.tumi.org/license*.

Capstone Curriculum

Module 10: God the Son
Reading Completion Sheet

Name _____

Date _____

For each assigned reading, write a brief summary (one or two paragraphs) of the author's main point. (For additional readings, use the back of this sheet.)

Reading 1

Title and Author: _____ Pages _____

Reading 2

Title and Author: _____ Pages _____

Jesus, the Messiah and Lord of All
He Died

Lesson Objectives

Welcome in the strong name of Jesus Christ! After your reading, study, discussion, and application of the materials in this lesson, you will be able to:

- Articulate with Scripture and concrete examples the significance of the *humiliation* of Jesus Christ, that is, his descent in his divine person and glory to come to earth and die on our behalf.

- Illustrate and state the major points of Jesus' humiliation in his Incarnation and in his life and ministry.

- Elaborate with Scripture and clear reasons how this humiliation of Jesus is specifically revealed in his death.

- Expand upon some of the key historical perspectives on Jesus' death and the way in which these dimensions enable us to understand the blessing our Lord's death was for humankind.

- These include the view of his death as a ransom for us, as a propitiation for our sins, as a substitutionary sacrifice in our place, as a victory over the devil and death itself, and as a reconciliation between God and humankind.

- Elaborate on how the Nicene Creed unequivocally confesses that our Lord Jesus Christ died and was buried, and how this act was the culmination of our Lord's humiliation upon earth in his descent from his heavenly, preexistent glory.

- Lay out theories of the atonement which have emerged through history, including his death: 1) as an example, 2) as a demonstration of God's love, 3) as a demonstration of God's justice, 4) as a victory over the forces of evil and sin, and 5) as a satisfaction of God's honor.

- Argue how no one historical theory of the atonement by itself can explain the richness of the meaning of Jesus' death, but rather they each contain dimensions of truth which can help us gain a comprehensive understanding and appreciation of the significance of Jesus' death for us.

The Iniquity of Us All   Devotion

Isa. 53.1-12 - Who has believed what they heard from us? And to whom has the arm of the Lord been revealed? [2] For he grew up before him like a young plant, and like a root out of dry ground; he had no form or majesty that we should look at him, and no beauty that we should desire him. [3] He was despised and rejected by men; a man of sorrows, and acquainted with grief; and as one from whom men hide their faces he was despised, and we esteemed him not. [4] Surely he has borne our griefs and carried our sorrows; yet we esteemed him stricken, smitten by God, and afflicted. [5] But he was wounded for our transgressions; he was crushed for our iniquities; upon him was the chastisement that brought us peace, and with his stripes we are healed. [6] All we like sheep have gone astray; we have turned every one to his own way; and the Lord has laid on him the iniquity of us all. [7] He was oppressed, and he was afflicted, yet he opened not his mouth; like a lamb that is led to the slaughter, and like a sheep that before its shearers is silent, so he opened not his mouth. [8] By oppression and judgment he was taken away; and as for his generation, who considered that he was cut off out of the land of the living, stricken for the transgression of my people? [9] And they made his grave with the wicked and with a rich man in his death, although he had done no violence, and there was no deceit in his mouth. [10] Yet it was the will of the Lord to crush him; he has put him to grief; when his soul makes an offering for sin, he shall see his offspring; he shall prolong his days; the will of the Lord shall prosper in his hand. [11] Out of the anguish of his soul he shall see and be satisfied; by his knowledge shall the righteous one, my servant, make many to be accounted righteous, and he shall bear their iniquities. [12] Therefore I will divide him a portion with the many, and he shall divide the spoil with the strong, because he poured out his soul to death and was numbered with the transgressors; yet he bore the sin of many, and makes intercession for the transgressors.

One of the greatest mysteries of the Christian faith relates to the profound humility of the Godhead as revealed in the death and passion of Jesus Christ. His lowliness and submission causes us to wonder and marvel at the *nature* of the divine. His willingness to follow the Father's command with such fierce loyalty and obedience, no matter what the cost, reveals the heart of a Savior which is boundless in virtue and grace. In this significant chapter of Messianic prophecy, Isaiah scripts out the contours of the one who would come in great humility for the sake of redeeming those who in fact were guilty and unconcerned. The lack of empathy and understanding for those who would receive his gift of grace makes the lowliness even more astounding.

One of the high points of the text leads us gently into the depths of the truth regarding the humility of our Lord and his death on our behalf. Isaiah 53.3-6 highlights his humiliation: "He was despised and rejected by men; a man of sorrows, and acquainted with grief; and as one from whom men hide their faces he was despised, and we esteemed him not. Surely he has borne our griefs and carried our sorrows; yet we esteemed him stricken, smitten by God, and afflicted. But he was wounded for our transgressions; he was crushed for our iniquities; upon him was the chastisement that brought us peace, and with his stripes we are healed. All we like sheep have gone astray; we have turned every one to his own way; and the Lord has laid on him the iniquity of us all." On close look at the text we are amazed at the *disposition* of people toward him. He was despised, rejected, a man of sorrows, acquainted with grief, unesteemed and unloved. Though ironically perceived as one who was stricken by the Lord, he was actually bearing our griefs, wounded for our transgressions, crushed for our iniquities, chastised for our peace, and beaten viciously for our healing. We like sheep have wandered and gone astray in directions that have nothing to do with the Lord, we've turned each one to our own way, *and the Lord has laid on him the iniquity of us all*.

This truth, that his humiliation was the result of our rebellion and sin, ought to produce in each of us a deep sense of sobriety and angst. Hymnody has captured these inclinations in surveying the wondrous cross, in seeing the sacred head wounded on account of our own foolishness and transgression. The Lord's love to reconcile, redeem, and restore led him to punish his own Servant in our place, laying on *him* the iniquity of us *all*.

No other truth, no other idea, can bring in us such a deep level of self-awareness of the real consequences our sin wrought upon our Lord. His blows, beatings, rejection, and despising was caused directly by our own disobedience, lies, lust, and greed. Our waste and hatreds, our irritations and jealousies and our foolishness and profanities are the reasons for our Lord's horrible treatment and death. When we come to understand just how responsible we are for his suffering, only then will we be able to truly empathize with our Lord, and bear daily the cross that we are to share with him.

We must admit our part in Calvary, that contribution that made his death necessary *for our redemption*. Yes, we have gone our own way; yes, we have gone astray like wandering sheep without a shepherd, and the Lord has laid on him the iniquity of us all.

Nicene Creed and Prayer

After reciting and/or singing the Nicene Creed (located in the Appendix), pray the following prayer:

Holy and everliving God who revealed the glory of your Son when he was exalted on the cross: Accept our praise and thanksgiving for the power of his victory and grant us never to be afraid to suffer or to die with him; our crucified King who is alive, and reigns in all eternity with you and the Holy Spirit one God for ever and ever.

~ The Church of the Province of South Africa.
Minister's Book for Use With the Holy Eucharist and Morning and Evening Prayer. Braamfontein: Publishing Department of the Church of the Province of South Africa. p. 47.

Quiz

Put away your notes, gather up your thoughts and reflections, and take the quiz for Lesson 2, *Jesus, the Messiah and Lord of All: He Lived.*

Scripture Memorization Review

Review with a partner, write out and/or recite the text for last class session's assigned memory verse: Hebrews 2.14-17.

Assignments Due

Turn in your summary of the reading assignment for last week, that is, your brief response and explanation of the main points that the authors were seeking to make in the assigned reading (Reading Completion Sheet).

The Cross in Your Pocket

The Cross is arguably one of the most visible symbols of the Christian faith, and least understood. Today, the Cross is represented in every conceivable way, from trinkets and lockets, on bracelets and T-shirts, to church art and architecture. It is a staple in the West and despised in many places of the world. One company makes a cross of coin-size that fits in the pocket to remind you of the price paid for our sin. What is your view of the commercialization of the cross, and how might such activities dull us to the true meaning of the passion of Christ?

The Passion of the Christ

In response to the blockbuster film, *The Passion of the Christ*, many evangelical churches held evangelistic meetings designed to share the Good News in conjunction with the debut of the film. The graphic nature of the sufferings of the Messiah shown in the film have produced wide ranging responses, from deep feelings of remorse and love to shock and horror. The film is perhaps the most dramatically violent depiction ever of the sufferings of Jesus. Some have said such showings simply go too far in highlighting the violence of Calvary without really dramatically revealing the underlying reasons for it. What is your opinion about such dramatic interpretations of the passion of Jesus. Ought we to produce more of these, or have we had enough of them for now?

A Strange Silence

In many of our more "seeker sensitive" churches, we are witnessing a strange silence to the stigma and passion of Calvary. Many of the sermons and homilies are on subjects of wide public interest, usually avoiding topics and themes which are overtly theological and doctrinal. When the cross is presented, it is usually done in a way that highlights the self-actualization of the hearer rather than as an explicit solution to the transgression of humankind. Teachings on the blood sacrifice of Messiah have been replaced by homilies on positive thinking and building family memories. Many of the old hymns which highlighted the wonder, power, and mystery of the cross have been replaced by a flood of choruses, all of which focus on the joy of the worshiper and not the underlying suffering that makes worship possible. While many churches continue to emphasize the cross as the central event in salvation history, our methods of evangelism and outreach tend to focus on more positive themes for the sake of attracting new visitors. What is your opinion as to the growing and strange silence of the cross in the preaching, teaching, and worship in our churches today?

Jesus, the Messiah and Lord of All: He Died

Segment 1: His Humiliation and Death

Rev. Dr. Don L. Davis

The humiliation of Jesus Christ, to use the theologian Oden's language, deals with his descent from the heavenly realms in his divine glory to come to earth and die on behalf of the world. This lowliness was reflected in every dimension of Jesus' Incarnation and earthly life, from his birth to his life and ministry. The culmination of this lowliness and humility is revealed in his passion and death on Calvary. His death may be understood through various dimensions which enable us to understand better the nature of our salvation in him: his death was a ransom for us, the propitiation for our sins, a substitutionary sacrifice in our place, a victory over the devil and death itself, and a reconciliation between God and humankind.

Our objective for this segment, *His Humiliation and Death*, is to enable you to see that:

- The humiliation of Jesus Christ is represented by his descent from the heavenly realms in his glory to come to earth to suffer and die on behalf of the world.

- Jesus revealed his lowliness and humility in every dimension of his Incarnation, in his birth and throughout his life and ministry.

- The culmination of this lowliness and humility is revealed in the passion and death of Jesus Christ.

- The death of Jesus may be understood through various dimensions which enable us to understand the blessings his suffering provided to the world. These include the concept of Jesus' death as a ransom for us, as a propitiation for our sins, as a substitutionary sacrifice in our place, as a victory over the devil and death itself, and as a reconciliation between God and humankind.

- The Nicene Creed unequivocally confesses that our Lord Jesus Christ died and was buried for our sins. This was the culmination of our Lord's humiliation upon earth in his descent from his heavenly, preexistent glory.

Summary of Segment 1

Video Segment 1 Outline

By means of a tree, we were made debtors to God. Likewise, by means of a tree [the cross], we can obtain the remission of our debt.
~ Irenaeus (c. 180, E/W), 1.545. David W. Bercot, ed. *A Dictionary of Early Christian Beliefs*. Peabody, MA: Hendrickson Publishers, 1998. p. 184.

I. **The *Humiliation* of Jesus Christ**

Phil. 2.6-8 - . . . who, though he was in the form of God, did not count equality with God a thing to be grasped, [7] but made himself nothing, taking the form of a servant,[a] being born in the likeness of men. [8] And being found in human form, he humbled himself by becoming obedient to the point of death, even death on a cross.

Gal. 4.4-5 - But when the fullness of time had come, God sent forth his Son, born of woman, born under the law, [5] to redeem those who were under the law, so that we might receive adoption as sons.

A. Humiliation in the Incarnation: the self-emptying of Jesus Christ

   1. He gave up his equality with God.

      a. Giving up the presence of the Father and the Spirit

      b. Form of spirit and infinite glory

   2. He made himself nothing and took the form of a servant (in human likeness).

      a. Born of a woman in dramatically humble surroundings

      b. Raised in anonymity (no one knew who he was for the majority of his life)

c. Yielded his will without limit to the Father

   (1) John 4.34

   (2) John 6.38

   (3) Matt. 26.39

3. As a human being, he humbled himself becoming obedient to the point of death on the cross.

   a. He was born under the law and lived subject to it.

      (1) He was circumcised.

         (a) Gen. 17.12

         (b) Lev. 12.3

         (c) Luke 2.21

      (2) He was brought to the Temple for his mother's time of purification, Luke 2.22-39.

      (3) He fulfilled both the letter and spirit of the Law in his own person, Matt. 5.17-18.

   b. He surrendered the independent use of his divine attributes.

      (1) He was wholly dependent on his Father, John 5.19-20.

      (2) He strictly and wholeheartedly obeyed the Father's commandment in every particular.

         (a) John 5.30

         (b) John 8.28

         (c) John 12.49

         (d) John 14.10

The cross was to express grace by the letter "T."
~ Barnabas (c. 70-130, E), 1.143. Ibid. p. 96.

B. Humiliation in his death: the significance of Jesus' death

Christ is called a Sheep and a Lamb who was to be slain. . . . Christ is also called a Stone. . . . He Himself is both Judge and King.
~ Cyprian (c. 250, W), 5.521-5.527. Ibid. p. 370.

1. It is critical as the *central doctrine in apostolic witness and spirituality*.

    a. 1 Cor. 15.3-8

    b. Gal. 6.14

    c. Rom. 1.16

    d. 1 Cor. 1.22-24

    e. 1 Cor. 2.2

    f. Gal. 2.20

    g. Gal. 5.24

    h. 2 Cor. 4.8-10

2. It is critical for its *dramatic preeminence in the Holy Scriptures*.

    a. Jesus claimed this was the heart of the OT scriptural theme.
        (1) Luke 24.27
        (2) Luke 24.44-45

b. It ranked among the critical subjects researched by the OT prophets, 1 Pet. 1.10-12.

3. It is critical as the *clear reason for his Incarnation*.

   a. Heb. 2.14-15

   b. 1 John 3.5

   c. Matt. 20.28

4. It is critical for it appears to be *the compelling theme of heaven*.

   a. Luke 9.30-31

   b. Rev. 5.8-12

II. The Meaning of Jesus' Death

A. Jesus died as *a ransom for many*.

   1. The biblical evidence

      a. Matt. 20.28

It is impossible to teach the Father except by His Son Jesus Christ.
~ Cyprian (c. 250, W), 5.542. Ibid. p. 574.

b. Gal. 3.13

c. 1 Tim. 2.5-6

d. 1 Pet. 1.18

2. Picture: lost souls as in a slave market, bound, subject to domination and abuse, held in bondage

   a. Ezek. 18.4

   b. Rom. 7.14

3. Through his death, Jesus liberates the captives from the tyranny of the devil and sin, purchases us by his own blood and becomes our new Owner and Master."

   a. 1 Cor. 7.23

   b. Heb. 9.12

   c. Rev. 5.9

B. Jesus died as *a propitiation for our sins*.

1. The biblical evidence

By believing in Him you will live. But by disbelieving, you will be punished. For "he that is disobedient to the Son will not see life."
~ Apostolic Constitutions (compiled c. 390, E), 7.449. Ibid. p. 575.

a. Rom. 3.25-26

b. Heb. 2.17

c. Heb. 9.5

d. 1 John 2.2

2. Picture: the Ark of the Covenant, which was called a propitiation ("mercy seat")

   a. Exod. 25.17-22 (cf. Heb. 9.5)

   b. Lev. 16.15

   c. The transgression of sin is covered, and pardoned because propitiation provides a way that a righteous God may justly forgive the transgressor.

   d. The propitiation affirmed God's righteous anger against sin, covered the sin of the transgressor, and allowed God to be merciful to the penitent sinner.

   e. The propitiation allows God to affirm his infinite holiness while, at the very same time, pardon the guilty sinner: his righteousness is not compromised in the display of mercy.

3. Through his death, Jesus becomes our propitiation, he himself in his own death becomes our all-sufficient sacrifice for propitiation.

   a. Rom. 5.9

   b. 1 John 2.2

   c. 1 John 4.10

C. Jesus died as *a substitutionary sacrifice (our Passover)*.

   1. The biblical evidence

      a. Isa. 53.5-6

      b. Rom. 8.3

      c. 2 Cor. 5.21

      d. Gal. 3.13

      e. Eph. 5.2

      f. Heb. 10.12-14

Because of the love He had for us, Jesus Christ our Lord gave His blood for us by the will of God. He gave His flesh for our flesh, and His soul for our souls.
~ Clement of Rome (c. 96, W), 1.18. Ibid. p. 42.

g. 1 Pet. 2.24

h. 1 Pet. 3.18

2. Picture

   a. The Passover Lamb of the Exodus story (Exod. 12) where the life of an innocent sacrifice is substituted for the life (*in the place of, instead of*) of the other, cf. Exod. 12.11-13

   b. The sacrifice of Isaac, where in the place of Isaac, a ram was substituted *in place of, instead of* Isaac, Gen. 22.13

3. Through his death, Jesus becomes our Paschal Lamb, the one whose own body absorbs and takes the punishment for our lawlessness, iniquity, and transgression, (*Christus Victum*: Christ, the Victim for us).

   a. 1 Cor. 5.7

   b. 1 Pet. 1.19-20

   c. Rev. 5.12

D. Jesus died in order to *destroy the devil and his work*.

   1. The biblical evidence

God had foretold that this seed would proceed from the woman, and that he would trample on the head of the devil.
~ Cyprian (c. 250, W), 5.553. Ibid. p. 594.

a. Ps. 68.18

b. Matt. 12.29

c. John 12.31-33

d. Rom. 14.7-9

e. Col. 2.15

f. Heb. 2.14-15

g. 1 John 3.8

2. Picture: through his own death, Jesus destroyed the one who has the power of death (the devil).

a. Isa. 25.8

b. Hos. 13.14

c. 1 Cor. 15.54-55

d. 2 Tim. 1.10

3. Through his death, Jesus destroys the devil, ending any legitimate right he has on humankind, being totally disarmed in his ability to lie, accuse, enslave, and destroy those who were legitimately blamed by him before the Father, Rev. 12.9-10.

E. Jesus died as *a reconciliation between God and creation (including humankind)*.

1. The biblical evidence

    a. Rom. 5.10

    b. 2 Cor. 5.18-21

    c. Eph. 2.16

    d. Col. 1.20

    e. Rom. 8.19-23

2. Picture: hostility and bitterness between two parties, having it removed by the settling of the accounts

    a. Isa. 52.7

    b. Isa. 57.19

Our Lord Jesus Christ endured man's condition on our behalf, so that He could destroy all sin and furnish us with the provision necessary for our entrance into eternal life.
~ Phileas (c. 307, E), 6.162. Ibid. p. 47.

3. Through his death, Jesus effects a reconciliation and peace between God and his creation; he brings to a final and lasting conclusion the alienation between God and humankind, 2 Cor. 5.18-20

Conclusion

» Jesus Christ in his descent from the heavenly realms humbled himself in his Incarnation and death.

» Through his work on the Cross, Jesus has laid the foundation for our faith, worship, and witness to the world.

» Jesus' death has been historically understood through the dimensions of a ransom sacrifice, a propitiation for our sins, a vicarious or substitutionary offering in our place, a triumph over Satan's hold on us through death, and a reconciliation between God and humankind.

Segue 1

Student Questions and Response

Please take as much time as you have available to answer these and other questions that the video brought out. In many ways, the humility and lowliness of our Lord constitutes the heart and soul of our personal ethic of the Kingdom of God. We are called to suffer with him, to bear our cross daily, and follow him. Only if we experience the fellowship of his sufferings can we fully be liberated as his vessels of worship and witness. The significance of the cross cannot be overestimated for Christian leadership or effective urban ministry. Answer the following questions with an eye to apply these truths as the Spirit leads. Be clear and concise in your reasoning and support your answers with biblical proofs.

1. What is the meaning of the phrase "self-emptying of Jesus Christ?" In other words, what specifically did Jesus "empty" himself of in his Incarnation and ministry on earth?

2. How did the life and ministry of Jesus demonstrate his servanthood, humility, and lowliness? What are the implications of this for our own lives of discipleship and ministry today?

3. What is the relationship between Jesus humbling himself and him surrendering the "independent use" of his divine attributes while on earth?

4. Why is the death of Jesus so important for an overall understanding of Incarnation?

5. How are we to understand the death of Jesus as a *ransom sacrifice* for the world? Explain your answer.

6. What does it mean that Jesus' death is a *propitiation* for our sins?

7. In what ways does Jesus' death parallel for us the meaning of the *Passover* and substitutionary sacrifice?

8. What are the characteristics of conflict and struggle shown between Jesus' death and the devil, in other words, in what way did the death of Jesus destroy the devil's work?

9. How does the death of Jesus reconcile God with his creation and with humankind, even as both have been so dramatically affected by sin and the curse?

Jesus, the Messiah and Lord of All: He Died

Segment 2: Alternate Views on the Meaning of Jesus' Death

Rev. Dr. Don L. Davis

The death of Jesus has been understood in various ways throughout Christian history. These theories of the atonement each focus on a particular dimension of salvation, and taken together they enable us to gain an even greater understanding and appreciation of the significance of Jesus' death for us. Jesus' death and its meaning has been viewed as 1) an example, 2) a demonstration of God's love, 3) a demonstration of God's justice, 4) a victory over the forces of evil and sin, and 5) a satisfaction of God's honor. While none of these theories in and of themselves fully explains Jesus' death, each contains truths which can enhance our understanding of its larger meaning and truth.

Our objective for this segment, *Alternate Views on the Meaning of Jesus' Death*, is to enable you to see that:

- The death of Jesus has been understood in various ways throughout Christian history.

Summary of Segment 2

- The various theories of the atonement which have developed in the Church over the centuries each focus on a particular dimension of salvation, and taken together they enable us to gain an even greater understanding and appreciation of the significance of Jesus' death for us.

- Some of the major theories regarding the meaning and implication of Jesus' death include seeing his death as 1) an example, 2) a demonstration of God's love, 3) a demonstration of God's justice, 4) a victory over the forces of evil and sin, and 5) a satisfaction of God's honor.

- While none of these theories in and of themselves fully explains Jesus' death, each contains truth which can enhance our understanding of its larger meaning and truth.

Video Segment 2 Outline

I. **View One: Jesus' Death Was an *Example* (Unitarians).**

In no other way could we have learned the things of God, unless our Master, existing as the Word, had become man. For no other being had the power of revealing to us the things of the Father.
~ Irenaeus (c. 180, E/W), 1.526. David W. Bercot, ed. *A Dictionary of Early Christian Beliefs.* Peabody, MA: Henrickson Publishers, 1998. p. 43.

A. Authors and arguments of those who hold *Example* view:

1. Faustus and Laelius Socinius, 16th century theologians, and modern-day Unitarians

2. Jesus' example is our pattern for what it means to have a total love for God, which is needed for salvation.

3. The central biblical text: 1 Pet. 2.21

4. We are inspired by Jesus' personal sense of sacrifice and love; this level of love which Jesus shows can be done by all of us–it is possible.

B. The case against the *Example* view:

1. It ignores all of the Scriptures which point to Jesus' death as propitiation, sacrifice, ransom, and so on.

2. It ignores the fact that Jesus' death can be displayed *both* as sacrificial offering *and* as an example for us to follow, 1 Pet. 2.21-25.

C. What truth can we glean from this view?

1. Jesus did die as an example for us to follow.

2. We are to be conformed to the death of Jesus for the sake of caring for others and preaching the Good News.

3. We ought never overly simplify Jesus' misery: he didn't die metaphorically to teach an object lesson, but personally to redeem us to God, 1 Pet. 3.18.

II. **View Two: Jesus' Death as a Demonstration of God's Love (*Moral Influence Theory*)**

A. Authors and arguments of those who hold the *Moral Influence* view:

1. Advocates of this view:

    a. Peter Abelard

My brothers, do not say any evil thing against the One who was crucified. Do not treat with scorn the stripes by which everyone may be healed, even as we [Christians] are healed.
~ Justin Martyr (c. 160, E), 1.268. Ibid. p. 42.

b. Horace Bushnell (1802-1876)

2. God is love: his justice, wrath, vengeance, and holiness are not our most fundamental problem, *but our attitude toward him.*

3. The difficulty in being in fellowship with God lies in us, *not in God himself.*

   a. We are unaware of his love for us.

   b. We do not understand that our sin has brought him grief.

   c. We may fear that he will never receive us again.

   d. We may blame God for the evil things that happens to us and others.

4. Christ's dying reveals just how much God truly loves us and desires to relate to us; it becomes clear evidence of his love and can then eliminate all excuses for not coming to him.

5. Biblical texts:

   a. John 15.13

   b. Rom. 5.8

c. Eph. 2.4-5

B. The case against the *Moral Influence* view:

1. It pretends that God's holiness and justice expresses no wrath.

2. It tends to be overly sentimental: "if people only knew how much God loved them, they would all run to him with open arms!"

3. It inflates the meaning of God's love at the expense of his holiness.

C. What truth can we glean from this view?

1. Jesus' death is a remarkable demonstration of God's love for us, John 3.16.

2. Jesus' death is simultaneously a demonstration of God's wrath against sin, 1 John 2.2.

3. The love of God demonstrated on the cross should move us to seek him, and not allow us to think we can go scot free if we ignore his offer, Rom. 2.3-5.

III. View Three: Jesus' Death as a Demonstration of Divine Justice (*Governmental Theory*)

A. Authors and arguments of those who hold *Governmental* view:

When our Lord arose from the place of the dead, and trampled death under foot, and bound the strong one, and set man free, then the whole creation saw clearly that for man's sake the Judge was condemned.
~ Melito (c. 170), 8.756. Ibid. p. 42.

1. Advocates of this view: Hugo Grotius, a lawyer (1583-1645)

2. The righteous God has established laws, and sin violates those laws.

3. Although God has a right to punish sin, he doesn't have to do so.

4. God acts in order to maintain "the interests of government," not necessarily to punish every specific disobedience of his laws.

    a. He acts with the best interests of humankind.

    b. He provides for the possibility of forgiveness (if he chooses to do so) and establishes a stable structure for him to rule.

5. Jesus' death shows us what God's righteous justice will do to us if we keep on sinning.

    a. Christ's misery can convince us that sin doesn't pay.

    b. We can be forgiven if we repent, and God's government of his world will be kept secure.

B. The case against the *Governmental* view:

1. No biblical or scriptural references to back it up (only a misapplication of Isa. 42.21).

2. Purely logical argument: claims made and other arguments given which flow from those claims

3. It inflates the meaning of God's love at the expense of his holiness.

C. What truth can we glean from this view?

1. Jesus' death did affect for him the rulership of the universe, Rom. 14.7-9.

2. The power of Satan's dominion has been shattered through the death of Jesus Christ, Heb. 2.14.

3. Unbiblical views which offer no scriptural understanding will never be able to explain adequately the meaning of Jesus' death, Isa. 8.20.

IV. View Four: Jesus' Death as a Victory over the Forces of Sin and Evil (*Ransom Theory*)

A. Authors and arguments of those who hold the *Ransom* view:

1. Advocates of this view:

   a. Early Church father, Origen; (his view dominated the earliest perspective of the Church; because of this early belief, it is called the "classic view")

In the last times, the Son was made a man among men, and He re-formed the human race. However, He destroyed and conquered man's enemy. So He gave to His handiwork victory against the adversary.
~ Irenaeus (c. 180, E/W), 1.495.
Ibid. p. 43.

b. Gustaf Aulen: *Christus Victor: An Historical Study of Three Main Types of the Idea of the Atonement*

2. The entire universe is caught up in a cosmic drama: the *forces of good* are doing battle against the *forces of evil*.

3. In this battle, Satan gained control of the world and its inhabitants.

4. The devil now has legal rights over humanity; a ransom must be paid to the devil to liberate its inhabitants.

   a. Biblical citations:
      (1) Matt. 20.28
      (2) Mark 10.45

   b. God does not require (nor would he accept such a ransom).

   c. The devil required the soul of Jesus as payment for the captives of the world.

5. The devil was mistaken; having released the souls of humanity through the payment of Jesus' soul, he was stunned because Jesus rose from the dead!

6. Satan misperceived Jesus' mighty power; he lost all humanity, and Jesus too, through his death and resurrection.

B. The case against the *Ransom* view:

1. The Bible does not teach that a ransom needed to be paid to the devil for the liberation of humankind.

2. Christ died *in our place* to liberate us from the penalty of our sins (i.e., the curse of the law), Gal. 3.13.

3. Christ's propitiation and suffering for our sin debt and punishment crushed the power of sin to hold us in every way (not as some debt that required payment to Satan), Heb. 2.14.

4. His substitution provided the redemption from the curse's bondage, not payment to the devil.

C. What truth can we glean from this view?

1. Jesus' death is the climax of God's warfare against evil, death, and the forces of the curse, 1 John 3.8.

2. Jesus' death does represent a complete destruction of the Devil's ability to accuse, control us through the power of death, and blame us as unworthy sinners in the presence of God, 1 Pet. 5.8-10.

3. We do triumph over the forces of evil through what Jesus accomplished on the cross; the devil simply had no rights to force anything upon us, 2 Cor. 2.14.

By His own passion, He rescued us from offenses and sins.
~ Clement of Alexandria (c. 195, E), 2.257. Ibid. p. 44.

V. View Five: Jesus' Death as Giving to God Due Compensation (*Satisfaction Theory*)

A. Authors and arguments of those who hold the *Satisfaction* view:

1. Advocates of this view: early Church father, Anselm. *Cur Deus Homo*? (Why God Human?)

    a. Sought to give an answer to why God became a human being

    b. Stresses that something in God's nature demanded it (not as a payment to the Devil, i.e., Ransom view)

2. Sin is not giving to God what he is worthy of; it is *dishonoring* God by not providing God with his due honor and glory.

3. Our problem: we must give God back what we've stolen from him.

    a. We have to restore what we have taken.

    b. We have injured him *on top of what we've taken*; we owe God *compensation* or *punitive damages* (those payments given *on top of what was originally owed*).

4. The solution: pay it ourselves (*by being punished*) or God accept compensation from another *for us*

5. Only God himself could pay such a satisfaction back: only a God-man could both *receive our punishment and make adequate compensation worthy of God himself.*

6. Biblical support:

    a. Heb. 2.17

    b. Lev. 6.30

    c. Rom. 5.10

    d. Eph. 2.16

    e. Col. 1.21

B. The case against the *Satisfaction* view:

1. Intriguing ideas: lines up with Christ's role as being a perfect mediator between God and humankind, able to satisfy God's demands for our sins

    a. He paid our debt voluntarily, John 10.17-18.

    b. He satisfied God's honor vicariously (as a substitute), Heb. 2.9.

2. Language is economic: the language of *satisfaction* is certainly a major element in the meaning of Christ's death, 1 John 2.2.

3. Tends to reduce Jesus' death down to legal-like requirements, many of the other dimensions of Christ's death do not seem to get as much coverage or attention in this view

C. What truth can we glean from this view?

1. Jesus' death satisfies once and for all the righteous demands of God against us because of our sins' offense to God, Rom. 5.9-11.

2. Jesus' death is infinite in its value; his death is so effective he could die once for all and cover the sacrifice needed for us, Heb. 10.10-14.

3. Only the death of Jesus can possibly settle the sin question for us; no amount of ethical reform or godly sorrow will suffice, Gal. 3.11-13.

VI. Concluding Thoughts on Differing Views of the Atonement

A. All views contain elements of truth.

1. Jesus' death *did* provide us with an example of what it means to live for God.

2. Jesus' death *did* demonstrate the love of God for us.

3. Jesus' death *did* reveal the terrible consequences of sin, and show God's holy demands in his law and rule.

4. Jesus' death *did* destroy the forces of Satan and death, and liberate God's people to live free in Christ.

5. Jesus' death *did* satisfy the holiness and honor of God in regard to our sin and transgression.

B. No single view captures the full breadth of revelation of what Jesus accomplished on Calvary.

C. Only the Scriptures can give a clear, final, and redemptive understanding of what the death of Jesus means.

D. Remember Paul's warning!

Gal. 1.6-9 - I am astonished that you are so quickly deserting him who called you in the grace of Christ and are turning to a different gospel– [7] not that there is another one, but there are some who trouble you and want to distort the gospel of Christ. [8] But even if we or an angel from heaven should preach to you a gospel contrary to the one we preached to you, let him be accursed. [9] As we have said before, so now I say again: If anyone is preaching to you a gospel contrary to the one you received, let him be accursed.

Conclusion

> » Throughout Church history different views of Jesus' death on the cross have emerged.

> » Five major views have dominated throughout Church history, each containing specific dimensions of truth regarding the meaning of his crucifixion for us.

> » Jesus' death offers us an example of our dedication to God, demonstrates God's love for us, reveals God's perfect justice, conquers the forces of evil and sin, satisfies God's honor, and reconciles creation and humankind to God.

> » No one theory or view can comprehend the majesty and blessing of his death for us.

Segue 2

Student Questions and Response

The following questions were designed to help you review the material in the second video segment. What will be important in your mastering this material is your ability to carefully and specifically review the theories of the atonement, understand the arguments and evidence of each, and be able to evaluate them according to the Scriptures. Use the questions to carefully review the various positions, and be charitable; listen to all positions and seek to understand them before you criticize them. Be clear, concise, and biblical.

1. In what sense does the death of Jesus Christ serve as an example to us? Why would it be insufficient to view his death *only* as an example?

2. Explain the arguments and evidence for the view of Jesus' death as a demonstration of God's love. What problems emerge if we seek to make this the *only* credible view of Jesus' death?

3. How does the death of Jesus demonstrate God's sense of justice and government in this world? Why is this view insufficient as the *only credible view* regarding Jesus' death?

4. In what way does the death of Jesus provide victory over the forces of evil, of the devil, and even death itself? Can this view, like the others, be understood as the *only credible* perspective or even *the major* perspective on the death of Jesus?

5. Outline the major elements in the *satisfaction theory* of the atonement. Can this view serve as the most accurate portrayal of the meaning of Jesus' death?

6. Why is it important to glean truth from each of the various views of the atonement to help us understand *the full meaning* of the death of Jesus Christ? What place should humility play in our consideration of the various views?

7. Discuss the statement: "No single view captures the full breadth of revelation of what Jesus accomplished on Calvary." Why must we always weigh any theory of the atonement against the Scriptures in order to understand its value as an explanation of the cross?

CONNECTION

This lesson focuses upon the humiliation of Jesus Christ in the Incarnation and ministry, and in the meaning of the death of Jesus Christ as it relates to our salvation and redemption. In some ways, the truths associated with these topics constitute both warp and woof of God's loom of the Kingdom of God. All threads of God's revelation of himself as Maker and Redeemer are connected to the person of Jesus on Nazareth, his perfect life and substitutionary death on the cross. Our obligation as Christian leaders on these matters is crystal clear: we must not only understand these truths from a biblical and historical perspective, we must also reflect and embody them in our lives and ministries. *We* are to die, even as he did, and we are to suffer, even as our Lord suffered for us. Carefully consider these implications as you review the key concepts below.

Summary of Key Concepts

- The humiliation of Jesus Christ, to use the theologian Oden's language, deals with his descent from the heavenly realms in his divine glory to come to earth and die on behalf of the world.

- The lowliness of Jesus was reflected in every dimension of his Incarnation and earthly life, from his birth to his life and ministry. The culmination of this lowliness and humility is revealed in his passion and death at Calvary.

- Jesus' death may be understood through various dimensions which enable us to understand better the nature of our salvation in him: his death was a ransom for us, the propitiation for our sins, a substitutionary sacrifice in our place, a victory over the devil and death itself, and a reconciliation between God and humankind.

- Various theories of the atonement of Jesus have been introduced and argued for throughout Christian history. These various theories focus on particular dimensions of salvation, and taken together they enable us to gain an even greater understanding and appreciation of the significance of Jesus' death for us.

- Jesus' death and its meaning has been viewed as 1) an example, 2) a demonstration of God's love, 3) a demonstration of God's justice, 4) a victory over the forces of evil and sin, and 5) a satisfaction of God's honor.

- While none of these theories in and of themselves fully explains Jesus' death, each contains truths which can enhance our understanding of its larger meaning and truth.

Student Application and Implications

Now is the time for you to discuss with your fellow students your questions about the humiliation of Jesus and the culmination of that humility and lowliness through his death on the cross. As mentioned above, it is arguably one of the most important topics that we as Christian leaders can pursue. Understanding the meaning of the death of Jesus is the heart of our Christian confession and the pulse of our Christian service. Undoubtedly, certain questions have come to mind as you have discussed and studied these ideas. What particular issues have come to the light as you have studied the death of Christ so far? The questions below are given to provoke your own, more contextualized questions about Jesus' death.

* How should the self-emptying of Jesus Christ affect our attitudes about our own lives and ministries as we go forth to answer God's call on our lives?

* To what extent is Jesus' lowliness and humility a model for us, and in what ways is his submission to the Father *unique to him alone*? Explain your answer.

* How do you currently apply the following instruction of Jesus to your own life and ministry? Luke 9.23-25 - And he said to all, "If anyone would come after me, let him deny himself and take up his cross daily and follow me. [24] For whoever would save his life will lose it, but whoever loses his life for my sake will save it. [25] For what does it profit a man if he gains the whole world and loses or forfeits himself?"

* In what way should we incorporate texts like Philippians 2.5-11 and 2 Corinthians 8.9 into our understanding of Christian discipleship and ministry?

* Of all of the pictures given of Jesus' death and its meaning for our lives, which do you personally find most powerful for your life and ministry?

* Finish the following statement: "The one thing that still troubles me about my own grasp of Jesus' death that I need to learn more about is _____."

* What are the ways in which you will seek to make the death of Jesus more real in your life and ministry? Why is the Lord's Supper such an important ongoing practice to help us appreciate the meaning of his passion and death on our behalf?

* How might we better teach the humility and death of Jesus in our discipling, preaching, and teaching? Brainstorm together ways you can reemphasize the passion of Christ in your church life.

A Bloodless Faith?

Many modern presentations of the Gospel tend to focus on the *ethics of Christian faith*, that is, on the character of relationships and virtues associated with the Christian faith and not on the passion of Christ, his humility, sufferings, and death on Calvary. Many mega-churches associated with church growth and more contemporary approaches to Christian worship and witness are explicit in their insistence that dealing constantly with the violent and tortuous themes of death and sacrifice is ineffective in winning others. Churches that are growing deal with "real" issues, address people's concrete personal anxieties and worries, and concentrate on the quality of life issues that most mainstream Westerners worry about day to day. Our entree into their lives will not begin, it is argued, with tough teachings on the shed blood of Christ but more ground-floor issues like work, family, and self-development. *At what point ought we to introduce to genuine seekers of God the teaching surrounding the cross of Christ?* Is it the ground floor or the end game of Christian witness? Explain your answer.

Politically Incorrect Theories

 In a world that is fragmented by political strife, many evangelical preachers have determined not to use the military metaphors of the NT to communicate the faith. Although much of Jesus' and the apostles' language uses military symbolism to make sense of Jesus' life and mission, including his death on the cross, few teachers seek to follow their example today. Some have gone so far as to suggest that using these pictures to communicate the nature of Christian faith would be a mistake at a time like this, where religious bigotry, *jihads*, and intolerance and violence is taking place in the name of gods and religion. The image of war is a horrible reality, and one that we ought not use without genuine caution. Others would argue that these images are *divinely inspired*, given in order to enable us to understand the *core meaning of redemption in Christ*. In other words, the image of war was selected because it communicates better than any other way the *true nature of spirituality*; Jesus came to *destroy the works of the devil* (1 John 3.8). The universe is *at war*, and no amount of squeamishness will change this fact. *Is using the image of war as a theory of atonement valid for us today?*

The Resurrection, Not the Passion

 It is clear that the NT focuses on the nature of the resurrection as the central teaching of the Christian faith. First Corinthians chapter fifteen is the Magna Carta of Christian doctrine: apart from the resurrection Christianity would be a futile and false affirmation that changes nothing practically or spiritually for those deluded enough to embrace it. Some have argued that our focus should be upon the triumph of the resurrection and the victory of our Lord's work, rather than on the death of Jesus and the humiliation and violence associated with it. *Easter*, not *Good Friday*, is the defining event of Christian witness, these would argue, and would further state that a kind of obsession with the death and violence of Calvary is neither spiritually helpful nor psychologically healthy. It is clear, however, that the apostles' challenged believers in the early Church to model their attitudes and conduct on the basis of the sufferings of Christ and his death (e.g., Phil. 2.5-11; 1 Pet. 2.21ff; Gal. 2.20). Still, many tend to focus on the abundance, prosperity, health, and riches of the Christian experience rather than the fellowship of his sufferings in order to be conformed to his death (Phil. 3.10). *What is the relationship between emphasizing the resurrection of our Lord and his sufferings as it relates to a true communication of the Christian faith?*

The humiliation of Jesus Christ, to use the theologian Oden's language, deals with his descent from the heavenly realms in his divine glory to come to earth and die on behalf of the world. This lowliness was reflected in every dimension of Jesus' Incarnation and earthly life, from his birth to his life and ministry. The culmination of this lowliness and humility is revealed in his passion and death on Calvary. His death may be understood through various dimensions which enable us to understand better the nature of our salvation in him: his death was a ransom for us, the propitiation for our sins, a substitutionary sacrifice in our place, a victory over the devil and death itself, and a reconciliation between God and humankind.	Restatement of the Lesson's Thesis
The death of Jesus has been understood in various ways throughout Christian history. These theories of the atonement each focus on a particular dimension of salvation, and taken together they enable us to gain an even greater understanding and appreciation of the significance of Jesus' death for us. Jesus' death and its meaning has been viewed as 1) an example, 2) a demonstration of God's love, 3) a demonstration of God's justice, 4) a victory over the forces of evil and sin, and 5) a satisfaction of God's honor. While none of these theories in and of themselves fully explains Jesus' death, each contains truth which can enhance our understanding of its larger meaning and truth.	

If you are interested in pursuing some of the ideas of *Jesus, the Messiah and Lord of All: He Died*, you might want to give these books a try:
 	
    Brown, Raymond E. *The Death of the Messiah*. New York: Doubleday, 1994.
 	
    Kiehl, Erich H. *The Passion of Our Lord*. Grand Rapids: Baker Book House, 1990.
 	
    Lohse, Eduard. *History of the Suffering and Death of Jesus Christ*. Philadelphia: Fortress Press, 1967.
 	
    Stott, John. *The Cross of Christ*. Downers Grove, IL: InterVarsity, 1986.
	Resources and Bibliographies

The humility and death of Jesus Christ is so central to faith and practice that we as Christian leaders must relate its insights and truths to our lives and ministries constantly. How you flesh this truth out in your own life will determine your effectiveness in articulating its relevance in your own church and witness. How God might want you to change or alter your ministry approach based on these truths is	Ministry Connections

largely dependent on your ability to hear what the Holy Spirit is saying to you about where you are, where your ministry and pastoral leadership is, where the members of your church are, and what specifically God is calling you to do right now, if anything, about these truths. Plan to spend good time this week meditating on the meaning of the death of Christ, and how your own life needs to become better informed and enriched by its truth. Furthermore, as you consider your ministry project for this module, you can possibly use it to connect it to the truth of Jesus' lowliness and death in a practical and direct way for your audience, whomever you choose to share your insights with.

Above all, we must seek the Lord's own application for us related to Christ's humility and death. Seek the Lord's face this week for his insight, and come back next week ready to share your insights with the other learners in your class.

Counseling and Prayer

As the Lord speaks to you, know that he will give you opportunity to pray and to be prayed for in the areas of growth that are needful for you today. Perhaps there are some specific needs which the Holy Spirit has surfaced through your study and discussion of this material on the death of Jesus. Seek out a partner in prayer who can share your burdens and heart, and lift up your burdens together before the Lord. Of course, your instructor is extremely open to walking with you on this, and your church leaders, especially your pastor, may be specially equipped to help you answer any difficult questions arising from your reflection on this study. Be open to God and allow him to lead you as he determines. Concentrate on your need to let the mind of Christ dwell in you, and for the death of Jesus to become more and more real in every dimension of your Christian character and witness.

Scripture Memory

1 Peter 2.21-24

Reading Assignment

To prepare for class, please visit *www.tumi.org/books* to find next week's reading assignment, or ask your mentor.

Other Assignments

As usual you ought to come with your reading assignment sheet containing your summary of the reading material for the week. *Also, you must have selected the text for your exegetical project, and turn in your proposal for your ministry project.*

Looking Forward to the Next Lesson

In this lesson, we looked at the humiliation of Jesus Christ in his Incarnation and death. We explored some of the critical dimensions of his death for salvation: as a ransom sacrifice, a propitiation for our sins, as a vicarious or substitutionary offering in our place, as a triumph over Satan's hold on us through death, and as a reconciliation between God and humankind. Jesus' death did offer to us an example of our dedication to God, a demonstration of God's love for us, a demonstration of God's perfect justice, a victory over the forces of evil and sin, and a satisfaction of God's honor. No one theory or view can comprehend the majesty and blessing of his death for us. In our next lesson, we will look at the center of Christology and Christian theology, the resurrection of Jesus, as well as the ascension, and his soon return. Praise God for our Savior and Lord, Jesus, who died and rose to bring salvation to the world, and will return soon to establish God's reign to us. Amen!

Capstone Curriculum

Module 10: God the Son
Reading Completion Sheet

Name _____

Date _____

For each assigned reading, write a brief summary (one or two paragraphs) of the author's main point. (For additional readings, use the back of this sheet.)

Reading 1

Title and Author: _____ Pages _____

Reading 2

Title and Author: _____ Pages _____

LESSON 4

Jesus, the Messiah and Lord of All
He Rose and Will Return

Lesson Objectives

Welcome in the strong name of Jesus Christ! After your reading, study, discussion, and application of the materials in this lesson, you will be able to:

- Explain with Scripture and worthy arguments the various aspects and implications of two events which mark the exaltation of Christ, the resurrection and the ascension.

- Elaborate the key points which show how the resurrection serves as a vindication of Jesus' Messiahship and position as God's Son.

- Articulate the importance and significance of Jesus' ascension which grants to our Savior a position of dignity and authority that allows him to fill all things with his glory.

- Show how the Nicene Creed and its confession gives a clear and persuasive summary of the teaching of the Scriptures on both the resurrection and the ascension, and give the major implications of these great events.

- Outline the final three Christological events referred to in the Nicene Creed on the present and coming ministry of the exalted Christ.

- Argue from both the Scriptures and the Creed about the Second Coming of Christ in glory, and lay out its character and its significance for us in ministry.

- Defend the biblical and creedal affirmations about Jesus' judgment of the nations, and the main elements in the coming reign of Jesus.

- Elaborate the key issues and implications of Christ's return and reign for us as we do ministry in the city.

Devotion

A Vision to Live By

Rom. 13.8-14 - Owe no one anything, except to love each other, for the one who loves another has fulfilled the law. [9] The commandments, "You shall not commit adultery, You shall not murder, You shall not steal, You shall not covet," and any other commandment, are summed up in this word: "You shall love your neighbor as yourself."

[10] Love does no wrong to a neighbor; therefore love is the fulfilling of the law. [11] Besides this you know the time, that the hour has come for you to wake from sleep. For salvation is nearer to us now than when we first believed. [12] The night is far gone; the day is at hand. So then let us cast off the works of darkness and put on the armor of light. [13] Let us walk properly as in the daytime, not in orgies and drunkenness, not in sexual immorality and sensuality, not in quarreling and jealousy. [14] But put on the Lord Jesus Christ, and make no provision for the flesh, to gratify its desires.

It is hard to overestimate how powerful the apostolic witness was in the Roman world shortly after the days of our Lord's resurrection and ascension. The message of Jesus dead, risen, ascended, and returning became more than the wishful thinking of a weird little Jewish sect of deluded followers of a failed rabbi. Instead, the message of the Nazarene became a blazing fire that ignited every village and city where followers of *Yeshua* (Jesus) gathered and spoke. The Holy Spirit transformed the little group of confused and cowering disciples into world-changing messengers of a new order which, at any time, was expected to be unveiled and revealed according to God's own timing and method. What was the vision that ignited the new fellowship, that made them combustible and ready to make the kinds of sacrifices that would propel an entire generation to give witness of Messiah and the hope of eternal life in his name?

Even a cursory read of the book of Acts and the Epistles reveals that the apostles' worldview was that of messengers of an age and its Lord which, at any moment, was about to be unveiled on a corrupt and dying era. They lived as if they believed that this Nazarene was in fact the divine Son of God who had come to make an end of sin, destroy the devil's work, and now was alive and pouring forth on his own his blessings, endowments, and gifts in order that they might represent him. For them, he was truly Lord. At any moment, he could decide to return (by the Father's leave and command), and consummate the work that he began here. They were, in the dry language of the theological schools an *eschatological community*. That is, their entire identity, value system, and worldview was shaped by their conviction that a new world was about to dawn, and that the time was imminent (close by) for its revelation. Any day might be *the* day.

"Besides this you know the time, that the hour has come for you to wake from sleep. For salvation is nearer to us now than when we first believed." Their vision was that Jesus was the Messiah, that he died and rose to ratchet down God's work for creation, that he ascended into heaven and would soon return to establish God's reign in the earth and rule as King. This vision ignited their imaginations and hearts, sustained them in trial, and motivated them to go to the then-known ends of the earth with the good news of Christ. It is an empowering, transforming, and igniting vision, and one which needs to be rediscovered in our day and time.

What we in urban ministry need today is to be captivated again by that life-sustaining and life-transforming vision. It is impossible to ignite someone else if our own embers are smouldering and smoking. Are you convinced that Jesus is the Messiah, that he died for our sins, and that he rose again the third day? Do you believe that he ascended into heaven and will soon return in power and glory to finish the task he began so many centuries ago? Does this story so control your heart and passions that you are willing to make any sacrifice necessary to see it broadcast to the very ends of the earth? If you are willing to receive it in this way, you will join in the wild adventure of the apostles, and extend the influence of their lives into your very home, place of work, and neighborhood. Only a vision so controlling and all-encompassing will give modern day urban disciples a vision that they can live–and die–by.

Nicene Creed and Prayer

After reciting and/or singing the Nicene Creed (located in the Appendix), pray the following prayer:

Eternal God, by raising Jesus from the dead you proclaimed his victory, and by his ascension, you declared him Lord of all. Lift up our hearts to heaven where he lives and reigns with you and the Holy Spirit, one God, now and forever. Amen.

~ Presbyterian Church (U.S.A.) and Cumberland Presbyterian Church.
The Theology and Worship Ministry Unit. **Book of Common Worship**.
Louisville, Ky: Westminster/John Knox Press, 1993. p. 333

Quiz

Put away your notes, gather up your thoughts and reflections, and take the quiz for Lesson 3, *Jesus, the Messiah and Lord of All: He Died.*

Scripture Memorization Review

Review with a partner, write out and/or recite the text for last class session's assigned memory verse: 1 Peter 2.21-24.

Assignments Due

Turn in your summary of the reading assignment for last week, that is, your brief response and explanation of the main points that the authors were seeking to make in the assigned reading (Reading Completion Sheet).

Don't Get Bit by the Prophecy Bug

The relative absence of sermons on the Second Coming of Christ is to be contrasted with the dominance of that message by the apostles. One would be hard-pressed to find a proclamation of Christ by the apostles that did not emphasize (let alone mention!) the coming of Christ. Today, it is possible for biblical preachers and teachers to go for months, even years, without spending any focused attention on the Second Coming of Christ, and, as a rule, it tends to be de-emphasized in our churches. Why do you think so many equate teaching about the coming of Christ with the "prophecy bug," those workshops and seminars which spend inordinate amounts of time trying to attribute biblical symbols to Russia, the Middle East current events, and the latest figure in the news who compares with biblical imagery?

Why "Ascension Sunday"?

In many Protestant churches today, the Ascension is never mentioned. While it is seen as a critical pre-Pentecost event, it is neither focused upon or celebrated as it is in more liturgical traditions like the Catholic, Orthodox, and Anglican traditions. Why haven't Protestant churches tended to recognize the theological and spiritual significance of the Ascension, unlike the more liturgical and sacramental traditions?

Back to the Future

Much of our preaching and teaching today focuses on the present day application of Christian theology and truth. We concentrate on *contemporary meanings*, that is, how can we apply this *today, right now*, in our *current living situation*? How are we as disciples to integrate our understanding of the past, the present, and the future, and as it applies to Christ, what he *did*, what he is *doing*, and what he will *do*? What role does a vision of the future play in Christian discipleship, and how should we as ministers of the Gospel *focus on the future*?

CONTENT

Jesus, the Messiah and Lord of All: He Rose and Will Return

Segment 1: The Resurrection and Ascension of Jesus Christ

Rev. Dr. Don L. Davis

Summary of Segment 1

The various aspects and implications of Christ's exaltation can be comprehended clearly on the basis of two critical salvific events; the resurrection and the ascension of Christ. The resurrection serves as a vindication of Jesus' Messiahship and sonship, and his ascension grants to our Savior a position of dignity and authority that allows him to fill all things with his glory. The *Christ event* (i.e., Jesus' preexistence, life, ministry, death, resurrection, and glory) can be thought of in terms of two movements, a movement of descent (into humiliation), and ascent (into exaltation). The resurrection and ascension are associated directly with Christ's exaltation and glory.

Our objectives for this segment, *The Resurrection and Ascension of Jesus Christ*, is to enable you to see that:

- The various aspects and implications of Christ's exaltation can be comprehended clearly on the basis of two critical salvific events; the resurrection and the ascension of Christ.

- The resurrection serves as a vindication of Jesus' Messiahship and sonship, and his ascension grants to our Savior a position of dignity and authority that allows him to fill all things with his glory.

- The *Christ event* (i.e., Jesus' preexistence, life, ministry, death, resurrection, and glory) can be thought of in terms of two movements, a movement of descent (into humiliation), and ascent (into exaltation). The resurrection and ascension are associated directly with Christ's exaltation and glory.

Let us begin by reciting the relevant portion of the Creed for Lesson four:

"*The third day he rose again according to the Scriptures, ascended into heaven and is seated at the right hand of the Father.* He will come again in glory to judge the living and the dead, and his Kingdom will have no end."

I. The Resurrection of Jesus Christ

A. The centrality of Jesus' resurrection in Christian faith and mission

1. It is the central doctrine in all of Christian faith: (cf. 1 Cor. 15.1-20, "If Christ has not been raised").

    a. The Apostles' proclamation is worthless and our faith in that preaching is worthless, v. 14.

    b. The Apostles misrepresented God, since they lied about God raising Christ from the dead, which in fact he did not do, v. 15.

    c. Our faith is utterly futile, and we are still in our sins, v. 17.

    d. Those who have died as believers in Christ (Greek, "*fallen asleep*") have actually perished.

    e. We are the most pathetic and most pitied of all people because of the deception and error of our hope, v. 19.

2. It was the central historical fact in the preaching of the Apostles.

Video Segment 1 Outline

God has made the Lord Jesus Christ the firstfruits by raising Him from the dead.
~ Clement of Rome (c. 96, W), 1.11. David W. Bercot, ed. *A Dictionary of Early Christian Beliefs*. Peabody, MA: Hendrickson Publishers, 1998. p. 558.

I give you thanks . . . that I can have a part . . . in the resurrection of eternal life, both of soul and body.
~ Martyrdom of Polycarp (c. 135, E), 1.42. Ibid. p. 96.

a. The Apostle Peter

   (1) Acts 2.24

   (2) Acts 2.32

   (3) Acts 3.15

   (4) Acts 5.30

   (5) Acts 10.40

   (6) 1 Pet. 1.21

b. The Apostle Paul

   (1) Acts 13.27-33

   (2) Acts 17.31

   (3) 1 Cor. 15.3-4

   (4) Phil. 3.20-21

3. It constituted the central burning hope which established the Christian community: it was the faith of the early Church, Acts 4.33.

4. It confirmed our Lord's identity as Lord and Christ, as he predicted.

   a. Matt. 12.39-40

   b. John 2.20-22

5. It established the authenticity of the Holy Scriptures, which prophesied of the Messiah's resurrection, Acts 2.23-28.

B. The creedal language and its biblical support

1. "He was resurrected on the Third Day": the historical evidence of the resurrection accounts, Matt. 28.1-15; Mark 16.1-11; Luke 24.1-12; John 20.1-18

   a. The historical evidence that *Jesus actually died is abundant and clear.*

      (1) Crucified and pierced, John 19.33-37

      (2) Joseph of Arimethea's request and granting of Jesus' dead body, Matt. 27.57-58

      (3) Pilate's confirmation through the centurion that Jesus of Nazareth had died, Mark 15.44-45

      (4) The soldier's testimony of Jesus' death, John 19.33

      (5) The testimony of the glorified Jesus, Rev. 1.17-18

2. "According to the Scriptures": the biblical prediction

   a. Paul's quotation of Psalm 2 and Psalm 16 as Scriptures pointing to the resurrection of Jesus Christ, Acts 13.30-37

   b. Paul's defense of his apostleship, Acts 26.22-23

   c. The suffering Servant of Yahweh's certain resurrection, Isa. 53.10-12

   d. An allusion to Jesus' resurrection? Hos. 6.2

e. Jesus compares his resurrection to Jonah's time in the great fish, Matt. 12.40.

f. Jesus explains his suffering and glory to the disciples and the Apostles after his resurrection.

   (1) Luke 24.26

   (2) Luke 24.46

g. Peter's explanation of Psalm 16 as biblical prophecy of Jesus' resurrection, Acts 2.25-32

C. The nature of Jesus' resurrection body

1. His body was an actual corporeal body, neither a phantom nor ghost.

   a. It could be touched and handled, John 20.20.

   b. It bore the marks of his suffering and crucifixion, John 20.24-29.

   c. He could eat food and have nourishment (food and drink), Luke 24.41-43.

2. His body had properties which go beyond our present natural bodies.

   a. Jesus appeared in the midst of the Apostles behind barred doors, John 20.19.

> *We profess our belief that [the flesh of Christ] is sitting at the right hand of the Father in heaven. And we further declare that it will come again from there in all the grandeur of the Father's glory. It is, therefore, just as impossible for us to say that [his flesh] was abolished, as it is for us to maintain that it was sinful.*
> ~ Tertullian (c. 210, W), 3.535. Ibid. p. 559.

b. He appeared unrecognizable to his friends and disciples at times, cf. Luke 24.13-16; John 20.14-15; Mark 16.12.

c. He disappeared from the presence of the disciples, Luke 24.31; John 20.19, 26; Luke 24.51.

d. His body could ascend into the heavenlies, Acts 1.9; Phil. 3.20-21.

3. His body, as the first fruits of the resurrection, is immortal (i.e., without any hint or quality of being able to be corrupted or die).

> *For I know that after His resurrection also, He was still possessed of flesh. And I believe that He is so now.*
> ~ Ignatius (c. 105, E), 1.87. Ibid. p. 558.

a. He cannot die again.

(1) Luke 20.36

(2) Rom. 6.9-10

(3) Rev. 1.18

b. He is the pattern for all who will believe after him.

(1) 1 Cor. 15.20

(2) Phil. 3.20-21

D. Theological implications of the resurrection

> *Jesus Christ, the faithful witness, the firstborn from the dead, Rev. 1.5*

1. While there is no direct testimony of Jesus' resurrection (eye-witness testimony who *witnessed the resurrection within the tomb with Jesus*) there is ample and satisfactory indirect evidence of its certainty.

a. The empty tomb: *wouldn't a simple credible explanation other than the resurrection account for the fact that it is still empty?*

b. The absence of Jesus' body: *why didn't opposition simply produce the body and crush this sect in one fatal blow?*

c. The abundance of witnesses who saw the Risen Jesus, cf. 1 Cor. 15.3-9: *how would so many arrange to harmonize the details of their lie about Jesus' rising?*

d. The transformation of the disciples: *why would the Apostles risk their very lives for a faith they knew to be false?*

e. The creation of Christian community and faith: *no reason for its existence seems to make sense if Christ did not raise.*

f. The formation of the New Testament: *if Jesus remained in the grave, shouldn't this story, so untrue and fanciful, have fizzled out long before now?*

2. The resurrection is outward sign of confirmation and validation for Jesus' triumph over death, the devil, and all the effects of the curse, 1 Cor. 15.24-28.

3. We ourselves will share in the very same corporeal glory that Jesus currently possesses: our body will be conformed to his pattern exactly.

a. Rom. 8.29

b. 1 Cor. 15.48-49

c. Phil. 3.20-21

d. 1 John 3.1-2

II. The Ascension of Jesus Christ

A. Its importance in Christian worship and mission

1. To fulfill his promise of his return to the Father (John 6.62; 14.2,12; 16.5,10, 28; 20.17) as a vindication of his Messiahship and sonship

2. To pour out the Holy Spirit upon the Church for worship and witness, John 16.7 with Acts 1.8

3. To spread abroad the "spoils" of his divine triumph over the devil and the forces of evil, Eph. 4.8-10

4. To prepare a place (i.e., the New Jerusalem) for his people, John 14.2-3,

5. The assurance of the ongoing presence of Jesus with his people, Matt. 28.20 cf. John 16.7-15

6. As a sign of his Second Coming in glory, Acts 1.9-11

Jesus is still sitting there at the right hand of the Father–man, yet God. He is the last Adam; yet, He is also the original Word. He is flesh and blood, yet His body is purer than ours.
~ Tertullian (c. 210, W), 3.535. Ibid. p. 559.

On the third day, He freely rose again from the dead. He appeared to His disciples as He had been. . . . However, He tarried for forty days, so that they might be instructed by Him in the precepts of life and so that they might learn what they were to teach. Then, in a cloud spread around Him, He was lifted up into heaven–so that as a conqueror, He might bring man to the Father.
~ Cyprian (c. 250, W), 5.468. Ibid. p. 559.

B. The creedal language and its biblical support

1. "He ascended into heaven": the exaltation of the glorified Christ

   a. Most extended accounts: Luke 24.50-51 and Acts 1.6-11

   b. Eph. 1.20

   c. Eph. 4.8-10

   d. Heb. 1.3

   e. Heb. 4.14

   f. Heb. 9.24

2. "Seated at the right hand of the Father": the high position of Messiah Jesus

   a. Matt. 26.64

   b. Acts 2.33-36

   c. Acts 5.31

       d. Eph. 1.20-22

       e. Heb. 10.12

       f. 1 Pet. 3.22

       g. Rev. 3.21

       h. Rev. 22.1

C. Theological implications of the ascension of Jesus Christ

   1. Jesus has been given an exalted place of distinction, authority, and honor before God: he is the Head over all things, Head of the Church.

       a. As the body of Christ, Eph. 1.20-23

       b. As the army of God, Matt. 28.18-20

       c. As Lord of the Harvest, Matt. 9.35-38

   2. Jesus ever lives to fulfill his high priestly role of intercession for us.

       a. His high priestly prayer, John 17

Following His resurrection from the tomb and ascension to the heavenly realm, Christ took His seat at the Father's right hand. Theologians call this "the session" of Christ. Of course, the biblical phrase, "right hand of God," is a human way of referring to God's universal dominion and power. In Eastern cultures the right hand of the sovereign was a position of honor and authority. So when the Bible says Christ is at God's right hand we know, as Calvin put it, that Christ is "installed in the government of heaven and earth" because the statement, "Christ is seated at God's side" is not suggesting that Jesus is resting from His labor. Rather it points to Christ's reign as King and His exercise of divine power over everyone and everything.
~ Bruce A. Demarest, Jesus Christ: The God-Man. Eugene, OR: Wipf and Stock Publishers, 1978, p. 125.

b. His intercession for believers today

   (1) Rom. 8.33-34

   (2) Heb. 7.25

   (3) Heb. 9.24

   (4) 1 John 2.1-2

3. Jesus is ruling all things now as Messiah and Lord, and must reign until all enemies have been placed under his feet at the Second Coming.

   a. The prophetic anticipation of the Messianic King

      (1) Gen. 49.10

      (2) Ps. 89.35-37

      (3) Dan. 7.13-14

      (4) Isa. 9.6-7

   b. Jesus is himself the fulfilment of OT prophecies of the coming King from David's line, Ps. 45.6-7 cf. Heb 1.8.

      (1) Luke 1.31-33

      (2) Heb. 1.1-3

      (3) Rev. 19.16

   c. He is currently reigning as Lord from his exalted place at God's right hand, subduing his enemies and reasserting God's rule through his people, the Church.

      (1) Rom. 14.7-9

      (2) Eph. 1.20-23

d. He is sustaining all things, and functioning as the head and source for all things to his body, the Church, Col. 1.17-18.

e. He must reign until all enemies have been placed under his feet, 1 Cor. 15.24-26.

III. Conclusion: Exalt the Risen and Ascended Lord!

Worship the exalted Christ as the Risen Lord and Christ and you will be *blessed*!

Heb. 1.1-11 - Long ago, at many times and in many ways, God spoke to our fathers by the prophets, [2] but in these last days he has spoken to us by his Son, whom he appointed the heir of all things, through whom also he created the world. [3] He is the radiance of the glory of God and the exact imprint of his nature, and he upholds the universe by the word of his power. After making purification for sins, he sat down at the right hand of the Majesty on high, [4] having become as much superior to angels as the name he has inherited is more excellent than theirs. [5] For to which of the angels did God ever say, "You are my Son, today I have begotten you"? Or again, "I will be to him a father, and he shall be to me a son"? [6] And again, when he brings the firstborn into the world, he says, "Let all God's angels worship him." [7] Of the angels he says, "He makes his angels winds, and his ministers a flame of fire." [8] But of the Son he says, "Your throne, O God, is forever and ever, the scepter of uprightness is the scepter of your kingdom. [9] You have loved righteousness and hated wickedness; therefore God, your God, has anointed you with the oil of gladness beyond your companions." [10] And, "You, Lord, laid the foundation of the earth in the beginning, and the heavens are the work of your hands; [11] they will perish, but you remain; they will all wear out like a garment,"

Confess that Jesus Christ is Lord and you will be *delivered*!

Rom. 10.9-10 - Because, if you confess with your mouth that Jesus is Lord and believe in your heart that God raised him from the dead, you will be saved. [10] For with the heart one believes and is justified, and with the mouth one confesses and is saved.

Acknowledge Jesus Christ as ascended and exalted and you will be *empowered*!

Eph.4.8-10 - Therefore it says, "When he ascended on high he led a host of captives, and he gave gifts to men." [9] (In saying, "He ascended," what does it mean but that he had also descended into the lower parts of the earth? [10] He who descended is the one who also ascended far above all the heavens, that he might fill all things.)

Conclusion

» Two momentous events of Jesus Christ mark the beginning of his exaltation and glory.

» Jesus' resurrection serves as a vindication of his Messiahship and sonship, and his ascension places our Lord in a position of glory, priestly representation, and kingship.

» Jesus must now reign until all enemies have been put under his feet.

Segue 1

Student Questions and Response

Please take as much time as you have available to answer these and other questions that the video brought out. As the central doctrine of the Christian faith, the resurrection stands as the bedrock confession for believers. As a defining symbol of Christ's kingship and victory, the ascension demonstrates the absolute character of Jesus' victory over the world, the flesh, and the devil. Carefully review the biblical teaching through the questions below, and support your objections and claims with Scripture.

1. According to Paul, the resurrection of Jesus is the central doctrine in Christian confession. In Paul's mind, what specifically is also true if Jesus in fact *did not rise from the dead*?

2. In what way did our Lord's resurrection confirm his identity as the Messiah and the Lord? Be specific and give scriptural proofs.

3. According to the language of the Nicene Creed, when precisely did Jesus rise, and what is the source which supports this testimony?

4. List some of the specific evidence included in the historical accounts of the resurrection in the Gospels that testify that Jesus died and rose from the grave. How do you explain some of the apparent differences in the various Gospel accounts regarding the *details of the resurrection*?

5. How do the Gospel accounts describe the various characteristics of Jesus' resurrection body? Why is it important to assert that Jesus rose *bodily* and not merely as *a spirit*? Explain your answer.

6. Why is the ascension important for our worship, devotion, and witness of the Lord Jesus? How does the creedal language correspond to the Bible's teaching about Christ's current session in heaven?

7. How does Jesus' headship over the Church relate to his ascension to the Father's right hand? In the same way, how does his current role as High Priest connect to his ascension?

8. How does Jesus' current reign in heaven relate to the hope we have that one day he will reign upon the earth? How did Jesus' ascension give confirmation that he is in fact the coming King from David's line?

9. How does Jesus' resurrection and ascension encourage us in our worship and celebration of Christ as Lord of all?

Jesus, the Messiah and Lord of All: He Rose and Will Return

Segment 2: The Return and Coming Reign of Jesus Christ

Rev. Dr. Don L. Davis

Three specific statements in the Nicene Creed speak of Jesus' *future work upon earth*. First, the Creed asserts that Jesus Christ will return again in glory, which will be dramatic in character and has present significance for our lives and ministry. Next, the Creed affirms that he will come to judge the nations, for all judgment has been given to the Son by the Father. Finally, the Creed confesses that he will reign and his Kingdom will have no end, fulfilling the prophesies of the OT and establishing God's rule in a new heavens and earth. These three affirmations (i.e., his coming in glory, his judgment of the nations, and his eternal Kingdom) carry significant meaning for our lives and ministries today.

Summary of Segment 2

Our objective for this segment, *The Return and Coming Reign of Jesus Christ*, is to enable you to see that:

- Three specific statements in the Nicene Creed speak of Jesus' *future work upon earth*.

- The Creed asserts that Jesus Christ will return again in glory, which will be dramatic in character and has present significance for our lives and ministry.

- The Creed also affirms that he will come to judge the nations, for all judgment has been given to the Son by the Father.

- Finally, the Creed also confesses that Jesus will reign and his Kingdom will have no end, implying that he will finally fulfill the prophesies of the OT, establishing God's rule in a new heavens and earth.

- These three affirmations of the Nicene Creed (i.e., his coming in glory, his judgment of the nations, and his eternal Kingdom) carry significant meaning for our lives and ministries today.

Video Segment 2 Outline

As in our last session, let's recite the relevant portion of the Creed for our final lesson:

"The third day he rose again according to the Scriptures, ascended into heaven and is seated at the right hand of the Father. *He will come again in glory to judge the living and the dead, and his Kingdom will have no end.*"

He speaks of the day of His appearing, when He will come and redeem us, each one according to his works.
~ Second Clement (c. 150), 7.522. David W. Bercot, ed. *A Dictionary of Early Christian Beliefs.* Peabody, MA: Hendrickson Publishers, 1998. p. 606.

I. **"He Will Come Again in Glory": the Second Coming of Jesus Christ**

A. His coming will be *personal* (Jesus Messiah himself will return).

1. He goes to take us to himself, John 14.3.

2. The Lord himself will descend, 1 Thess. 4.16-17.

3. No proxies, substitutes, or messengers will come to consummate God's Kingdom. Jesus will come himself, personally, and we will see his glory, John 17.24.

B. His coming will be *bodily and physical*.

1. It will be corporeal, not merely spiritual or psychic.

2. Acts 1.11

3. Dan. 7.13-14

C. His coming will be *visible*.

1. Matt. 24.30

2. Mark 13.26

3. 1 Thess. 4.16

4. 2 Thess. 1.7-8

5. Rev. 1.7

D. His coming will be *full of splendor, majesty, and glory*.

1. Luke 21.27

Already His Second Coming draws near to us.
~ Cyprian (c. 250, W), 5.363. Ibid. p. 606.

When He comes from heaven with His mighty angels, the whole earth will be shaken, as He Himself declares.
~ Irenaeus (c. 180, E/W), 1.510. Ibid. p. 606.

2. Coming on the clouds with great power and glory, Matt. 24.30; Mark 13.26; Luke 21.27

3. Heralded by the archangel's trumpet blast, 1 Thess. 4.16

4. Accompanied by angels, Matt. 24.31

5. Associated with his consummation of his kingly reign, assuming his kingly throne, judging and reigning over the nations, Matt. 25.31-46

E. His coming will be completely *unexpected*.

1. It will be swift, like a thief in the night, with many being completely unaware of his return, Matt. 24.42-44

2. The parable of the ten virgins in Matthew 25 suggests this truth.

3. 2 Pet. 3.10

4. The problem of delay: 2 Pet. 3.3-4

5. *Don't be mistaken at the delay*: 2 Pet. 3.8-10.

   a. Noah: Luke 17.20-27

   b. Remember Lot's wife: Luke 17.32

II. "To Judge the Living and Dead"

A. All judgment has been given over to the Son.

1. John 5.22-23

2. John 5.27

3. Rom. 14.10-12

4. 2 Cor. 5.9-10

B. He will judge all human beings on the basis of their deeds.

1. Ps. 62.12

2. Prov. 24.12

3. Eccles. 12.14

4. Jer. 17.10

5. Jer. 32.19

6. Matt. 16.27

7. Rom. 2.6

8. Rev. 22.12

C. Jesus will judge all believers and award "crowns" for their faithful service to the Lord (cf. 1 Cor. 3.9-15).

1. Crown of life

   a. James 1.12

   b. Rev. 2.10

2. Crown of glory

   a. 1 Pet. 5.4

   b. Cf. John 17.22

   c. Heb. 2.9

3. Crown of righteousness, 2 Tim. 4.8

4. Crown of rejoicing, 1 Thess. 2.19

5. Crown incorruptible, 1 Cor. 9.25

But be ready, for you do not know the hour in which our Lord comes.
~ Didache
(c. 80-140, E), 7.382.
Ibid. p. 606.

D. Only those found written in the Lamb's book of Life will enter into God's new kingdom order.

1. The terrifying vision of judgment, Rev. 20.12-15

2. The devil and all the wicked will be consigned to everlasting punishment (the place of separation from the presence of Almighty God).

   a. The judgment of Satan, Rev. 20.10

   b. The judgment of the unbelieving, 2 Thess. 1.6-10

III. "And His Kingdom Will Have No End"

A. In the Kingdom of our Lord Jesus Christ, the knowledge of the Lord will be global and universal.

1. Isa. 11.9 (cf. Hab. 2.14)

2. A direct knowledge of the Lord, 1 John 3.2

3. Ps. 16.11

4. Matt. 5.8

5. John 17.24

B. The saints of God will enter into the glorious freedom of the children of God.

1. A new creation will emerge: the glorious freedom of the children of God.

    a. Rom. 8.19-22

    b. Isa. 65.17

    c. 2 Pet. 3.11-13

2. A new city will be revealed: the New Jerusalem

    a. The vision of St. John, Rev. 21.1-5

    b. God's abode comes down to dwell with humankind.

    c. Uninterrupted communion and service to God in the glory of the new creation

3. A new age and identity will dawn: our co-regency in Christ.

    a. 1 Cor. 2.9

    b. Rom. 8.16-17

c. 1 Cor. 3.22-23

d. Rev. 2.26-27

e. Rev. 3.21

C. Once all enemies have been subdued under Christ's feet, including death, then Christ will transfer the Kingdom to God, who will then become the universe's All in all.

1 Cor. 15.24-25, 28 - Then comes the end, when he delivers the kingdom to God the Father after destroying every rule and every authority and power. [25] For he must reign until he has put all his enemies under his feet. [28] When all things are subjected to him, then the Son himself will also be subjected to him who put all things in subjection under him, that God may be all in all.

1. Christ will entrust the kingdom rule to God.

2. God will become All-in-all.

IV. The Implications of the Return of Jesus Christ

Isa. 62.11 - Behold, the LORD has proclaimed to the end of the earth: Say to the daughter of Zion, "Behold, your salvation comes; behold, his reward is with him, and his recompense before him."

Rev. 22.12-13 - Behold, I am coming soon, bringing my recompense with me, to repay everyone for what he has done. [13] I am the Alpha and the Omega, the first and the last, the beginning and the end.

A. His coming is *certain*.

B. The judgment is *awesome*.

C. The kingdom stakes are *unbelievably high*.

D. Our mission is *clear*: go and make disciples of Jesus among all nations as quickly as possible, Matt. 28.18-20.

Conclusion

» The last three clauses in the Christological section of the Nicene Creed speak of Christ's coming in glory, his coming judgment of all people, and his coming eternal reign.

» Because our Lord Jesus is risen and exalted, he deserves our highest worship and best service.

» We must strive to make him known, both in his humiliation and exaltation to our neighborhoods, cities, and world for he alone is Lord, and he alone shall reign.

All glory to his name. Amen!

At His coming, only the righteous will rejoice. For they look for the things that have been promised them. And the subsistence of the affairs of this world will no longer be maintained. Rather, all things will be destroyed.
~ Disputation of Archelaus and Manes (c. 320, E), 6.2111. Ibid. p. 606.

Segue 2

Student Questions and Response

The following questions were designed to help you review the material in the second video segment. The Nicene Creed supplies us with a clear and compelling summary of the biblical witness of Christ's coming in glory, his coming judgment of all people, and his coming eternal reign. Your grasp of this material is crucial, both in terms of your own personal discipleship, and just as importantly, for your witness and ministry. Review the material in the segment through these questions, and highlight your answer with solid biblical support.

1. What are the characteristics of the Second Coming of Jesus Christ? Why must we assert that his coming will be both *personal* and *visible* (cf. Acts 1.11)? What role will angelic beings play in his glorious coming?

2. What are the implications that the Lord's coming will be *unexpected*? What does this suggest about current trends in prophecy conferences and seminars to predict the coming of Christ?

3. How are we to understand the apparent delay in the coming of Christ–why has so much time elapsed since the resurrection and the ascension? What should our current attitude be as we await the coming of the Lord?

4. How do the Scriptures describe the divine task of judgment, i.e., what member of the Trinity has been given this honor?

5. What will be the criteria that the Righteous Judge will use as he passes judgment on all humankind?

6. What will be the reward given to believers as they are judged in connection to their faithful service to the Lord? List the various "crowns" mentioned in the NT associated with the judgment seat of Christ and the reward of believers?

7. What will be the fate of those whose names are not found written in the Lamb's book of life? What are the major differences between the Judge's judgment on believers versus unbelievers?

8. In what sense will the Kingdom of Jesus as exalted Lord be both *global* and *universal*? Cite Scripture. What will be the status of the saints of God in the eternal Kingdom of Christ?

9. In the revelation of the new city, the New Jerusalem, how will the dwelling place of God and Christ be connected to the saints? What role will they play in the new age?

10. What will Christ do with the Kingdom once all enemies have been subdued under his feet? What place will God then have in the aeons of time to come?

CONNECTION

Summary of Key Concepts

This lesson focuses upon the exaltation of Christ in the resurrection and the ascension, as well as the last three statements of the Christological section of the Nicene Creed which testify of Christ's coming in glory, his judgment of humankind, and his coming eternal reign. The concepts listed below highlight some of the critical issues and truths associated with the exalted Christ, and the coming work he will accomplish upon earth.

- The various aspects and implications of Christ's exaltation can be comprehended clearly on the basis of two critical salvific events; the resurrection and the ascension of Christ.

- The resurrection serves as a vindication of Jesus' Messiahship and sonship, and his ascension grants to our Savior a position of dignity and authority that allows him to fill all things with his glory.

- The *Christ event* (i.e., Jesus' preexistence, life, ministry, death, resurrection, and glory) can be thought of in terms of two movements, a movement of descent (into humiliation), and ascent (into exaltation). The resurrection and ascension are associated directly with Christ's exaltation and glory.

- Three specific statements in the Nicene Creed speak of Jesus' *future work upon earth*.

- The Creed asserts that Jesus Christ will return again in glory, which will be dramatic in character and has present significance for our lives and ministry.

- The Creed also affirms that he will come to judge the nations, for all judgment has been given to the Son by the Father.

- Finally, the Creed also confesses that Jesus will reign and his Kingdom will have no end, implying that he will finally fulfill the prophesies of the OT, establishing God's rule in a new heavens and earth.

- These three affirmations of the Nicene Creed (i.e., his coming in glory, his judgment of the nations, and his eternal Kingdom) carry significant meaning for our lives and ministries today.

Student Application and Implications

Now is the time for you to discuss with your fellow students your questions about the resurrection, ascension, and return of the Lord. This teaching provides us as Christian leaders with the confidence and assurance we need as share the Good News with those who do not know Christ, as well as to grow disciples which we are establishing and equipping in the Church. What questions have come to mind as we have covered this exciting biblical testimony on our Lord's exaltation and return? Use the questions below to spark your own questions about the implications of the exaltation of Christ for your life and ministry.

* Why is the doctrine of the resurrection so important to the doctrine of the resurrection of *Christ*?

* How can the doctrine of Jesus' resurrection give us comfort and assurance during seasons of ministry which are less than effective, even unfruitful and difficult?

* How might our worship of Christ be enhanced if we were to rediscover the doctrine of the ascension in our worship, lectionary, and Church calendar?

* How often is the glorious return of Christ mentioned or referred to in your own devotional reading and prayer, Bible study and teaching, and your preaching and exposition? When is the last time you studied this material in depth for your edification's sake?

* How should the prospect of Christ's future judgment of your service influence both your motive and your methods of ministry today? What is likely to happen if you ignore this important truth as you minister in Christ's name?

* In what ways might you integrate the teaching about Christ's eternal Kingdom into your daily life and faith? What kinds of activities and practices might you adopt to help those whom you lead and teach to be more aware of the Second Coming of Christ, and the implications of that event for their lives?

His Body Did Not Rise

Using 1 Corinthians 15.45 as a pretext, Jehovah's Witnesses do not believe that the body of Jesus *physically rose from the dead*. The verse reads, "Thus it is written, 'The first man Adam became a living being'; the last Adam became *a life-giving spirit*." Asserting that this text reveals that Jesus was raised *a spirit*, the Witnesses affirm that the body of Jesus is gone; they make no theological assertion as to where it may be today, i.e., where it was buried for good, but their own theology does not require that Jesus rose visibly, nor that he return in a *body, visibly, in immortal glory*. How would you refute this long-standing doctrine of the Witnesses?

More than One Second Coming?

According to one popular view of the Second Coming, there will be a series of appearances where Christ will come first for his own at the Rapture of the Church (1 Thess. 4.13-17), followed by a period of great tribulation of seven years, and then, the Second Coming proper, where Christ will appear in full glory, judging the wicked world system, and establishing his Kingdom upon it. (This view is prominent in the current *Left Behind* series by Timothy LaHaye). In regards to the Second Coming of Christ, what is essential for us to believe about it? For instance, must we take a position on the specific nature of the coming, or merely confess wholeheartedly that the Second Coming will occur? Another way of asking this question is this: does the Creed's simple affirmation that he will come again in glory give too little information to really encourage the hearts of Christians awaiting Christ's return? Defend your answer with Scripture.

There'll Be No Real Kingdom

In a series at church on the Second Coming of Christ, a heated discussion has been brewing among several of the key teachers in the church. One of the leaders, deeply influenced by teaching that suggests the millennial Kingdom of Revelation 20 is a *literal Kingdom on earth* has begun to dialogue with one of her colleague who believes the Kingdom to be merely *a symbolic and not a literal reign on the earth*. These two are respected, well-learned, biblical people who both possess a fine heart for the Lord and deep walk with God. Yet, their discussion has become public and intense enough that it is plain that some kind of resolution of their dialogue must occur soon. How would your understanding of the "big picture" of the coming reign of Christ help you to resolve this more specific disagreement about the details of his coming?

Restatement of the Lesson's Thesis

The various aspects and implications of Christ's exaltation can be comprehended clearly on the basis of two critical salvific events; the resurrection and the ascension of Christ. The resurrection serves as a vindication of Jesus' Messiahship and sonship, and his ascension grants to our Savior a position of dignity and authority that allows him to fill all things with his glory. The *Christ event* (i.e., Jesus' preexistence, life, ministry, death, resurrection, and glory) can be thought of in terms of two movements, a movement of descent (into humiliation), and ascent (into exaltation). The resurrection and ascension are associated directly with Christ's exaltation and glory.

Three specific statements in the Nicene Creed speak of Jesus' *future work upon earth*. First, the Creed asserts that Jesus Christ will return again in glory, which will be dramatic in character and has present significance for our lives and ministry. Next, the Creed affirms that he will come to judge the nations, for all judgment has been given to the Son by the Father. Finally, the Creed confesses that he will reign and his Kingdom will have no end, fulfilling the prophesies of the OT, establishing God's rule in a new heavens and earth. These three affirmations (i.e., his coming in glory, his judgment of the nations, and his eternal Kingdom) carry significant meaning for our lives and ministries today.

Resources and Bibliographies

If you are interested in pursuing some of the ideas of *Jesus, the Messiah and Lord of All: He Rose and Will Return*, you might want to give these books a try:

> Craig, William Lane. *The Son Risen: The Historical Evidence for the Resurrection of Jesus*. Chicago: Moody Press, 1981.
>
> Ladd, George Eldon. *I Believe in the Resurrection of Jesus*. Grand Rapids: Eerdmans, 1975.
>
> ------. *The Last Things*. Grand Rapids: Eerdmans, 1978.
>
> Wenham, John. *Easter Enigma: Are the Resurrection Accounts in Conflict?* Grand Rapids: Baker Book House, 1992.

Ministry Connections

You have now reached a point in your studies where you will be called upon to apply the insights of your module investigation in a practicum that you and your mentor agree to. You are responsible to make real in your life and ministry the ramifications of the exaltation of Christ, the testimony regarding his resurrection and ascension, and the certainty of the hope of his return. Begin to consider all the numberless ways that this teaching can influence your devotional life, your prayers, your response to your church, your attitude at work, and on and on and on.

What is important now in your studies is to apply one of these implications to an actual issue and area in your life, work, and ministry. The ministry project is designed to help you practice the Word you have learned, and in the next days you will have the opportunity to share these insights in real-life, ministry environments. Pray that God will give you insight into his ways as you share your insights in your projects.

Counseling and Prayer	As you conclude your studies in this module, are there any issues, persons, situations, or opportunities that need to be prayed for as a result of your studies in this lesson? What particular issues or people has God laid upon your heart that require focused supplication and prayer for in this lesson? Take the time to ponder this, and receive the necessary support in counsel and prayer for what the Spirit has shown you.

Scripture Memory	No assignment due.
Reading Assignment	No assignment due.
Other Assignments	Your ministry project and your exegetical project should now be outlined, determined, and accepted by your instructor. Make sure that you plan ahead, so you will not be late in turning in your assignments.
Final Exam Notice	The final will be a take home exam, and will include questions taken from the first three quizzes, new questions on material drawn from this lesson, and essay questions which will ask for your short answer responses to key integrating questions. Also, you should plan on reciting or writing out the verses memorized for the course on the exam. When you have completed your exam, please notify your mentor and make certain that they get your copy.
	Please note: Your module grade cannot be determined if you do not take the final exam and turn in all outstanding assignments to your mentor (ministry project, exegetical project, and final exam).
The Last Word about this Module	In this final lesson we have examined two of the events which dramatically mark the exaltation of Christ, his resurrection which serves to vindicate his identity as Messiah and God's son, and his ascension, which establishes our Lord in a position of glory, priestly representation, and kingship. The risen and exalted Lord will and must reign until all enemies have been put under his feet. At God's own time he will return in glory, to judge the living and the dead and establish God's eternal Kingdom on earth.

Our sincere prayer as those who prepared this material is that these theological affirmations will become your personal cries of the heart, and that God would so ignite and inspire you that you can become a fire-brand of our Lord to declare our risen Savior and his Kingdom in your world, or wherever he might lead. Even so, come, Lord Jesus!

May the grace of God strengthen you as your flesh out your discipleship in following our Lord Jesus Christ, God's only begotten Son, and may your life bring glory and honor to him, to whom be all the glory and praise. Amen!

Appendices

159	Appendix 1: **The Nicene Creed** *(with Scripture memory passages)*
160	Appendix 2: **We Believe: Confession of the Nicene Creed (Common Meter)**
161	Appendix 3: **The Story of God: Our Sacred Roots**
162	Appendix 4: **The Theology of Christus Victor**
163	Appendix 5: **Christus Victor: An Integrated Vision for the Christian Life**
164	Appendix 6: **Old Testament Witness to Christ and His Kingdom**
165	Appendix 7: **Summary Outline of the Scriptures**
167	Appendix 8: **From Before to Beyond Time**
169	Appendix 9: **There Is a River**
170	Appendix 10: **A Schematic for a Theology of the Kingdom and the Church**
171	Appendix 11: **Living in the Already and the Not Yet Kingdom**
172	Appendix 12: **Jesus of Nazareth: The Presence of the Future**
173	Appendix 13: **Traditions**
181	Appendix 14: **Representin': Jesus as God's Chosen Representative**
182	Appendix 15: **Picking Up on Different Wavelengths: Integrated vs. Fragmented Mindsets**
186	Appendix 16: **Toward a Hermeneutic of Critical Engagement**
187	Appendix 17: **Spiritual Gifts Specifically Mentioned in the New Testament**
189	Appendix 18: **Fit to Represent**
190	Appendix 19: **Hindrances to Christlike Servanthood**
191	Appendix 20: **Understanding Leadership as Representation**
192	Appendix 21: **A Sociology of Urban Leadership Development**
193	Appendix 22: **Messianic Prophecies Cited in the New Testament**
199	Appendix 23: **Ethics of the New Testament: Living in the Upside-Down Kingdom of God**

Page	Appendix	Title
200	Appendix 24:	**Preaching and Teaching Jesus of Nazareth as Messiah and Lord**
201	Appendix 25:	**Summary of Messianic Interpretations in the Old Testament**
206	Appendix 26:	**Suffering: The Cost of Discipleship and Servant-Leadership**
207	Appendix 27:	**Old Testament Names, Titles, and Epithets for the Messiah**
209	Appendix 28:	**Messiah Jesus: Fulfillment of the Old Testament Types**
213	Appendix 29:	**Portrayals of Jesus in the New Testament Books**
214	Appendix 30:	**A Harmony of the Ministry of Jesus**
215	Appendix 31:	**Communicating Messiah: The Relationship of the Gospels**
216	Appendix 32:	**Appearances of the Resurrected Messiah**
217	Appendix 33:	**The Shadow and the Substance**
218	Appendix 34:	**In Christ**
219	Appendix 35:	**The Miracles of Jesus**
220	Appendix 36:	**The Parables of Jesus**
221	Appendix 37:	**Union with Christ: The Christocentric Paradigm**
224	Appendix 38:	**The Life of Christ according to Seasons and Years**
226	Appendix 39:	**Faithfully Re-Presenting Jesus of Nazareth**
227	Appendix 40:	**Apostolicity**
228	Appendix 41:	**The Self-Consciousness of Jesus Christ**
229	Appendix 42:	**I Find My Lord in the Book**
230	Appendix 43:	**The Center and Circumference: Christianity Is Jesus Christ**
241	Appendix 44:	**Jesus and the Poor**
247	Appendix 45:	**Documenting Your Work**

APPENDIX 1
The Nicene Creed

Memory Verses ⇩

Rev. 4.11 (ESV) *Worthy are you, our Lord and God, to receive glory and honor and power, for you created all things, and by your will they existed and were created.*

John 1.1 (ESV) *In the beginning was the Word, and the Word was with God, and the Word was God.*

1 Cor.15.3-5 (ESV) *For what I received I passed on to you as of first importance: that Christ died for our sins according to the Scriptures, that he was buried, that he was raised on the third day according to the Scriptures, and that he appeared to Peter, and then to the Twelve.*

Rom. 8.11 (ESV) *If the Spirit of him who raised Jesus from the dead dwells in you, he who raised Christ Jesus from the dead will also give life to your mortal bodies through his Spirit who dwells in you.*

1 Pet. 2.9 (ESV) *But you are a chosen race, a royal priesthood, a holy nation, a people for his own possession, that you may proclaim the excellencies of him who called you out of darkness into his marvelous light.*

1 Thess. 4.16-17 (ESV) *For the Lord himself will descend from heaven with a cry of command, with the voice of an archangel, and with the sound of the trumpet of God. And the dead in Christ will rise first. Then we who are alive, who are left, will be caught up together with them in the clouds to meet the Lord in the air, and so we will always be with the Lord.*

We believe in one God,   (Deut. 6.4-5; Mark 12.29; 1 Cor. 8.6)
    the Father Almighty,   (Gen. 17.1; Dan. 4.35; Matt. 6.9; Eph. 4.6; Rev. 1.8)
    Maker of heaven and earth   (Gen 1.1; Isa. 40.28; Rev. 10.6)
    and of all things visible and invisible.   (Ps. 148; Rom. 11.36; Rev. 4.11)

We believe in one Lord Jesus Christ, the only Begotten Son of God,
    begotten of the Father before all ages,
    God from God, Light from Light, True God from True God,
    begotten not created,
    of the same essence as the Father,   (John 1.1-2; 3.18; 8.58; 14.9-10; 20.28; Col. 1.15, 17; Heb. 1.3-6)
    through whom all things were made.   (John 1.3; Col. 1.16)

Who for us men and for our salvation came down from heaven
    and was incarnate by the Holy Spirit and the virgin Mary
    and became human.   (Matt. 1.20-23; John 1.14; 6.38; Luke 19.10)
    Who for us too, was crucified under Pontius Pilate,
    suffered, and was buried.   (Matt. 27.1-2; Mark 15.24-39, 43-47; Acts 13.29; Rom. 5.8; Heb. 2.10; 13.12)
    The third day he rose again
    according to the Scriptures,   (Mark 16.5-7; Luke 24.6-8; Acts 1.3; Rom. 6.9; 10.9; 2 Tim. 2.8)
    ascended into heaven,
    and is seated at the right hand of the Father.   (Mark 16.19; Eph. 1.19-20)
    He will come again in glory
    to judge the living and the dead,
    and his Kingdom will have no end.
      (Isa. 9.7; Matt. 24.30; John 5.22; Acts 1.11; 17.31; Rom. 14.9; 2 Cor. 5.10; 2 Tim. 4.1)

We believe in the Holy Spirit, the Lord and life-giver,
      (Gen. 1.1-2; Job 33.4; Ps. 104.30; 139.7-8; Luke 4.18-19; John 3.5-6; Acts 1.1-2; 1 Cor. 2.11; Rev. 3.22)
    who proceeds from the Father and the Son,   (John 14.16-18, 26; 15.26; 20.22)
    who together with the Father and Son
    is worshiped and glorified,   (Isa. 6.3; Matt. 28.19; 2 Cor. 13.14; Rev. 4.8)
    who spoke by the prophets.   (Num. 11.29; Mic. 3.8; Acts 2.17-18; 2 Pet. 1.21)

We believe in one holy, catholic, and apostolic Church.
    (Matt. 16.18; Eph. 5.25-28; 1 Cor. 1.2; 10.17; 1 Tim. 3.15; Rev. 7.9)

We acknowledge one baptism for the forgiveness of sin,   (Acts 22.16; 1 Pet. 3.21; Eph. 4.4-5)
    And we look for the resurrection of the dead
    And the life of the age to come.   (Isa. 11.6-10; Mic. 4.1-7; Luke 18.29-30; Rev. 21.1-5; 21.22-22.5)

Amen.

APPENDIX 2

We Believe: Confession of the Nicene Creed (Common Meter*)

Rev. Dr. Don L. Davis, 2007. All Rights Reserved.

* This song is adapted from the Nicene Creed, and set to Common Meter (8.6.8.6.), meaning it can be sung to tunes of the same meter, such as: O, for a Thousand Tongues to Sing; Alas, and Did My Savior Bleed?; Amazing Grace; All Hail the Power of Jesus' Name; There Is a Fountain; Joy to the World

The Father God Almighty rules, Maker of earth and heav'n.
Yes, all things seen and those unseen, by him were made, and given!

We hold to one Lord Jesus Christ, God's one and only Son,
Begotten, not created, too, he and our Lord are one!

Begotten from the Father, same, in essence, God and Light;
Through him all things were made by God, in him were given life.

Who for us all, for salvation, came down from heav'n to earth,
Was incarnate by the Spirit's pow'r, and the Virgin Mary's birth.

Who for us too, was crucified, by Pontius Pilate's hand,
Suffered, was buried in the tomb, on third day rose again.

According to the Sacred text all this was meant to be.
Ascended to heav'n, to God's right hand, now seated high in glory.

He'll come again in glory to judge all those alive and dead.
His Kingdom rule shall never end, for he will reign as Head.

We worship God, the Holy Spirit, our Lord, Life-giver known,
With Fath'r and Son is glorified, Who by the prophets spoke.

And we believe in one true Church, God's people for all time,
Cath'lic in scope, and built upon the apostolic line.

Acknowledging one baptism, for forgiv'ness of our sin,
We look for Resurrection day–the dead shall live again.

We look for those unending days, life of the Age to come,
When Christ's great Reign shall come to earth, and God's will shall be done!

APPENDIX 3
The Story of God: Our Sacred Roots
Rev. Dr. Don L. Davis

The Alpha and the Omega	Christus Victor	Come, Holy Spirit	Your Word Is Truth	The Great Confession	His Life in Us	Living in the Way	Reborn to Serve
The LORD God is the source, sustainer, and end of all things in the heavens and earth. All things were formed and exist by his will and for his eternal glory, the triune God, Father, Son, and Holy Spirit, Rom. 11.36.							
The Triune God's Unfolding Drama — God's Self-Revelation in Creation, Israel, and Christ				**The Church's Participation in God's Unfolding Drama** — Fidelity to the Apostolic Witness to Christ and His Kingdom			
The Objective Foundation: The Sovereign Love of God — God's Narration of His Saving Work in Christ				**The Subjective Practice: Salvation by Grace through Faith** — The Redeemed's Joyous Response to God's Saving Work in Christ			
The Author of the Story	*The Champion of the Story*	*The Interpreter of the Story*	*The Testimony of the Story*	*The People of the Story*	*Re-enactment of the Story*	*Embodiment of the Story*	*Continuation of the Story*
The Father as Director	Jesus as Lead Actor	The Spirit as Narrator	Scripture as Script	As Saints, Confessors	As Worshipers, Ministers	As Followers, Sojourners	As Servants, Ambassadors
Christian Worldview	Communal Identity	Spiritual Experience	Biblical Authority	Orthodox Theology	Priestly Worship	Congregational Discipleship	Kingdom Witness
Theistic and Trinitarian Vision	Christ-centered Foundation	Spirit-Indwelt and -Filled Community	Canonical and Apostolic Witness	Ancient Creedal Affirmation of Faith	Weekly Gathering in Christian Assembly	Corporate, Ongoing Spiritual Formation	Active Agents of the Reign of God
Sovereign Willing	Messianic Representing	Divine Comforting	Inspired Testifying	Truthful Retelling	Joyful Excelling	Faithful Indwelling	Hopeful Compelling
Creator True Maker of the Cosmos	Recapitulation Typos and Fulfillment of the Covenant	Life-Giver Regeneration and Adoption	Divine Inspiration God-breathed Word	The Confession of Faith Union with Christ	Song and Celebration Historical Recitation	Pastoral Oversight Shepherding the Flock	Explicit Unity Love for the Saints
Owner Sovereign Disposer of Creation	Revealer Incarnation of the Word	Teacher Illuminator of the Truth	Sacred History Historical Record	Baptism into Christ Communion of Saints	Homilies and Teachings Prophetic Proclamation	Shared Spirituality Common Journey through the Spiritual Disciplines	Radical Hospitality Evidence of God's Kingdom Reign
Ruler Blessed Controller of All Things	Redeemer Reconciler of All Things	Helper Endowment and the Power	Biblical Theology Divine Commentary	The Rule of Faith Apostles' Creed and Nicene Creed	The Lord's Supper Dramatic Re-enactment	Embodiment Anamnesis and Prolepsis through the Church Year	Extravagant Generosity Good Works
Covenant Keeper Faithful Promisor	Restorer Christ, the Victor over the powers of evil	Guide Divine Presence and Shekinah	Spiritual Food Sustenance for the Journey	The Vincentian Canon Ubiquity, antiquity, universality	Eschatological Foreshadowing The Already/Not Yet	Effective Discipling Spiritual Formation in the Believing Assembly	Evangelical Witness Making Disciples of All People Groups

APPENDIX 4
The Theology of Christus Victor
A Christ-Centered Biblical Motif for Integrating and Renewing the Urban Church
Rev. Dr. Don L. Davis

	The Promised Messiah	The Word Made Flesh	The Son of Man	The Suffering Servant	The Lamb of God	The Victorious Conqueror	The Reigning Lord in Heaven	The Bridegroom and Coming King
Biblical Framework	Israel's hope of Yahweh's anointed who would redeem his people	In the person of Jesus of Nazareth, the Lord has come to the world	As the promised king and divine Son of Man, Jesus reveals the Father's glory and salvation to the world	As Inaugurator of the Kingdom of God, Jesus demonstrates God's reign present through his words, wonders, and works	As both High Priest and Paschal Lamb, Jesus offers himself to God on our behalf as a sacrifice for sin	In his resurrection from the dead and ascension to God's right hand, Jesus is proclaimed as Victor over the power of sin and death	Now reigning at God's right hand till his enemies are made his footstool, Jesus pours out his benefits on his body	Soon the risen and ascended Lord will return to gather his Bride, the Church, and consummate his work
Scripture References	Isa. 9.6-7 Jer. 23.5-6 Isa. 11.1-10	John 1.14-18 Matt. 1.20-23 Phil. 2.6-8	Matt. 2.1-11 Num. 24.17 Luke 1.78-79	Mark 1.14-15 Matt. 12.25-30 Luke 17.20-21	2 Cor. 5.18-21 Isa. 52-53 John 1.29	Eph. 1.16-23 Phil. 2.5-11 Col. 1.15-20	1 Cor. 15.25 Eph. 4.15-16 Acts. 2.32-36	Rom. 14.7-9 Rev. 5.9-13 1 Thess. 4.13-18
Jesus' History	The pre-incarnate, only begotten Son of God in glory	His conception by the Spirit, and birth to Mary	His manifestation to the Magi and to the world	His teaching, exorcisms, miracles, and mighty works among the people	His suffering, crucifixion, death, and burial	His resurrection, with appearances to his witnesses, and his ascension to the Father	The sending of the Holy Spirit and his gifts, and Christ's session in heaven at the Father's right hand	His soon return from heaven to earth as Lord and Christ: the Second Coming
Description	The biblical promise for the seed of Abraham, the prophet like Moses, the son of David	In the Incarnation, God has come to us; Jesus reveals the Father's glory to humankind in fullness	In Jesus, God has shown his salvation to the entire world, including the Gentiles	In Jesus, the promised Kingdom of God has come visibly to earth, demonstrating his binding of Satan and rescinding the Curse	As God's perfect Lamb, Jesus offers himself up to God as a sin offering on behalf of the entire world	In his resurrection and ascension, Jesus destroyed death, disarmed Satan, and rescinded the Curse	Jesus is installed at the Father's right hand as Head of the Church, Firstborn from the dead, and supreme Lord in heaven	As we labor in his harvest field in the world, so we await Christ's return, the fulfillment of his promise
Church Year	Advent	Christmas	Season after Epiphany Baptism and Transfiguration	Lent	Holy Week Passion	Eastertide Easter, Ascension Day, Pentecost	Season after Pentecost Trinity Sunday	Season after Pentecost All Saints Day, Reign of Christ the King
	The Coming of Christ	*The Birth of Christ*	*The Manifestation of Christ*	*The Ministry of Christ*	*The Suffering and Death of Christ*	*The Resurrection and Ascension of Christ*	*The Heavenly Session of Christ*	*The Reign of Christ*
Spiritual Formation	As we await his Coming, let us proclaim and affirm the hope of Christ	O Word made flesh, let us every heart prepare him room to dwell	Divine Son of Man, show the nations your salvation and glory	In the person of Christ, the power of the reign of God has come to earth and to the Church	May those who share the Lord's death be resurrected with him	Let us participate by faith in the victory of Christ over the power of sin, Satan, and death	Come, indwell us, Holy Spirit, and empower us to advance Christ's Kingdom in the world	We live and work in expectation of his soon return, seeking to please him in all things

APPENDIX 5
Christus Victor
An Integrated Vision for the Christian Life
Rev. Dr. Don L. Davis

For the Church
- The Church is the primary extension of Jesus in the world
- Ransomed treasure of the victorious, risen Christ
- *Laos:* The people of God
- God's new creation: presence of the future
- Locus and agent of the Already/Not Yet Kingdom

For Gifts
- God's gracious endowments and benefits from *Christus Victor*
- Pastoral offices to the Church
- The Holy Spirit's sovereign dispensing of the gifts
- Stewardship: divine, diverse gifts for the common good

For Theology and Doctrine
- The authoritative Word of Christ's victory: the Apostolic Tradition: the Holy Scriptures
- Theology as commentary on the grand narrative of God
- *Christus Victor* as core theological framework for meaning in the world
- The Nicene Creed: the Story of God's triumphant grace

Christus Victor
Destroyer of Evil and Death
Restorer of Creation
Victor o'er Hades and Sin
Crusher of Satan

For Spirituality
- The Holy Spirit's presence and power in the midst of God's people
- Sharing in the disciplines of the Spirit
- Gatherings, lectionary, liturgy, and our observances in the Church Year
- Living the life of the risen Christ in the rhythm of our ordinary lives

For Worship
- People of the Resurrection: unending celebration of the people of God
- Remembering, participating in the Christ event in our worship
- Listen and respond to the Word
- Transformed at the Table, the Lord's Supper
- The presence of the Father through the Son in the Spirit

For Evangelism and Mission
- Evangelism as unashamed declaration and demonstration of *Christus Victor* to the world
- The Gospel as Good News of kingdom pledge
- We proclaim God's Kingdom come in the person of Jesus of Nazareth
- The Great Commission: go to all people groups making disciples of Christ and his Kingdom
- Proclaiming Christ as Lord and Messiah

For Justice and Compassion
- The gracious and generous expressions of Jesus through the Church
- The Church displays the very life of the Kingdom
- The Church demonstrates the very life of the Kingdom of heaven right here and now
- Having freely received, we freely give (no sense of merit or pride)
- Justice as tangible evidence of the Kingdom come

APPENDIX 6
Old Testament Witness to Christ and His Kingdom
Rev. Dr. Don L. Davis

Christ Is Seen in the OT's:	Covenant Promise and Fulfillment	Moral Law	Christophanies	Typology	Tabernacle, Festival, and Levitical Priesthood	Messianic Prophecy	Salvation Promises
Passage	Gen. 12.1-3	Matt. 5.17-18	John 1.18	1 Cor. 15.45	Heb. 8.1-6	Mic. 5.2	Isa. 9.6-7
Example	The Promised Seed of the Abrahamic covenant	The Law given on Mount Sinai	Commander of the Lord's army	Jonah and the great fish	Melchizedek, as both High Priest and King	The Lord's Suffering Servant	Righteous Branch of David
Christ As	Seed of the woman	The Prophet of God	God's present Revelation	Antitype of God's drama	Our eternal High Priest	The coming Son of Man	Israel's Redeemer and King
Where Illustrated	Galatians	Matthew	John	Matthew	Hebrews	Luke and Acts	John and Revelation
Exegetical Goal	To see Christ as heart of God's sacred drama	To see Christ as fulfillment of the Law	To see Christ as God's revealer	To see Christ as antitype of divine typos	To see Christ in the Temple *cultus*	To see Christ as true Messiah	To see Christ as coming King
How Seen in the NT	As fulfillment of God's sacred oath	As *telos* of the Law	As full, final, and superior revelation	As substance behind the historical shadows	As reality behind the rules and roles	As the Kingdom made present	As the One who will rule on David's throne
Our Response in Worship	God's veracity and faithfulness	God's perfect righteousness	God's presence among us	God's inspired Scripture	God's ontology: his realm as primary and determinative	God's anointed servant and mediator	God's resolve to restore his kingdom authority
How God Is Vindicated	God does not lie: he's true to his word	Jesus fulfills all righteousness	God's fulness is revealed to us in Jesus of Nazareth	The Spirit spoke by the prophets	The Lord has provided a mediator for humankind	Every jot and tittle written of him will occur	Evil will be put down, creation restored, under his reign

APPENDIX 7
Summary Outline of the Scriptures
Rev. Dr. Don L. Davis

1. GENESIS - Beginnings
   a. Adam
   b. Noah
   c. Abraham
   d. Isaac
   e. Jacob
   f. Joseph

2. EXODUS - Redemption, (out of)
   a. Slavery
   b. Deliverance
   c. Law
   d. Tabernacle

3. LEVITICUS - Worship and Fellowship
   a. Offerings, sacrifices
   b. Priests
   c. Feasts, festivals

4. NUMBERS - Service and Walk
   a. Organized
   b. Wanderings

5. DEUTERONOMY - Obedience
   a. Moses reviews history and law
   b. Civil and social laws
   c. Palestinian Covenant
   d. Moses' blessing and death

6. JOSHUA - Redemption (into)
   a. Conquer the land
   b. Divide up the land
   c. Joshua's farewell

7. JUDGES - God's Deliverance
   a. Disobedience and judgment
   b. Israel's twelve judges
   c. Lawless conditions

8. RUTH - Love
   a. Ruth chooses
   b. Ruth works
   c. Ruth waits
   d. Ruth rewarded

9. 1 SAMUEL - Kings, Priestly Perspective
   a. Eli
   b. Samuel
   c. Saul
   d. David

10. 2 SAMUEL - David
    a. King of Judah
       (9 years - Hebron)
    b. King of all Israel
       (33 years - Jerusalem)

11. 1 KINGS - Solomon's Glory, Kingdom's Decline
    a. Solomon's glory
    b. Kingdom's decline
    c. Elijah the prophet

12. 2 KINGS- Divided Kingdom
    a. Elisha
    b. Israel (N. Kingdom falls)
    c. Judah (S. Kingdom falls)

13. 1 CHRONICLES - David's Temple Arrangements
    a. Genealogies
    b. End of Saul's reign
    c. Reign of David
    d. Temple preparations

14. 2 CHRONICLES - Temple and Worship Abandoned
    a. Solomon
    b. Kings of Judah

15. EZRA - The Minority (Remnant)
    a. First return from exile - Zerubbabel
    b. Second return from exile - Ezra (priest)

16. NEHEMIAH - Rebuilding by Faith
    a. Rebuild walls
    b. Revival
    c. Religious reform

17. ESTHER - Female Savior
    a. Esther
    b. Haman
    c. Mordecai
    d. Deliverance: Feast of Purim

18. JOB - Why the Righteous Suffer
    a. Godly Job
    b. Satan's attack
    c. Four philosophical friends
    d. God lives

19. PSALMS - Prayer and Praise
    a. Prayers of David
    b. Godly suffer; deliverance
    c. God deals with Israel
    d. Suffering of God's people - end with the Lord's reign
    e. The Word of God (Messiah's suffering and glorious return)

20. PROVERBS - Wisdom
    a. Wisdom versus folly
    b. Solomon
    c. Solomon - Hezekiah
    d. Agur
    e. Lemuel

21. ECCLESIASTES - Vanity
    a. Experimentation
    b. Observation
    c. Consideration

22. SONG OF SOLOMON - Love Story

23. ISAIAH - The Justice (Judgment) and Grace (Comfort) of God
    a. Prophecies of punishment
    b. History
    c. Prophecies of blessing

24. JEREMIAH - Judah's Sin Leads to Babylonian Captivity
    a. Jeremiah's call; empowered
    b. Judah condemned; predicted Babylonian captivity
    c. Restoration promised
    d. Prophesied judgment inflicted
    e. Prophesies against Gentiles
    f. Summary of Judah's captivity

25. LAMENTATIONS - Lament over Jerusalem
    a. Affliction of Jerusalem
    b. Destroyed because of sin
    c. The prophet's suffering
    d. Present desolation versus past splendor
    e. Appeal to God for mercy

26. EZEKIEL - Israel's Captivity and Restoration
    a. Judgment on Judah and Jerusalem
    b. Judgment on Gentile nations
    c. Israel restored; Jerusalem's future glory

27. DANIEL - The Time of the Gentiles
    a. History; Nebuchadnezzar, Belshazzar, Daniel
    b. Prophecy

28. HOSEA - Unfaithfulness
    a. Unfaithfulness
    b. Punishment
    c. Restoration

29. JOEL - The Day of the Lord
    a. Locust plague
    b. Events of the future day of the Lord
    c. Order of the future day of the Lord

30. AMOS - God Judges Sin
    a. Neighbors judged
    b. Israel judged
    c. Visions of future judgment
    d. Israel's past judgment blessings

31. OBADIAH - Edom's Destruction
    a. Destruction prophesied
    b. Reasons for destruction
    c. Israel's future blessing

32. JONAH - Gentile Salvation
    a. Jonah disobeys
    b. Other suffer
    c. Jonah punished
    d. Jonah obeys; thousands saved
    e. Jonah displeased, no love for souls

33. MICAH - Israel's Sins, Judgment, and Restoration
    a. Sin and judgment
    b. Grace and future restoration
    c. Appeal and petition

34. NAHUM - Nineveh Condemned
    a. God hates sin
    b. Nineveh's doom prophesied
    c. Reasons for doom

35. HABAKKUK - The Just Shall Live by Faith
    a. Complaint of Judah's unjudged sin
    b. Chaldeans will punish
    c. Complaint of Chaldeans' wickedness
    d. Punishment promised
    e. Prayer for revival; faith in God

36. ZEPHANIAH - Babylonian Invasion Prefigures the Day of the Lord
    a. Judgment on Judah foreshadows the Great Day of the Lord
    b. Judgment on Jerusalem and neighbors foreshadows final judgment of all nations
    c. Israel restored after judgments

37. HAGGAI - Rebuild the Temple
    a. Negligence
    b. Courage
    c. Separation
    d. Judgment

38. ZECHARIAH - Two Comings of Christ
    a. Zechariah's vision
    b. Bethel's question; Jehovah's answer
    c. Nation's downfall and salvation

39. MALACHI - Neglect
    a. The priest's sins
    b. The people's sins
    c. The faithful few

Summary Outline of the Scriptures (continued)

1. MATTHEW - Jesus the King
   a. The Person of the King
   b. The Preparation of the King
   c. The Propaganda of the King
   d. The Program of the King
   e. The Passion of the King
   f. The Power of the King

2. MARK - Jesus the Servant
   a. John introduces the Servant
   b. God the Father identifies the Servant
   c. The temptation initiates the Servant
   d. Work and word of the Servant
   e. Death, burial, resurrection

3. LUKE - Jesus Christ the Perfect Man
   a. Birth and family of the Perfect Man
   b. Testing of the Perfect Man; hometown
   c. Ministry of the Perfect Man
   d. Betrayal, trial, and death of the Perfect Man
   e. Resurrection of the Perfect Man

4. JOHN - Jesus Christ is God
   a. Prologue - the Incarnation
   b. Introduction
   c. Witness of Jesus to his Apostles
   d. Passion - witness to the world
   e. Epilogue

5. ACTS - The Holy Spirit Working in the Church
   a. The Lord Jesus at work by the Holy Spirit through the Apostles at Jerusalem
   b. In Judea and Samaria
   c. To the uttermost parts of the Earth

6. ROMANS - The Righteousness of God
   a. Salutation
   b. Sin and salvation
   c. Sanctification
   d. Struggle
   e. Spirit-filled living
   f. Security of salvation
   g. Segregation
   h. Sacrifice and service
   i. Separation and salutation

7. 1 CORINTHIANS - The Lordship of Christ
   a. Salutation and thanksgiving
   b. Conditions in the Corinthian body
   c. Concerning the Gospel
   d. Concerning collections

8. 2 CORINTHIANS - The Ministry in the Church
   a. The comfort of God
   b. Collection for the poor
   c. Calling of the Apostle Paul

9. GALATIANS - Justification by Faith
   a. Introduction
   b. Personal - Authority of the Apostle and glory of the Gospel
   c. Doctrinal - Justification by faith
   d. Practical - Sanctification by the Holy Spirit
   e. Autographed conclusion and exhortation

10. EPHESIANS - The Church of Jesus Christ
    a. Doctrinal - the heavenly calling of the Church
       A Body
       A Temple
       A Mystery
    b. Practical - The earthly conduct of the Church
       A New Man
       A Bride
       An Army

11. PHILIPPIANS - Joy in the Christian Life
    a. Philosophy for Christian living
    b. Pattern for Christian living
    c. Prize for Christian living
    d. Power for Christian living

12. COLOSSIANS - Christ the Fullness of God
    a. Doctrinal - In Christ believers are made full
    b. Practical - Christ's life poured out in believers, and through them

13. 1 THESSALONIANS - The Second Coming of Christ:
    a. Is an inspiring hope
    b. Is a working hope
    c. Is a purifying hope
    d. Is a comforting hope
    e. Is a rousing, stimulating hope

14. 2 THESSALONIANS - The Second Coming of Christ
    a. Persecution of believers now; judgment of unbelievers hereafter (at coming of Christ)
    b. Program of the world in connection with the coming of Christ
    c. Practical issues associated with the coming of Christ

15. 1 TIMOTHY - Government and Order in the Local Church
    a. The faith of the Church
    b. Public prayer and women's place in the Church
    c. Officers in the Church
    d. Apostasy in the Church
    e. Duties of the officer of the Church

16. 2 TIMOTHY - Loyalty in the Days of Apostasy
    a. Afflictions of the Gospel
    b. Active in service
    c. Apostasy coming; authority of the Scriptures
    d. Allegiance to the Lord

17. TITUS - The Ideal New Testament Church
    a. The Church is an organization
    b. The Church is to teach and preach the Word of God
    c. The Church is to perform good works

18. PHILEMON - Reveal Christ's Love and Teach Brotherly Love
    a. Genial greeting to Philemon and family
    b. Good reputation of Philemon
    c. Gracious plea for Onesimus
    d. Guiltless illustration of Imputation
    e. General and personal requests

19. HEBREWS - The Superiority of Christ
    a. Doctrinal - Christ is better than the Old Testament economy
    b. Practical - Christ brings better benefits and duties

20. JAMES - Ethics of Christianity
    a. Faith tested
    b. Difficulty of controlling the tongue
    c. Warning against worldliness
    d. Admonitions in view of the Lord's coming

21. 1 PETER - Christian Hope in the Time of Persecution and Trial
    a. Suffering and security of believers
    b. Suffering and the Scriptures
    c. Suffering and the sufferings of Christ
    d. Suffering and the Second Coming of Christ

22. 2 PETER - Warning Against False Teachers
    a. Addition of Christian graces gives assurance
    b. Authority of the Scriptures
    c. Apostasy brought in by false testimony
    d. Attitude toward Return of Christ: test for apostasy
    e. Agenda of God in the world
    f. Admonition to believers

23. 1 JOHN - The Family of God
    a. God is Light
    b. God is Love
    c. God is Life

24. 2 JOHN - Warning against Receiving Deceivers
    a. Walk in truth
    b. Love one another
    c. Receive not deceivers
    d. Find joy in fellowship

25. 3 JOHN - Admonition to Receive True Believers
    a. Gaius, brother in the Church
    b. Diotrephes
    c. Demetrius

26. JUDE - Contending for the Faith
    a. Occasion of the epistle
    b. Occurrences of apostasy
    c. Occupation of believers in the days of apostasy

27. REVELATION - The Unveiling of Christ Glorified
    a. The person of Christ in glory
    b. The possession of Jesus Christ - the Church in the World
    c. The program of Jesus Christ - the scene in Heaven
    d. The seven seals
    e. The seven trumpets
    f. Important persons in the last days
    g. The seven vials
    h. The fall of Babylon
    i. The eternal state

APPENDIX 8

From Before to Beyond Time:
The Plan of God and Human History

Adapted from: Suzanne de Dietrich. **God's Unfolding Purpose.** *Philadelphia: Westminster Press, 1976.*

I. Before Time (Eternity Past) 1 Cor. 2.7
A. The Eternal Triune God
B. God's Eternal Purpose
C. The Mystery of Iniquity
D. The Principalities and Powers

II. Beginning of Time (Creation and Fall) Gen. 1.1
A. Creative Word
B. Humanity
C. Fall
D. Reign of Death and First Signs of Grace

III. Unfolding of Time (God's Plan Revealed Through Israel) Gal. 3.8
A. Promise (Patriarchs)
B. Exodus and Covenant at Sinai
C. Promised Land
D. The City, the Temple, and the Throne (Prophet, Priest, and King)
E. Exile
F. Remnant

IV. Fullness of Time (Incarnation of the Messiah) Gal. 4.4-5
A. The King Comes to His Kingdom
B. The Present Reality of His Reign
C. The Secret of the Kingdom: the Already and the Not Yet
D. The Crucified King
E. The Risen Lord

V. The Last Times (The Descent of the Holy Spirit) Acts 2.16-18
A. Between the Times: the Church as Foretaste of the Kingdom
B. The Church as Agent of the Kingdom
C. The Conflict Between the Kingdoms of Darkness and Light

VI. The Fulfillment of Time (The Second Coming) Matt. 13.40-43
A. The Return of Christ
B. Judgment
C. The Consummation of His Kingdom

VII. Beyond Time (Eternity Future) 1 Cor. 15.24-28
A. Kingdom Handed Over to God the Father
B. God as All in All

From Before to Beyond Time
Scriptures for Major Outline Points

I. Before Time (Eternity Past)

1 Cor. 2.7 (ESV) - But we impart a secret and hidden wisdom of God, *which God decreed before the ages* for our glory (cf. Titus 1.2).

II. Beginning of Time (Creation and Fall)

Gen. 1.1 (ESV) - *In the beginning*, God created the heavens and the earth.

III. Unfolding of Time (God's Plan Revealed Through Israel)

Gal. 3.8 (ESV) - And the Scripture, foreseeing that God would justify the Gentiles by faith, *preached the Gospel beforehand to Abraham*, saying, "In you shall all the nations be blessed" (cf. Rom. 9.4-5).

IV. Fullness of Time (The Incarnation of the Messiah)

Gal. 4.4-5 (ESV) - *But when the fullness of time had come*, God sent forth his Son, born of woman, born under the law, to redeem those who were under the law, so that we might receive adoption as sons.

V. The Last Times (The Descent of the Holy Spirit)

Acts 2.16-18 (ESV) - But this is what was uttered through the prophet Joel: "'*And in the last days it shall be*,' God declares, 'that I will pour out my Spirit on all flesh, and your sons and your daughters shall prophesy, and your young men shall see visions, and your old men shall dream dreams; even on my male servants and female servants in those days I will pour out my Spirit, and they shall prophesy.'"

VI. The Fulfillment of Time (The Second Coming)

Matt. 13.40-43 (ESV) - Just as the weeds are gathered and burned with fire, *so will it be at the close of the age*. The Son of Man will send his angels, and they will gather out of his kingdom all causes of sin and all lawbreakers, and throw them into the fiery furnace. In that place there will be weeping and gnashing of teeth. Then the righteous will shine like the sun in the Kingdom of their Father. He who has ears, let him hear.

VII. Beyond Time (Eternity Future)

1 Cor. 15.24-28 (ESV) - Then comes the end, when he delivers the Kingdom to God the Father after destroying every rule and every authority and power. For he must reign until he has put all his enemies under his feet. The last enemy to be destroyed is death. For "God has put all things in subjection under his feet." But when it says, "all things are put in subjection," it is plain that he is excepted who put all things in subjection under him. When all things are subjected to him, then the Son himself will also be subjected to him who put all things in subjection under him, that God may be all in all.

APPENDIX 9
"There Is a River"
Identifying the Streams of a Revitalized Authentic Christian Community in the City[1]
Rev. Dr. Don L. Davis • Psalm 46.4 (ESV) - There is a river whose streams make glad the city of God, the holy habitation of the Most High.

Tributaries of Authentic Historic Biblical Faith			
Recognized Biblical Identity	*Revived Urban Spirituality*	*Reaffirmed Historical Connectivity*	*Refocused Kingdom Authority*
The Church Is **One**	The Church Is **Holy**	The Church Is **Catholic**	The Church Is **Apostolic**
A Call to Biblical Fidelity — Recognizing the Scriptures as the anchor and foundation of the Christian faith and practice	**A Call to the Freedom, Power, and Fullness of the Holy Spirit** — Walking in the holiness, power, gifting, and liberty of the Holy Spirit in the body of Christ	**A Call to Historic Roots and Continuity** — Confessing the common historical identity and continuity of authentic Christian faith	**A Call to the Apostolic Faith** — Affirming the apostolic tradition as the authoritative ground of the Christian hope
A Call to Messianic Kingdom Identity — Rediscovering the story of the promised Messiah and his Kingdom in Jesus of Nazareth	**A Call to Live as Sojourners and Aliens as the People of God** — Defining authentic Christian discipleship as faithful membership among God's people	**A Call to Affirm and Express the Global Communion of Saints** — Expressing cooperation and collaboration with all other believers, both local and global	**A Call to Representative Authority** — Submitting joyfully to God's gifted servants in the Church as undershepherds of true faith
A Call to Creedal Affinity — Embracing the Nicene Creed as the shared rule of faith of historic orthodoxy	**A Call to Liturgical, Sacramental, and Catechetical Vitality** — Experiencing God's presence in the context of the Word, sacrament, and instruction	**A Call to Radical Hospitality and Good Works** — Expressing kingdom love to all, and especially to those of the household of faith	**A Call to Prophetic and Holistic Witness** — Proclaiming Christ and his Kingdom in word and deed to our neighbors and all peoples

[1] This schema is an adaptation and is based on the insights of the **Chicago Call** statement of May 1977, where various leading evangelical scholars and practitioners met to discuss the relationship of modern evangelicalism to the historic Christian faith.

APPENDIX 10
A Schematic for a Theology of the Kingdom and the Church
The Urban Ministry Institute

The Reign of the One, True, Sovereign, and Triune God, the LORD God, Yahweh, God the Father, Son, and Holy Spirit

The Father	The Son	The Spirit
Love - 1 John 4.8 Maker of heaven and earth and of all things visible and invisible	Faith - Heb. 12.2 Prophet, Priest, and King	Hope - Rom. 15.13 Lord of the Church
Creation All that exists through the creative action of God.	**Kingdom** The Reign of God expressed in the rule of his Son Jesus the Messiah.	**Church** The one, holy, apostolic community which functions as a witness to (Acts 28.31) and a foretaste of (Col. 1.12; James 1.18; 1 Pet. 2.9; Rev. 1.6) the Kingdom of God.
The eternal God, sovereign in power, infinite in wisdom, perfect in holiness, and steadfast in love, is the source and goal of all things.	**Freedom** (Slavery) Jesus answered them, "Truly, truly, I say to you, everyone who commits sin is a slave to sin. The slave does not remain in the house forever; the Son remains forever. So if the Son sets you free, you will be free indeed." John 8.34-36 (ESV)	*The Church is an Apostolic Community Where the Word is Rightly Preached. Therefore it is a Community of:* **Calling** - For freedom Christ has set us free; stand firm therefore, and do not submit again to a yoke of slavery. - Gal. 5.1 (ESV) (cf. Rom. 8.28-30; 1 Cor. 1.26-31; Eph. 1.18; 2 Thess. 2.13-14; Jude 1.1) **Faith** - ". . . for unless you believe that I am he you will die in your sins". . . . So Jesus said to the Jews who had believed in him, "If you abide in my word, you are truly my disciples, and you will know the truth, and the truth will set you free." - John 8.24b, 31-32 (ESV) (cf. Ps. 119.45; Rom. 1.17; 5.1-2; Eph. 2.8-9; 2 Tim. 1.13-14; Heb. 2.14-15; James 1.25) **Witness** - The Spirit of the Lord is upon me, because he has anointed me to proclaim good news to the poor. He has sent me to proclaim liberty to the captives and recovering of sight to the blind, to set at liberty those who are oppressed, to proclaim the year of the Lord's favor. - Luke 4.18-19 (ESV) (cf. Lev. 25.10; Prov. 31.8; Matt. 4.17, 28.18-20; Mark 13.10; Acts 1.8, 8.4, 12; 13.1-3; 25.20; 28.30-31)
Rom. 8.18-21 →	**Wholeness** (Sickness) But he was wounded for our transgressions; he was crushed for our iniquities; upon him was the chastisement that brought us peace, and with his stripes we are healed. - Isa. 53.5 (ESV)	*The Church is One Community Where the Sacraments are Rightly Administered. Therefore it is a Community of:* **Worship** - You shall serve the Lord your God, and he will bless your bread and your water, and I will take sickness away from among you. - Exod. 23.25 (ESV) (cf. Ps. 147.1-3; Heb. 12.28; Col. 3.16; Rev. 15.3-4; 19.5) **Covenant** - And the Holy Spirit also bears witness to us, for after the saying, "This is the covenant that I will make with them after those days, declares the Lord: I will put my laws on their hearts, and write them on their minds," then he adds, "I will remember their sins and their lawless deeds no more." - Heb. 10.15-17 (ESV) (cf. Isa. 54.10-17; Ezek. 34.25-31; 37.26-27; Mal. 2.4-5; Luke 22.20; 2 Cor. 3.6; Col. 3.15; Heb. 8.7-13; 12.22-24; 13.20-21) **Presence** - In him you also are being built together into a dwelling place for God by his Spirit. - Eph. 2.22 (ESV) (cf. Exod. 40.34-38; Ezek. 48.35; Matt. 18.18-20)
Rev. 21.1-5 →	**Justice** (Selfishness) Behold, my servant whom I have chosen, my beloved with whom my soul is well pleased. I will put my Spirit upon him, and he will proclaim justice to the Gentiles. He will not quarrel or cry aloud, nor will anyone hear his voice in the streets; a bruised reed he will not break, and a smoldering wick he will not quench, until he brings justice to victory. - Matt. 12.18-20 (ESV)	*The Church is a Holy Community Where Discipline is Rightly Ordered. Therefore it is a Community of:* **Reconciliation** - For he himself is our peace, who has made us both one and has broken down in his flesh the dividing wall of hostility by abolishing the law of commandments and ordinances, that he might create in himself one new man in place of the two, so making peace, and might reconcile us both to God in one body through the cross, thereby killing the hostility. And he came and preached peace to you who were far off and peace to those who were near. For through him we both have access in one Spirit to the Father. - Eph. 2.14-18 (ESV) (cf. Exod. 23.4-9; Lev. 19.34; Deut. 10.18-19; Ezek. 22.29; Mic. 6.8; 2 Cor. 5.16-21) **Suffering** - Since therefore Christ suffered in the flesh, arm yourselves with the same way of thinking, for whoever has suffered in the flesh has ceased from sin, so as to live for the rest of the time in the flesh no longer for human passions but for the will of God. - 1 Pet. 4.1-2 (ESV) (cf. Luke 6.22; 10.3; Rom. 8.17; 2 Tim. 2.3; 3.12; 1 Pet. 2.20-24; Heb. 5.8; 13.11-14) **Service** - But Jesus called them to him and said, "You know that the rulers of the Gentiles lord it over them, and their great ones exercise authority over them. It shall not be so among you. But whoever would be great among you must be your servant, and whoever would be first among you must be your slave even as the Son of Man came not to be served but to serve, and to give his life as a ransom for many." - Matt. 20.25-28 (ESV) (cf. 1 John 4.16-18; Gal. 2.10)
Isa. 11.6-9 →		

O, the depth of the riches and wisdom and knowledge of God! How unsearchable are his judgments, and how inscrutable his ways! For who has known the mind of the Lord, or who has been his counselor? Or who has ever given a gift to him, that he might be repaid?" For from him and through him and to him are all things. To him be glory forever! Amen! - Rom. 11.33-36 (ESV) (cf. 1 Cor. 15.23-28; Rev.)

APPENDIX 11
Living in the Already and the Not Yet Kingdom
Rev. Dr. Don L. Davis

The Spirit: The pledge of the inheritance (*arrabon*)
The Church: The foretaste (*aparche*) of the Kingdom
"In Christ": The rich life (*en Christos*) we share as citizens of the Kingdom

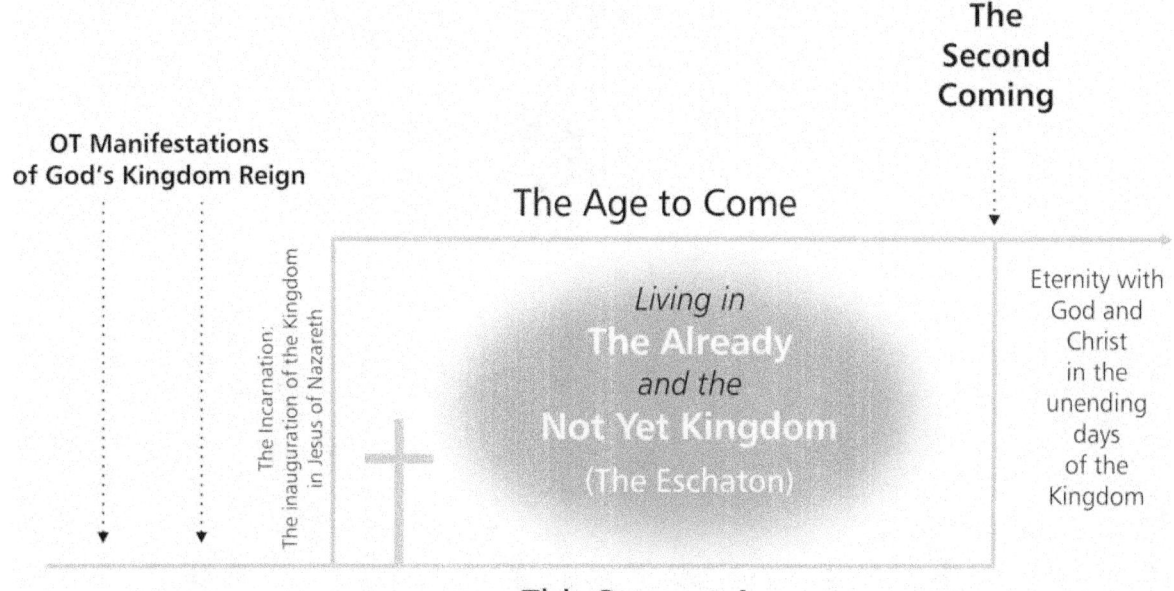

Internal enemy: The flesh (*sarx*) and the sin nature
External enemy: The world (*kosmos*) the systems of greed, lust, and pride
Infernal enemy: The devil (*kakos*) the animating spirit of falsehood and fear

Jewish View of Time

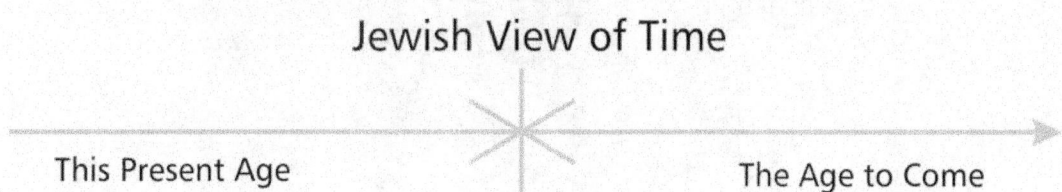

The Coming of Messiah
The restoration of Israel
The end of Gentile oppression
The return of the earth to Edenic glory
Universal knowledge of the Lord

APPENDIX 12
Jesus of Nazareth: The Presence of the Future
Rev. Dr. Don L. Davis

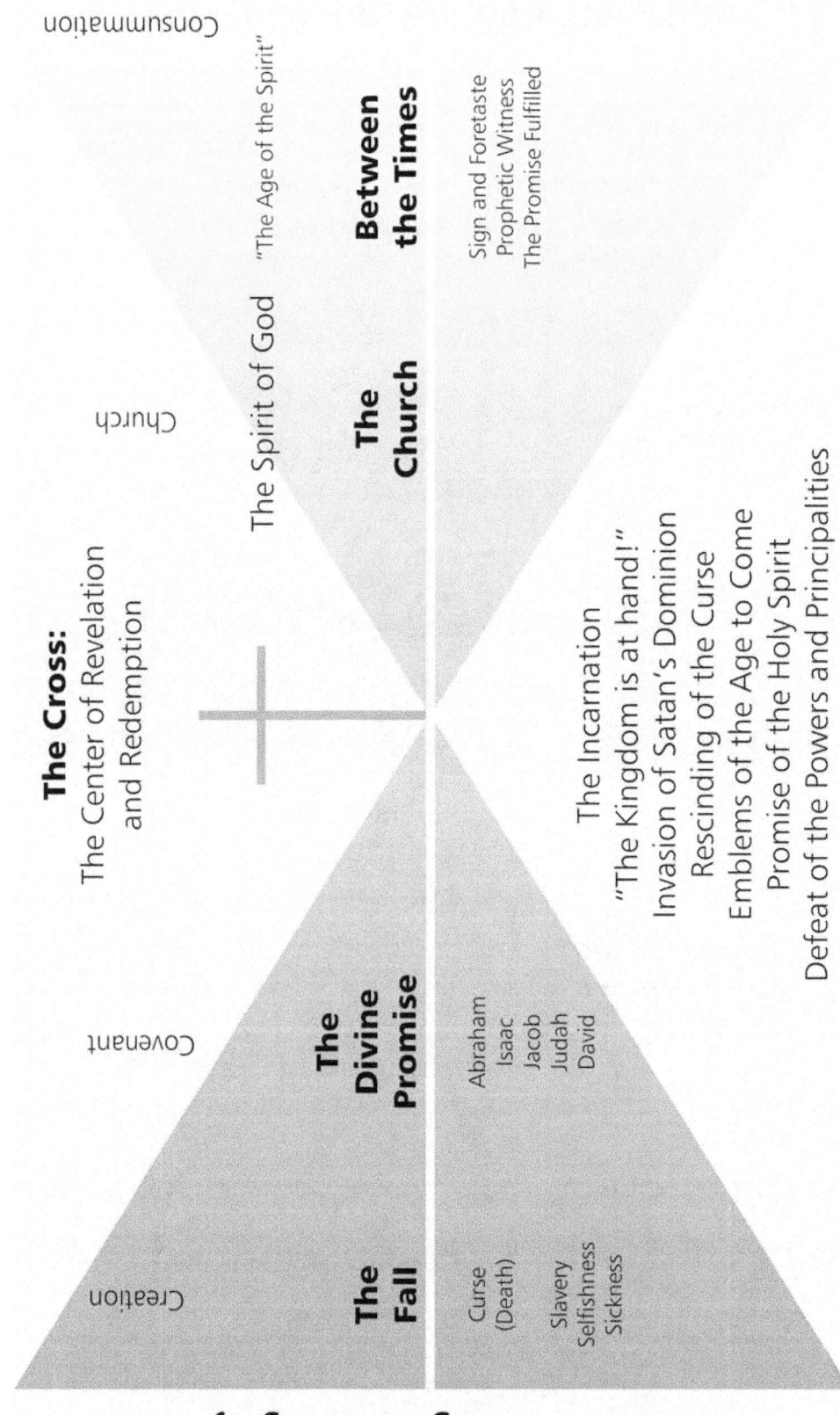

APPENDIX 13

Traditions

(Paradosis)

Dr. Don L. Davis and Rev. Terry G. Cornett

Strong's Definition

Paradosis. Transmission, i.e. (concretely) a precept; specifically, the Jewish traditionary law

Vine's Explanation

denotes "a tradition," and hence, by metonymy, (a) "the teachings of the rabbis," . . . (b) "apostolic teaching," . . . of instructions concerning the gatherings of believers, of Christian doctrine in general . . . of instructions concerning everyday conduct.

1. **The concept of tradition in Scripture is essentially positive.**

   Jer. 6.16 (ESV) - Thus says the Lord: "Stand by the roads, and look, and ask for the ancient paths, where the good way is; and walk in it, and find rest for your souls. But they said, 'We will not walk in it'" (cf. Exod. 3.15; Judg. 2.17; 1 Kings 8.57-58; Ps. 78.1-6).

   2 Chron. 35.25 (ESV) - Jeremiah also uttered a lament for Josiah; and all the singing men and singing women have spoken of Josiah in their laments to this day. They made these a rule in Israel; behold, they are written in the Laments (cf. Gen. 32.32; Judg. 11.38-40).

   Jer. 35.14-19 (ESV) - The command that Jonadab the son of Rechab gave to his sons, to drink no wine, has been kept, and they drink none to this day, for they have obeyed their father's command. I have spoken to you persistently, but you have not listened to me. I have sent to you all my servants the prophets, sending them persistently, saying, 'Turn now every one of you from his evil way, and amend your deeds, and do not go after other gods to serve them, and then you shall dwell in the land that I gave to you and your fathers.' But you did not incline your ear or listen to me. The sons of Jonadab the son of Rechab have kept the command that their father gave them, but this people has not obeyed me. Therefore, thus says the

Traditions (continued)

Lord, the God of hosts, the God of Israel: Behold, I am bringing upon Judah and all the inhabitants of Jerusalem all the disaster that I have pronounced against them, because I have spoken to them and they have not listened, I have called to them and they have not answered." But to the house of the Rechabites Jeremiah said, "Thus says the Lord of hosts, the God of Israel: Because you have obeyed the command of Jonadab your father and kept all his precepts and done all that he commanded you, therefore thus says the Lord of hosts, the God of Israel: Jonadab the son of Rechab shall never lack a man to stand before me."

2. **Godly tradition is a wonderful thing, but not all tradition is godly.**

   Any individual tradition must be judged by its faithfulness to the Word of God and its usefulness in helping people maintain obedience to Christ's example and teaching.[1] In the Gospels, Jesus frequently rebukes the Pharisees for establishing traditions that nullify rather than uphold God's commands.

   Mark 7.8 (ESV) - You leave the commandment of God and hold to the tradition of men" (cf. Matt. 15.2-6; Mark 7.13).

   Col. 2.8 (ESV) - See to it that no one takes you captive by philosophy and empty deceit, according to human tradition, according to the elemental spirits of the world, and not according to Christ.

3. **Without the fullness of the Holy Spirit, and the constant edification provided to us by the Word of God, tradition will inevitably lead to dead formalism.**

   Those who are spiritual are filled with the Holy Spirit, whose power and leading alone provides individuals and congregations a sense of freedom and vitality in all they practice and believe. However, when the practices and teachings of any given tradition are no longer infused by the power of the Holy Spirit and the Word of God, tradition loses its effectiveness, and may actually become counterproductive to our discipleship in Jesus Christ.

   Eph. 5.18 (ESV) - And do not get drunk with wine, for that is debauchery, but be filled with the Spirit.

---

[1] *"All Protestants insist that these traditions must ever be tested against Scripture and can never possess an independent apostolic authority over or alongside of Scripture." (J. Van Engen, "Tradition,"* Evangelical Dictionary of Theology, *Walter Elwell, Gen. ed.) We would add that Scripture is itself the "authoritative tradition" by which all other traditions are judged. See "Appendix A, The Founders of Tradition: Three Levels of Christian Authority," p. 4.*

Traditions (continued)

Gal. 5.22-25 (ESV) - But the fruit of the Spirit is love, joy, peace, patience, kindness, goodness, faithfulness, gentleness, self-control; against such things there is no law. And those who belong to Christ Jesus have crucified the flesh with its passions and desires. If we live by the Spirit, let us also walk by the Spirit.

2 Cor. 3.5-6 (ESV) - Not that we are sufficient in ourselves to claim anything as coming from us, but our sufficiency is from God, who has made us competent to be ministers of a new covenant, not of the letter but of the Spirit. For the letter kills, but the Spirit gives life.

4. **Fidelity to the Apostolic Tradition (teaching and modeling) is the essence of Christian maturity.**

    2 Tim. 2.2 (ESV) - and what you have heard from me in the presence of many witnesses entrust to faithful men who will be able to teach others also.

    1 Cor. 11.1-2 (ESV) - Be imitators of me, as I am of Christ. Now I commend you because you remember me in everything and maintain the traditions even as I delivered them to you (cf. 1 Cor. 4.16-17, 2 Tim. 1.13-14, 2 Thess. 3.7-9, Phil. 4.9).

    1 Cor. 15.3-8 (ESV) - For I delivered to you as of first importance what I also received: that Christ died for our sins in accordance with the Scriptures, that he was buried, that he was raised on the third day in accordance with the Scriptures, and that he appeared to Cephas, then to the twelve. Then he appeared to more than five hundred brothers at one time, most of whom are still alive, though some have fallen asleep. Then he appeared to James, then to all the apostles. Last of all, as to one untimely born, he appeared also to me.

5. **The Apostle Paul often includes an appeal to the tradition for support in doctrinal practices.**

    1 Cor. 11.16 (ESV) - If anyone is inclined to be contentious, we have no such practice, nor do the churches of God (cf. 1 Cor. 1.2, 7.17, 15.3).

Traditions (continued)

> 1 Cor. 14.33-34 (ESV) - For God is not a God of confusion but of peace. As in all the churches of the saints, the women should keep silent in the churches. For they are not permitted to speak, but should be in submission, as the Law also says.

6. **When a congregation uses received tradition to remain faithful to the "Word of God," they are commended by the apostles.**

    > 1 Cor. 11.2 (ESV) - Now I commend you because you remember me in everything and maintain the traditions even as I delivered them to you.

    > 2 Thess. 2.15 (ESV) - So then, brothers, stand firm and hold to the traditions that you were taught by us, either by our spoken word or by our letter.

    > 2 Thess. 3.6 (ESV) - Now we command you, brothers, in the name of our Lord Jesus Christ, that you keep away from any brother who is walking in idleness and not in accord with the tradition that you received from us.

Appendix A

The Founders of Tradition: Three Levels of Christian Authority

Exod. 3.15 (ESV) - God also said to Moses, "Say this to the people of Israel, 'The Lord, the God of your fathers, the God of Abraham, the God of Isaac, and the God of Jacob, has sent me to you.' This is my name forever, and thus I am to be remembered throughout all generations."

1. **The Authoritative Tradition: The Apostles and the Prophets (The Holy Scriptures)**

    Eph. 2.19-21 (ESV) - So then you are no longer strangers and aliens, but you are fellow citizens with the saints and members of the household of God, built on the foundation of the apostles and prophets, Christ Jesus himself being the cornerstone, in whom the whole structure, being joined together, grows into a holy temple in the Lord.

    ~ The Apostle Paul

Traditions (continued)

Those who gave eyewitness testimony to the revelation and saving acts of Yahweh, first in Israel, and ultimately in Jesus Christ the Messiah. This testimony is binding for all people, at all times, and in all places. It is the authoritative tradition by which all subsequent tradition is judged.

2. **The Great Tradition: The Ecumenical Councils and their Creeds[2]**

What has been believed everywhere, always, and by all.

~ Vincent of Lerins

The Great Tradition is the core dogma (doctrine) of the Church. It represents the teaching of the Church as it has understood the Authoritative Tradition (the Holy Scriptures), and summarizes those essential truths that Christians of all ages have confessed and believed. To these doctrinal statements the whole Church, (Catholic, Orthodox, and Protestant)[3] gives its assent. The worship and theology of the Church reflects this core dogma, which finds its summation and fulfillment in the person and work of Jesus Christ. From earliest times, Christians have expressed their devotion to God in its Church calendar, a yearly pattern of worship which summarizes and reenacts the events of Christ's life.

3. **Specific Church Traditions: the Founders of Denominations and Orders**

The Presbyterian Church (U.S.A.) has approximately 2.5 million members, 11,200 congregations and 21,000 ordained ministers. Presbyterians trace their history to the 16th century and the Protestant Reformation. Our heritage, and much of what we believe, began with the French lawyer John Calvin (1509-1564), whose writings crystallized much of the Reformed thinking that came before him.

~ The Presbyterian Church, U.S.A.

Christians have expressed their faith in Jesus Christ in various ways through specific movements and traditions which embrace and express the Authoritative Tradition and the Great Tradition in unique ways. For instance,

---

[2] See Appendix B, "Defining the Great Tradition."

[3] Even the more radical wing of the Protestant reformation (Anabaptists) who were the most reluctant to embrace the creeds as dogmatic instruments of faith, did not disagree with the essential content found in them. "They assumed the Apostolic Creed–they called it 'The Faith,' *Der Glaube*, as did most people." See John Howard Yoder, **Preface to Theology: Christology and Theological Method**. Grand Rapids: Brazos Press, 2002. pp. 222-223.

Traditions (continued)

Catholic movements have arisen around people like Benedict, Francis, or Dominic, and among Protestants people like Martin Luther, John Calvin, Ulrich Zwingli, and John Wesley. Women have founded vital movements of Christian faith (e.g., Aimee Semple McPherson of the Foursquare Church), as well as minorities (e.g., Richard Allen of the African Methodist Episcopal Church or Charles H. Mason of the Church of God in Christ, who also helped to spawn the Assemblies of God), all which attempted to express the Authoritative Tradition and the Great Tradition in a specific way consistent with their time and expression.

The emergence of vital, dynamic movements of the faith at different times and among different peoples reveal the fresh working of the Holy Spirit throughout history. Thus, inside Catholicism, new communities have arisen such as the Benedictines, Franciscans, and Dominicans; and outside Catholicism, new denominations have emerged (Lutherans, Presbyterians, Methodists, Church of God in Christ, etc.). Each of these specific traditions have "founders," key leaders whose energy and vision helped to establish a unique expression of Christian faith and practice. Of course, to be legitimate, these movements must adhere to and faithfully express both the Authoritative Tradition and the Great Tradition. Members of these specific traditions embrace their own unique practices and patterns of spirituality, but these unique features are not necessarily binding on the Church at large. They represent the unique expressions of that community's understanding of and faithfulness to the Authoritative and Great Traditions.

Specific traditions seek to express and live out this faithfulness to the Authoritative and Great Traditions through their worship, teaching, and service. They seek to make the Gospel clear within new cultures or sub-cultures, speaking and modeling the hope of Christ into new situations shaped by their own set of questions posed in light of their own unique circumstances. These movements, therefore, seek to contextualize the Authoritative tradition in a way that faithfully and effectively leads new groups of people to faith in Jesus Christ, and incorporates those who believe into the community of faith that obeys his teachings and gives witness of him to others.

Traditions (continued)

Appendix B

Defining the "Great Tradition"

The Great Tradition (sometimes called the "classical Christian tradition") is defined by Robert E. Webber as follows:

> *[It is] the broad outline of Christian belief and practice developed from the Scriptures between the time of Christ and the middle of the fifth century*
>
> ~ Webber. **The Majestic Tapestry**.
> Nashville: Thomas Nelson Publishers, 1986. p. 10.

This tradition is widely affirmed by Protestant theologians both ancient and modern.

> *Thus those ancient Councils of Nicea, Constantinople, the first of Ephesus, Chalcedon, and the like, which were held for refuting errors, we willingly embrace, and reverence as sacred, in so far as relates to doctrines of faith, for they contain nothing but the pure and genuine interpretation of Scripture, which the holy Fathers with spiritual prudence adopted to crush the enemies of religion who had then arisen.*
>
> ~ John Calvin. **Institutes**. IV, ix. 8.

> *. . . most of what is enduringly valuable in contemporary biblical exegesis was discovered by the fifth century.*
>
> ~ Thomas C. Oden. **The Word of Life**.
> San Francisco: HarperSanFrancisco, 1989. p. xi

> *The first four Councils are by far the most important, as they settled the orthodox faith on the Trinity and the Incarnation.*
>
> ~ Philip Schaff. **The Creeds of Christendom**. Vol. 1.
> Grand Rapids: Baker Book House, 1996. p. 44.

Our reference to the Ecumenical Councils and Creeds is, therefore, focused on those Councils which retain a widespread agreement in the Church among Catholics, Orthodox, and Protestants. While Catholic and Orthodox share common agreement on the first seven councils, Protestants tend to affirm and use primarily the first four. Therefore, those councils which continue to be shared by the whole Church are completed with the Council of Chalcedon in 451.

Traditions (continued)

It is worth noting that each of these four Ecumenical Councils took place in a pre-European cultural context and that none of them were held in Europe. They were councils of the whole Church and they reflected a time in which Christianity was primarily an eastern religion in it's geographic core. By modern reckoning, their participants were African, Asian, and European. The councils reflected a church that ". . . has roots in cultures far distant from Europe and preceded the development of modern European identity, and [of which] some of its greatest minds have been African" (Oden, *The Living God*, San Francisco: HarperSanFrancisco, 1987, p. 9).

Perhaps the most important achievement of the Councils was the creation of what is now commonly called the Nicene Creed. It serves as a summary statement of the Christian faith that can be agreed on by Catholic, Orthodox, and Protestant Christians.

The first four Ecumenical Councils are summarized in the following chart:

Name/Date/Location	Purpose
First Ecumenical Council 325 A.D. Nicea, Asia Minor	Defending against: *Arianism* Question answered: *Was Jesus God?* Action: *Developed the initial form of the Nicene Creed to serve as a summary of the Christian faith*
Second Ecumenical Council 381 A.D. Constantinople, Asia Minor	Defending against: *Macedonianism* Question answered: *Is the Holy Spirit a personal and equal part of the Godhead?* Action: *Completed the Nicene Creed by expanding the article dealing with the Holy Spirit*
Third Ecumenical Council 431 A.D. Ephesus, Asia Minor	Defending against: *Nestorianism* Question answered: *Is Jesus Christ both God and man in one person?* Action: *Defined Christ as the Incarnate Word of God and affirmed his mother Mary as* **theotokos** *(God-bearer)*
Fourth Ecumenical Council 451 A.D. Chalcedon, Asia Minor	Defending against: *Monophysitism* Question answered: *How can Jesus be both God and man?* Action: *Explained the relationship between Jesus' two natures (human and Divine)*

APPENDIX 14
Representin'
Jesus as God's Chosen Representative
Rev. Dr. Don L. Davis

To represent another

Is to be selected to stand in the place of another, and thereby fulfill the assigned duties, exercise the rights and serve as deputy for, as well as to speak and act with another's authority on behalf of their interests and reputation.

Jesus Fulfills The Duties Of Being an Emissary

1. Receiving an *Assignment*, **John 10.17-18**
2. Resourced with an *Entrustment*, **John 3.34; Luke. 4.18**
3. Launched into *Engagement*, **John 5.30**
4. Answered with an *Assessment*, **Matthew 3.16-17**
5. New assignment after *Assessment*, **Philippians 2.9-11**

The Temptation of Jesus Christ
Challenge to and Contention with God's Rep

Mark 1.12-13 (ESV) The Spirit immediately drove him out into the wilderness. [13] And he was in the wilderness forty days, being tempted by Satan. And he was with the wild animals, and the angels were ministering to him.

The Baptism of Jesus Christ
Commissioning and Confirmation of God's Rep

Mark 1.9-11 (ESV) In those days Jesus came from Nazareth of Galilee and was baptized by John in the Jordan. [10] And when he came up out of the water, immediately he saw the heavens opening and the Spirit descending on him like a dove. [11] And a voice came from heaven, "You are my beloved Son; with you I am well pleased."

The Public Preaching Ministry of Jesus Christ
Communication and Conveyance by God's Rep

Mark 1.14-15 (ESV) Now after John was arrested, Jesus came into Galilee, proclaiming the gospel of God, [15] and saying, "The time is fulfilled, and the kingdom of God is at hand; repent and believe in the gospel."

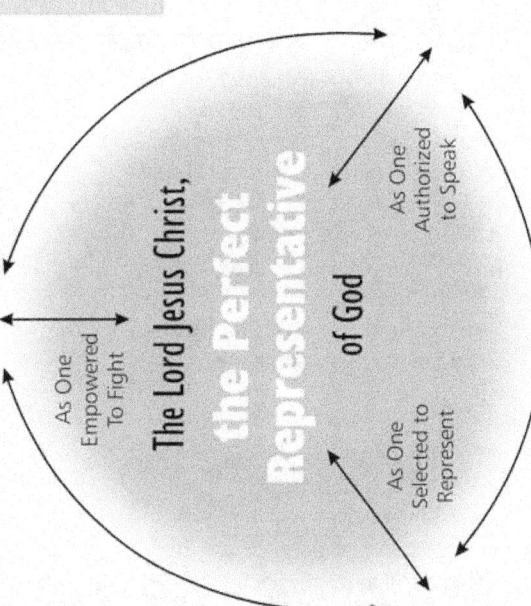

The Lord Jesus Christ, the Perfect Representative of God

- As One Empowered To Fight
- As One Authorized to Speak
- As One Selected to Represent

APPENDIX 15
Picking Up on Different Wavelengths
Integrated vs. Fragmented Mindsets and Lifestyles
Dr. Don L. Davis

A Fragmented Mindset and Lifestyle	An Integrated Lifestyle and Mindset
Sees things primarily in relation to one's own needs	Sees all things as one and whole
Sees something other than God as a substitute point of reference and coordination for meaning and truth	Sees God in Christ as the ultimate point of reference and coordination for all meaning and truth
Seeks God's blessing upon one's own personal enhancement	Aligns personal goals with God's ultimate plan and purposes
Understands the purpose of life to experience the greatest level of personal fulfillment and enhancement possible	Understands the purpose of life to make the maximum contribution possible to God's purpose in the world
Only relates to others in connection to their effect upon and place within one's individual personal space	Deeply identifies with all people and things as an integral part of God's great plan for his own glory
Defines theology as seeking to express someone's perspective on some religious idea or concept	Defines theology as seeking to comprehend God's ultimate designs and plans for himself in Jesus Christ
Applications are rooted in seeking right responses to particular issues and situations	Applications are byproducts of understanding what God is doing for himself in the world
Focuses on the style of analysis (to discern the processes and make-up of things)	Focuses on the style of synthesis (to discern the connection and unity of all things)
Seeks to understand biblical revelation primarily from the standpoint of one's private life ("God's plan for my life")	Seeks to understand biblical revelation primarily from the standpoint of God's plan for whole ("God's plan for the ages")
Governed by pressing concerns to ensure one's own security and significance in one's chosen endeavors ("My personal life plan")	Decision making is governed by commitment to participate as co-workers with God in the overall vision ("God's working in the world")
Coordinates itself around personal need as a working paradigm and project	Connects and correlates itself around God's vision and plan as a working paradigm
Sees mission and ministry as the expression of one's personal giftedness and burden, bringing personal satisfaction and security	Sees mission and ministry as the present, practical expression of one's identity vis-a-vis the panoramic vision of God
Relates knowledge, opportunity, and activity to the goals of personal enhancement and fulfillment	Relates knowledge, opportunity, and activity to a single, integrated vision and purpose
All of life is perceived to revolve around the personal identity and needs of the individual	All of life is perceived to revolve around a single theme: the revelation of God in Jesus of Nazareth

Picking Up on Different Wavelengths (continued)

Scriptures on the Validity of Seeing All Things as Unified and Whole

Ps. 27.4 (ESV) - One thing have I asked of the Lord, that will I seek after: that I may dwell in the house of the Lord all the days of my life, to gaze upon the beauty of the Lord and to inquire in his temple.

Luke 10.39-42 (ESV) - And she had a sister called Mary, who sat at the Lord's feet and listened to his teaching. [40] But Martha was distracted with much serving. And she went up to him and said, "Lord, do you not care that my sister has left me to serve alone? Tell her then to help me." [41] But the Lord answered her, "Martha, Martha, you are anxious and troubled about many things, [42] but one thing is necessary. Mary has chosen the good portion, which will not be taken away from her."

Phil. 3.13-14 (ESV) - Brothers, I do not consider that I have made it my own. But one thing I do: forgetting what lies behind and straining forward to what lies ahead [14] I press on toward the goal for the prize of the upward call of God in Christ Jesus.

Ps. 73.25 (ESV) - Whom have I in heaven but you? And there is nothing on earth that I desire besides you.

Mark 8.36 (ESV) - For what does it profit a man to gain the whole world and forfeit his life?

Luke 18.22 (ESV) - When Jesus heard this, he said to him, "One thing you still lack. Sell all that you have and distribute to the poor, and you will have treasure in heaven; and come, follow me."

John 17.3 (ESV) - And this is eternal life, that they know you the only true God, and Jesus Christ whom you have sent.

1 Cor. 13.3 (ESV) - If I give away all I have, and if I deliver up my body to be burned, but have not love, I gain nothing.

Gal. 5.6 (ESV) - For in Christ Jesus neither circumcision nor uncircumcision counts for anything, but only faith working through love.

Picking Up on Different Wavelengths (continued)

Col. 2.8-10 (ESV) - See to it that no one takes you captive by philosophy and empty deceit, according to human tradition, according to the elemental spirits of the world, and not according to Christ. [9] For in him the whole fullness of deity dwells bodily, [10] and you have been filled in him, who is the head of all rule and authority.

1 John 5.11-12 (ESV) - And this is the testimony, that God gave us eternal life, and this life is in his Son. [12] Whoever has the Son has life; whoever does not have the Son of God does not have life.

Ps. 16.5 (ESV) - The Lord is my chosen portion and my cup; you hold my lot.

Ps. 16.11 (ESV) - You make known to me the path of life; in your presence there is fullness of joy; at your right hand are pleasures forevermore.

Ps. 17.15 (ESV) - As for me, I shall behold your face in righteousness; when I awake, I shall be satisfied with your likeness.

Eph. 1.9-10 (ESV) - making known to us the mystery of his will, according to his purpose, which he set forth in Christ [10] as a plan for the fullness of time, to unite all things in him, things in heaven and things on earth.

John 15.5 (ESV) - I am the vine; you are the branches. Whoever abides in me and I in him, he it is that bears much fruit, for apart from me you can do nothing.

Ps. 42.1 (ESV) - As a deer pants for flowing streams, so pants my soul for you, O God.

Hab. 3.17-18 (ESV) - Though the fig tree should not blossom, nor fruit be on the vines, the produce of the olive fail and the fields yield no food, the flock be cut off from the fold and there be no herd in the stalls, [18] yet I will rejoice in the Lord; I will take joy in the God of my salvation.

Matt. 10.37 (ESV) - Whoever loves father or mother more than me is not worthy of me, and whoever loves son or daughter more than me is not worthy of me.

Ps. 37.4 (ESV) - Delight yourself in the Lord, and he will give you the desires of your heart.

Ps. 63.3 (ESV) - Because your steadfast love is better than life, my lips will praise you.

Picking Up on Different Wavelengths (continued)

Ps. 89.6 (ESV) - For who in the skies can be compared to the Lord? Who among the heavenly beings is like the Lord

Phil. 3.8 (ESV) - Indeed, I count everything as loss because of the surpassing worth of knowing Christ Jesus my Lord. For his sake I have suffered the loss of all things and count them as rubbish, in order that I may gain Christ

1 John 3.2 (ESV) - Beloved, we are God's children now, and what we will be has not yet appeared; but we know that when he appears we shall be like him, because we shall see him as he is.

Rev. 21.3 (ESV) - And I heard a loud voice from the throne saying, "Behold, the dwelling place of God is with man. He will dwell with them, and they will be his people, and God himself will be with them as their God.

Rev. 21.22-23 (ESV) - And I saw no temple in the city, for its temple is the Lord God the Almighty and the Lamb. [23] And the city has no need of sun or moon to shine on it, for the glory of God gives it light, and its lamp is the Lamb.

Ps. 115.3 (ESV) - Our God is in the heavens; he does all that he pleases.

Jer. 32.17 (ESV) - Ah, Lord God! It is you who has made the heavens and the earth by your great power and by your outstretched arm! Nothing is too hard for you.

Dan. 4.35 (ESV) - all the inhabitants of the earth are accounted as nothing, and he does according to his will among the host of heaven and among the inhabitants of the earth; and none can stay his hand or say to him, "What have you done?"

Eph. 3.20-21 (ESV) - Now to him who is able to do far more abundantly than all that we ask or think, according to the power at work within us, [21] to him be glory in the Church and in Christ Jesus throughout all generations, forever and ever. Amen.

APPENDIX 16
Toward a Hermeneutic of Critical Engagement
Rev. Dr. Don L. Davis

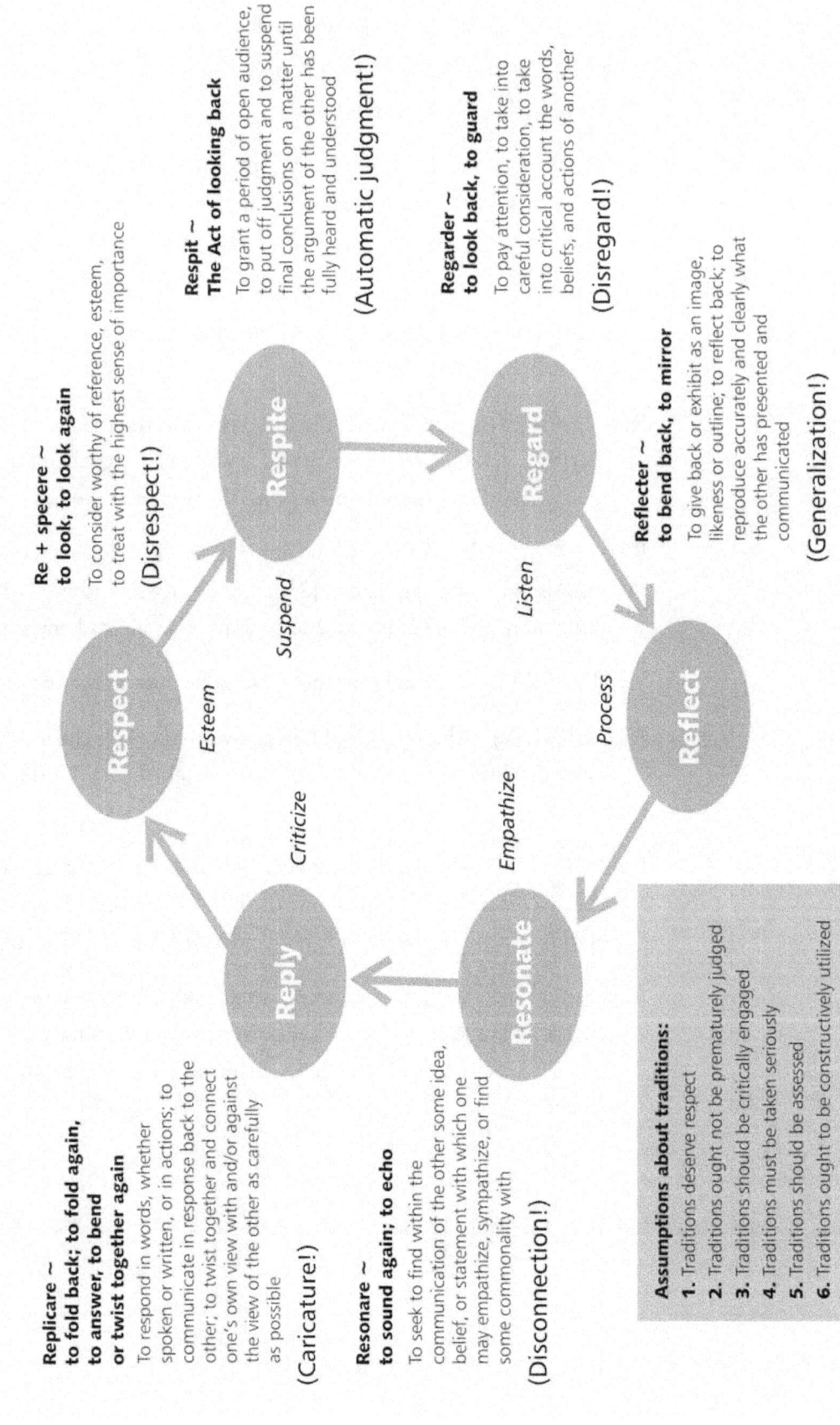

APPENDIX 17
Spiritual Gifts Specifically Mentioned in the New Testament
Rev. Terry G. Cornett

Administration	1 Cor. 12.28	The ability to bring order to Church life.
Apostleship	1 Cor. 12.28; Eph. 4.11	The ability to establish new churches among the unreached, nurture them to maturity, and exercise the authority and wisdom necessary to see them permanently established and able to reproduce; and/or A gift unique to the founding of the Church age which included the reception of special revelation and uniquely binding leadership authority
Discernment	1 Cor. 12.10	The ability to serve the Church through a Spirit-given ability to distinguish between God's truth (his presence, working, and doctrine) and fleshly error or satanic counterfeits
Evangelism	Eph. 4.11	The passion and the ability to effectively proclaim the Gospel so that people understand it
Exhortation	Rom. 12.8	The ability to give encouragement or rebuke that helps others obey Christ
Faith	1 Cor. 12.9	The ability to build up the Church through a unique ability to see the unrealized purposes of God and unwaveringly trust God to accomplish them
Giving	Rom. 12.8	The ability to build up a church through taking delight in the consistent, generous sharing of spiritual and physical resources
Healing	1 Cor. 12.9; 12.28	The ability to exercise faith that results in restoring people to physical, emotional, and spiritual health
Interpretation	1 Cor. 12.10	The ability to explain the meaning of an ecstatic utterance so that the Church is edified
Knowledge	1 Cor. 12.8	The ability to understand scriptural truth, through the illumination of the Holy Spirit, and speak it out to edify the body; and/or The supernatural revelation of the existence, or nature, of a person or thing which would not be known through natural means

Spiritual Gifts Specifically Mentioned in the New Testament (continued)

Leadership	Rom. 12.8	Spiritually-inspired courage, wisdom, zeal, and hard work which motivate and guide others so that they can effectively participate in building the Church
Mercy	Rom. 12.8	Sympathy of heart which enables a person to empathize with and cheerfully serve those who are sick, hurting, or discouraged
Ministering (or Service, or Helping, or Hospitality)	Rom. 12.7; 1 Pet. 4.9	The ability to joyfully perform any task which benefits others and meets their practical and material needs (especially on behalf of the poor or afflicted)
Miracles	1 Cor. 12.10; 12.28	The ability to confront evil and do good in ways that make visible the awesome power and presence of God
Pastoring	Eph. 4.11	The desire and ability to guide, protect, and equip the members of a congregation for ministry
Prophecy	1 Cor. 12.28; Rom. 12.6	The ability to receive and proclaim openly a revealed message from God which prepares the Church for obedience to him and to the Scriptures
Teaching	1 Cor. 12.28; Rom. 12.7; Eph. 4.11	The ability to explain the meaning of the Word of God and its application through careful instruction
Tongues	1 Cor. 12.10; 12.28	Ecstatic utterance by which a person speaks to God (or others) under the direction of the Holy Spirit
Wisdom	1 Cor. 12.8	Spirit-revealed insight that allows a person to speak godly instruction for solving problems; and/or Spirit-revealed insight that allows a person to explain the central mysteries of the Christian faith

APPENDIX 18
Fit to Represent
Multiplying Disciples of the Kingdom of God

Rev. Dr. Don L. Davis • Luke 10.16 (ESV) - The one who hears you hears me, and the one who rejects you rejects me, and the one who rejects me rejects him who sent me.

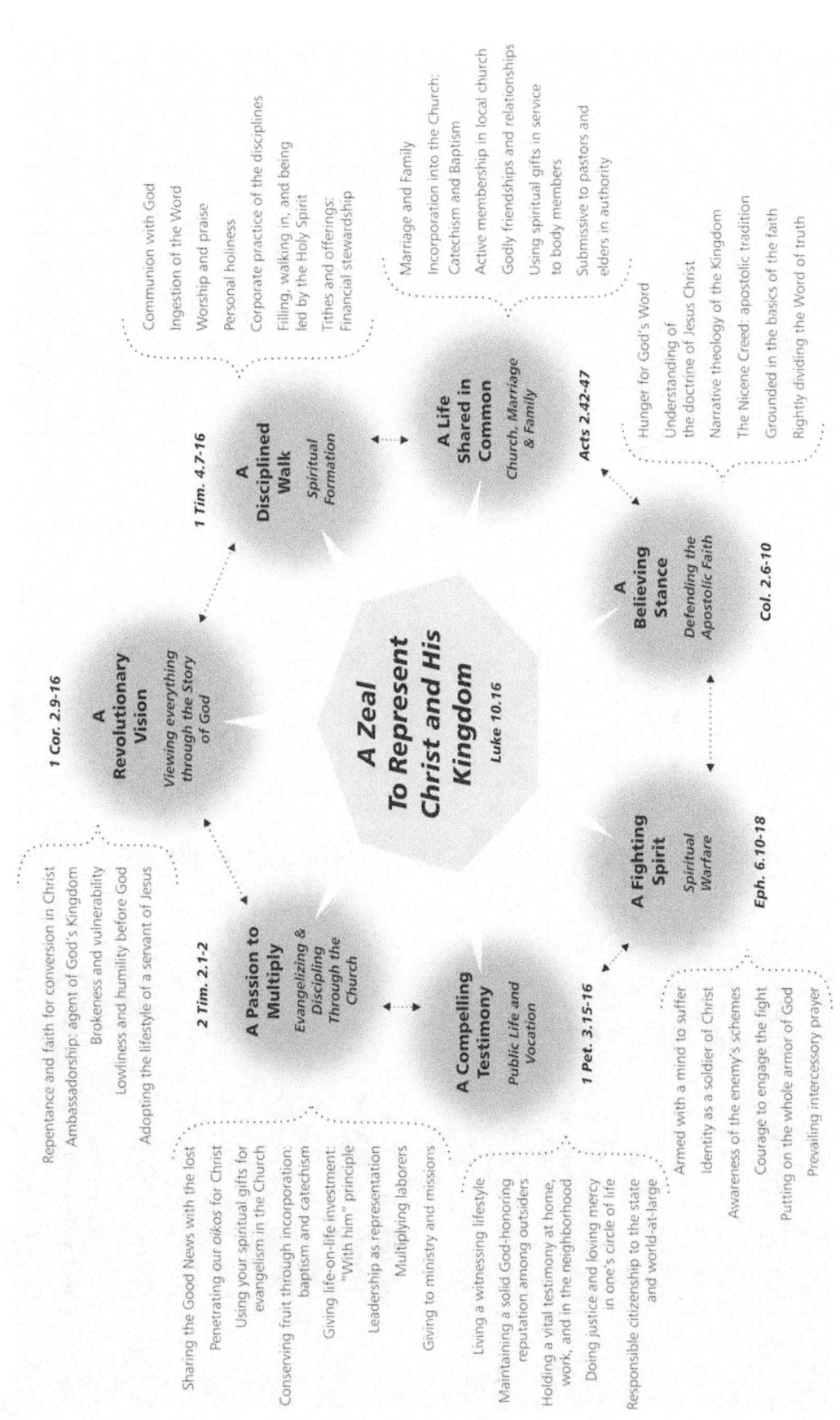

APPENDIX 19
Hindrances to Christ-Like Servanthood
Don L. Davis

Hindrances to Christ-like Servanthood

Worldly-mindedness
2 Tim. 4.10a (ESV)
For Demas, in love with this present world, has deserted me and gone to Thessalonica.

Seeking approval from people and not from God
Gal. 1.10 (ESV)
For am I now seeking the approval of man, or of God? Or am I trying to please man? If I were still trying to please man, I would not be a servant of Christ.

Scripting out the order and extent of our service
Luke 17.9-10 (ESV)
Does he thank the servant because he did what was commanded? [10] So you also, when you have done all that you were commanded, say, "We are unworthy servants; we have only done what was our duty."

A Competitive, prideful spirit
Luke 18.11-12 (ESV)
The Pharisee, standing by himself, prayed thus: "God I thank you that I am not like other men, extortioners, unjust, adulterers, or even like this tax collector. [12] I fast twice a week; I give tithes of all that I get."

Giving only to be seen by others
Acts 5.1-2 (ESV)
But a man named Ananias, with his wife Sapphira, sold a piece of property, [2] and with his wife's knowledge he kept back for himself some of the proceeds and brought only a part of it and laid it at the apostles' feet.

Responding with touchiness and defensiveness
2 Cor. 12.19 (ESV)
Have you been thinking all along that we have been defending ourselves to you? It is in the sight of God that we have been speaking in Christ, and all for your upbuilding, beloved.

Insistence on others not doing their fair share
Luke 10.40 (ESV)
But Martha was distracted with much serving. And she went up to him and said, "Lord, do you not care that my sister has left me to serve alone? Tell her then to help me."

Preoccupation with self-interest
Phil. 2.21 (ESV)
They all seek their own interests, not those of Jesus Christ.

APPENDIX 20

Understanding Leadership as Representation
The Six Stages of Formal Proxy
Don L. Davis

Commissioning (1)
Formal Selection and Call to Represent
- Chosen to be an emissary, envoy, or proxy
- Confirmed by appropriate other who recognize the call
- Is recognized to be a member of a faithful community
- Calling out of a group to a particular role of representation
- Calling to a particular task or mission
- Delegation of position or responsibility

> Luke 10.1 (ESV) After this the Lord appointed seventy-two others and sent them on ahead of him, two by two, into every town and place where he himself was about to go...
>
> Luke 10.16 (ESV) "The one who hears you hears me, and the one who rejects you rejects me, and the one who rejects me rejects him who sent me."
>
> John 20.21 (ESV) Jesus said to them again, "Peace be with you. As the Father has sent me, even so I am sending you."

Equipping (2)
Appropriate Resourcing and Training to Fulfill the Call
- Assignment to a supervisor, superior, mentor, or instructor
- Disciplined instruction of principles underlying the call
- Constant drill, practice, and exposure to appropriate skills
- Recognition of gifts and strengths
- Expert coaching and ongoing feedback

Entrustment (3)
Corresponding Authorization and Empowerment to Act
- Delegation of authority to act and speak on commissioner's behalf
- Scope and limits of representative power provided
- Formal deputization (right to enforce and represent)
- Permission given to be an emissary (to stand in stead of)
- Release to fulfill the commission and task received

Leadership As Representation

CONVICTION — The Revealed Will of God
CHARACTER — The Fulfillment of the Task and Mission
CONSCIENCE — Consent of Your Leaders

Mission (4)
Faithful and Disciplined Engagement of the Task
- Subordination of one's will to accomplish the assignment
- Obedience: carrying out the orders of those who sent you
- Fulfilling the task that was given to you
- Maintaining loyalty to those who sent you
- Freely acting within one's delegated authority to fulfill the task
- Using all means available to do one's duty, whatever the cost
- Full recognition of one's answerability to the one(s) who commissioned

Reckoning (5)
Official Evaluation and Review of One's Execution
- Reporting back to sending authority for critical review
- Formal comprehensive assessment of one's execution and results
- Judgment of one's loyalties and faithfulness
- Sensitive analysis of what we accomplished
- Readiness to ensure that our activities and efforts produce results

Reward (6)
Public Recognition and Continuing Response
- Formal publishing of assessment's results
- Acknowledgment and recognition of behavior and conduct
- Corresponding reward or rebuke for execution
- Review made basis for possible reassignment or recommissioning
- Assigning new projects with greater authority

APPENDIX 21
A Sociology of Urban Leadership Development
A Tool for Assessment and Training
Rev. Dr. Don L. Davis

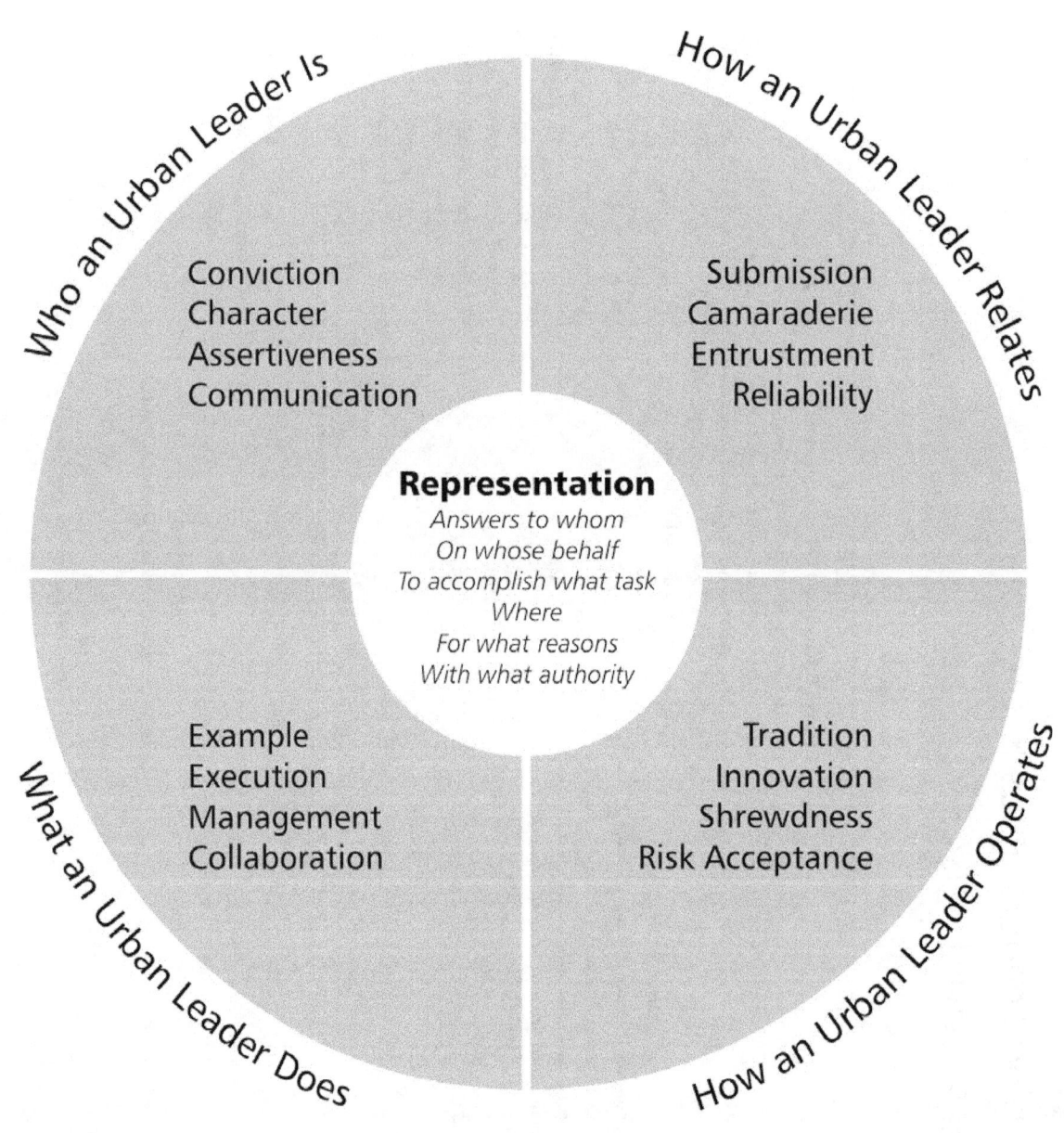

APPENDIX 22
Messianic Prophecies Cited in the New Testament
Rev. Dr. Don L. Davis

	NT Citation	OT Reference	Indication of the Fulfillment of the Messianic Prophecy
1	Matt. 1.23	Isa. 7.14	The virgin birth of Jesus of Nazareth
2	Matt. 2.6	Mic. 5.2	The birth of Messiah in Bethlehem
3	Matt. 2.15	Hos. 11.1	That Yahweh would call Messiah out of Egypt, the second Israel
4	Matt. 2.18	Jer. 31.15	Rachel weeping over infants slain by Herod seeking to destroy Messianic seed
5	Matt. 3.3	Isa. 40.3	John the Baptist's preaching fulfills the Messianic forerunner of Isaiah
6	Matt. 4.15-16	Isa. 9.1-2	Galilean ministry of Jesus fulfills Isaiah's prophecy of Messiah's light to the Gentiles
7	Matt. 8.17	Isa. 53.4	Healing ministry of Jesus fulfills Isaiah prophecy regarding Messiah's power to exorcize and heal
8	Matt. 11.14-15	Isa. 35.5-6; 61.1	Jesus' healing ministry confirms his identity as Yahweh's anointed Messiah
9	Matt. 11.10	Mal. 3.1	Jesus confirms John the Baptist's identity as the messenger of Yahweh in Malachi
10	Matt. 12.18-21	Isa. 42.1-4	Jesus' healing ministry fulfills Isaiah's prophecy of Messiah's compassion for the weak
11	Matt. 12.40	Jon. 1.17	As Jonah was three days and nights in the belly of the sea monster, so Jesus would be in the earth
12	Matt. 13.14-15	Isa. 6.9-10	The spiritual dullness of Jesus' audience
13	Matt. 13.35	Ps. 78.2	Messiah would teach in parables to the people
14	Matt. 15.8-9	Isa. 29.13	Hypocritical nature of the audience of Jesus
15	Matt. 21.5	Zech. 9.9	Triumphal entry of Messiah the King into Jerusalem upon the foal of a donkey
16	Matt. 21.9	Ps. 118.26-27	Hosannas to the King of Jerusalem
17	Matt. 21.16	Ps. 8.2	Out of the mouth of babes Yahweh declares salvation
18	Matt. 21.42	Ps. 118.22	The Stone which the builders rejected has become the Capstone
19	Matt. 23.39	Ps. 110.1	The enthronement of Yahweh's Lord

Messianic Prophecies Cited in the New Testament (continued)

	NT Citation	OT Reference	Indication of the Fulfillment of the Messianic Prophecy
20	Matt. 24.30	Dan. 7.13	The Son of Man to come, of Daniel's prophecy, is none other than Jesus of Nazareth
21	Matt. 26.31	Zech. 13.7	The Shepherd smitten by Yahweh and the sheep scattered
22	Matt. 26.64	Ps. 110.1	Jesus of Nazareth is the fulfillment of Daniel's Messianic Son of Man
23	Matt. 26.64	Dan. 7.3	Jesus will come in the clouds of heaven as Daniel's exalted ruler
24	Matt. 27.9-10	Zech. 11.12-13	Messiah is betrayed for thirty pieces of silver
25	Matt. 27.34-35	Ps. 69.21	God's anointed is given wine mingled with gall
26	Matt. 27.43	Ps. 22.18	The soldiers cast lots for the garments of the Messiah
27	Matt. 27.43	Ps. 22.8	Messiah receives mockery and derision upon the cross
28	Matt. 27.46	Ps. 22.1	Messiah forsaken by God for the sake of others
29	Mark 1.2	Mal. 3.1	John the Baptist is the fulfillment of the prophecy regarding the Lord's messenger
30	Mark 1.3	Isa. 40.3	John the Baptist is the voice calling in the wilderness to prepare the Lord's way
31	Mark 4.12	Isa. 6.9	The spiritual dullness of the audience in regards to Messiah's message
32	Mark 7.6	Isa. 29.13	Hypocrisy of the audience in their response to Messiah
33	Mark 11.9	Ps. 118.25	Hosanna's given to Messiah's entry as King into Jerusalem
34	Mark 12.10-11	Ps. 118.25	The stone which the builders rejected has become the chief cornerstone
35	Mark 12.36	Ps. 110.1	The Lord enthrones the Lord of David upon his throne in Zion
36	Mark 13.26	Dan. 7.13	Jesus is the prophesied Son of Man who will return in glory in the clouds
37	Mark 14.27	Zech. 13.7	Jesus will be forsaken by his own, for the shepherd will be smitten and the sheep scattered
38	Mark 14.62	Dan. 7.13	Jesus is the Messiah, the Son of Man of Daniel's vision
39	Mark 14.62	Ps. 110.1	The Son of Man, who is Jesus, will come from the right hand of Yahweh
40	Mark 15.24	Ps. 22.18	Lots are cast for the garments of Messiah during his passion
41	Mark 15.34	Ps. 22.1	Messiah is forsaken by God for the redemption of the world

Messianic Prophecies Cited in the New Testament (continued)

	NT Citation	OT Reference	Indication of the Fulfillment of the Messianic Prophecy
42	Luke 1.17	Mal. 4.6	John the Baptist will come in the power and the spirit of Elijah
43	Luke 1.76	Mal. 3.1	John goes before the Lord to prepare the way
44	Luke 1.79	Isa. 9.1-2	Messiah will give light to those who dwell in darkness
45	Luke 2.32	Isa. 42.6; 49.6	Messiah will be a light to the Gentiles
46	Luke 3.4-5	Isa. 40.3	John is Isaiah's voice that cries in the wilderness to prepare the Lord's way
47	Luke 4.18-19	Isa. 61.1-2	Jesus is Yahweh's servant, anointed by his Spirit to bring the good news of the Kingdom
48	Luke 7.27	Mal. 3.1	Jesus confirms John's identity as the preparer of the Lord's way
49	Luke 8.10	Isa. 6.9	The dullness of the audience to Messiah Jesus
50	Luke 19.38	Ps. 118.26	Jesus fulfills in his entry into Jerusalem the Messianic prophecy of the King of Israel
51	Luke 20.17	Ps. 118.26	Jesus is Yahweh's stone which the builders rejected, which has become the Capstone
52	Luke 20.42-43	Ps. 110.1	David calls his lord the Messiah and Lord, who is enthroned in Zion by Yahweh
53	Luke 22.37	Isa. 53.12	Messiah is classed among criminals
54	Luke 22.69	Ps. 110.1	Jesus will return from the right hand of God, from where he has been enthroned
55	Luke 23.34	Ps. 22.18	Lots are cast for the garments of Messiah
56	John 1.23	Isa. 40.3	John's preaching is the fulfillment of Isaiah's prophecy about the forerunner of the Messiah
57	John 2.17	Ps. 69.17	Zeal for the house of the Lord will consume the Messiah
58	John 6.45	Isa. 54.13	All those whom God teaches will come to Messiah
59	John 7.42	Ps. 89.4; Mic. 5.2	Messiah, the seed of David, will be from Bethlehem
60	John 12.13	Ps. 118.25-26	Hosannas are given to Israel's triumphant Messiah King
61	John 12.15	Zech. 9.9	The King of Israel enters Jerusalem upon the foal of a donkey
62	John 12.38	Isa. 53.1	As Isaiah prophesied, few believed the report of Yahweh about his anointed One
63	John 12.40	Isa. 6.10	Isaiah saw the glory of Messiah and spoke of the dullness of his audience to him

Messianic Prophecies Cited in the New Testament (continued)

	NT Citation	OT Reference	Indication of the Fulfillment of the Messianic Prophecy
64	John 13.18; cf. 17.12	Ps. 41.9	Betrayal of Messiah by one of his intimate followers
65	John 15.25	Pss. 35.19; 69.4	Messiah will be hated without cause
66	John 19.24	Ps. 22.18	The garments of Messiah will be divided
67	John 19.28	Ps. 69.21	Messiah will be offered wine upon the cross
68	John 19.36	Exod. 12.46; Num. 9.12; Ps. 34.20	Not one bone of the Messiah will be broken
69	John 19.37	Zech. 12.10	The repentant nation of Israel will look upon him whom they have pierced
70	Acts 1.20	Pss. 69.25; 109.8	Judas is to be replaced with another
71	Acts 2.16-21	Joel 2.28-32	The Spirit is to be poured out in the last days upon all flesh
72	Acts 2.25-28	Ps. 16.8-11	Messiah could not undergo decay or corruption in Sheol
73	Acts 2.34-35	Ps. 110.1	Messiah is enthroned at Yahweh's right hand until his enemies are defeated
74	Acts 3.22-23	Deut. 18.15, 19	God would raise up for the people a prophet like Moses
75	Acts 3.25	Gen. 22.18	All nations of the earth would be blessed in the seed of Abraham
76	Acts 4.11	Ps. 118.22	Messiah Jesus is the rejected stone whom God has made the cornerstone
77	Acts 4.25	Ps. 2.1	Yahweh will laugh at the opposition given by the nations to him and his anointed
78	Acts 7.37	Deut. 18.15	Yahweh will give to Israel a prophet like Moses
79	Acts 8.32-33	Isa. 53.7-9	Messiah Jesus is the Suffering Servant of Yahweh
80	Acts 13.33	Ps. 2.7	God has fulfilled the promise to Israel in Jesus by raising him from the dead
81	Acts 13.34	Isa. 53.3	Messiah Jesus is the fulfillment of the sure mercies of David
82	Acts 13.35	Ps. 16.10	Messiah would not undergo corruption in the grave
83	Acts 13.47	Isa. 49.6	Through Paul, the message of Messiah becomes a light to the nations
84	Acts 15.16-18	Amos 9.11-12	The dynasty of David is restored in Jesus, and Gentiles are welcomed into the Kingdom
85	Rom. 9.25-26	Hos. 2.23; 1.10	Gentiles are to become the people of God

Messianic Prophecies Cited in the New Testament (continued)

	NT Citation	OT Reference	Indication of the Fulfillment of the Messianic Prophecy
86	Rom. 9.33; 10.11	Isa. 28.16	Messiah becomes a stone of stumbling to those who reject God's salvation
87	Rom. 10.13	Joel 2.32	Anyone calling on the name of the Lord will be saved
88	Rom. 11.8	Isa. 29.10	Israel through unbelief has been hardened to Messiah
89	Rom. 11.9-10	Ps. 69.22-23	Judgment has hardened upon Israel
90	Rom. 11.26	Isa. 59.20-21	A deliverer will come from Zion
91	Rom. 11.27	Isa. 27.9	Forgiveness of sins will be given through a new covenant
92	Rom. 14.11	Isa. 45.23	All will be finally judged by Yahweh
93	Rom. 15.9	Ps. 18.49	Gentiles praise God through faith in Messiah
94	Rom. 15.10	Deut. 32.43	God receives praise from the nations
95	Rom. 15.11	Ps. 117.1	The peoples of the earth give God glory
96	Rom. 15.12	Isa. 11.10	Gentiles will hope in the root of Jesse
97	Rom. 15.21	Isa. 52.15	The Good News will be preached to those without understanding
98	1 Cor. 15.27	Ps. 8.7	All things are under the feet of God's representative head
99	1 Cor. 15.54	Isa. 25.8	Death will be swallowed up in victory
100	1 Cor. 15.55	Hos. 13.14	Death will one day lose its sting altogether
101	2 Cor. 6.2	Isa. 49.8	Now is the day of salvation through faith in Messiah Jesus
102	2 Cor. 6.16	Ezek. 37.27	God will dwell with his people
103	2 Cor. 6.18	Hos. 1.10; Isa 43.6	Believers in Messiah Jesus are the sons and daughters of God
104	Gal. 3.8, 16	Gen. 12.3; 13.15; 17.8	The Scriptures, foreseeing Gentile justification by faith, preached the Gospel beforehand through the promise to Abraham, that all nations would be blessed in his seed
105	Gal. 4.27	Isa. 54.1	Jerusalem is the mother of us all
106	Eph. 2.17	Isa. 57.19	Peace of Messiah Jesus is preached both to the Jew and the Gentile
107	Eph. 4.8	Ps. 68.18	Messiah in his ascension has conquered and given gifts to us all by his grace
108	Eph. 5.14	Isa. 26.19; 51.17; 52.1; 60.1	The regeneration of the Lord has occurred; his light has shined on us

Messianic Prophecies Cited in the New Testament (continued)

	NT Citation	OT Reference	Indication of the Fulfillment of the Messianic Prophecy
109	Heb. 1.5	Ps. 2.7	Messiah is God's Son
110	Heb. 1.5	2 Sam. 7.14	Messiah Jesus is the anointed Son of God
111	Heb. 1.6	Deut. 32.43	Angels worshiped Messiah when he entered the world
112	Heb. 1.8-9	Ps. 45.6-7	Messiah Jesus is referred to as God by Yahweh in direct address
113	Heb. 1.10-12	Ps. 102.25-27	The Son is the agent of God's creation and is eternal
114	Heb. 1.13	Ps. 110.1	Messiah Jesus is enthroned at the Father's right hand
115	Heb. 2.6-8	Ps. 8.4-6	All things have been made subject to the Son's authority
116	Heb. 2.12	Ps. 22.22	Messiah Jesus is a brother to all of the redeemed
117	Heb. 2.13	Isa. 8.17-18	Messiah puts his trust in Yahweh God
118	Heb. 5.5	Ps. 2.7	Messiah is God's Son
119	Heb. 5.6	Ps. 110.4	Messiah is an eternal priest after the order of Melchizedek
120	Heb. 7.17, 21	Ps. 110.4	Messiah Jesus is an eternal High Priest
121	Heb. 8.8-12	Jer. 31.31-34	A new covenant has been made in the blood of Jesus
122	Heb. 10.5-9	Ps. 40.6	The death of Messiah Jesus replaces the atoning system of temple sacrifice
123	Heb. 10.13	Ps. 110.1	Yahweh has enthroned Messiah Jesus as Lord
124	Heb. 10.16-17	Jer. 31.33-34	The Holy Spirit bears witness of the sufficiency of the New Covenant
125	Heb. 10.37-38	Hab. 2.3-4	He who will come will do so, in a little while
126	Heb. 12.26	Hag. 2.6	All heaven and earth will be shaken
127	1 Pet. 2.6	Isa. 28.16	God lays a cornerstone in Zion
128	1 Pet. 2.7	Ps. 118.22	The stone which the builders rejected, God has made the Capstone
129	1 Pet. 2.8	Isa. 8.14	Messiah is a stone of stumbling to those who do not believe
130	1 Pet. 2.10	Hos. 1.10; 2.23	Gentiles through Messiah are now invited to become the people of God
131	1 Pet. 2.22	Isa. 53.9	The sinless Messiah Jesus was sacrificed for us

APPENDIX 23

Ethics of the New Testament: Living in the Upside-Down Kingdom of God
True Myth and Biblical Fairy Tale
Dr. Don L. Davis

The Principle of Reversal

The Principle Expressed	Scripture
The poor shall become rich, and the rich shall become poor	Luke 6.20-26
The law breaker and the undeserving are saved	Matt. 21.31-32
Those who humble themselves shall be exalted	1 Pet. 5.5-6
Those who exalt themselves shall be brought low	Luke 18.14
The blind shall be given sight	John 9.39
Those claiming to see shall be made blind	John 9.40-41
We become free by being Christ's slave	Rom. 12.1-2
God has chosen what is foolish in the world to shame the wise	1 Cor. 1.27
God has chosen what is weak in the world to shame the strong	1 Cor. 1.27
God has chosen the low and despised to bring to nothing things that are	1 Cor. 1.28
We gain the next world by losing this one	1 Tim. 6.7
Love this life and you'll lose it; hate this life, and you'll keep the next	John 12.25
You become the greatest by being the servant of all	Matt. 10.42-45
Store up treasures here, you forfeit heaven's reward	Matt. 6.19
Store up treasures above, you gain heaven's wealth	Matt. 6.20
Accept your own death to yourself in order to live fully	John 12.24
Release all earthly reputation to gain heaven's favor	Phil. 3.3-7
The first shall be last, and the last shall become first	Mark 9.35
The grace of Jesus is perfected in your weakness, not your strength	2 Cor. 12.9
God's highest sacrifice is contrition and brokenness	Ps. 51.17
It is better to give to others than to receive from them	Acts 20.35
Give away all you have in order to receive God's best	Luke 6.38

APPENDIX 24

Preaching and Teaching Jesus of Nazareth as Messiah and Lord Is the Heart of All Biblical Ministry

Don L. Davis

Phil. 3.8 (ESV) - Indeed, I count everything as loss because of the surpassing worth of *knowing Christ [Messiah] Jesus my Lord*. For his sake I have suffered the loss of all things and count them as rubbish, in order *that I may gain Christ [Messiah]*.

Acts 5.42 (ESV) - And every day, in the temple and from house to house, they *did not cease teaching and preaching Jesus as the Christ [Messiah]*.

1 Cor. 1.23 (ESV) - but we preach *Christ [Messiah] crucified*, a stumbling block to Jews and folly to Gentiles.

2 Cor. 4.5 (ESV) - For what we proclaim is not ourselves, but *Jesus Christ [Messiah] as Lord*, with ourselves as your servants for Jesus' sake.

1 Cor. 2.2 (ESV) - For I decided to know nothing among you except *Jesus Christ [Messiah] and him crucified*.

Eph. 3.8 (ESV) - To me, though I am the very least of all the saints, this grace was given, *to preach to the Gentiles the unsearchable riches of Christ [Messiah]*.

Phil. 1.18 (ESV) - What then? Only that in every way, whether in pretense or in truth, *Christ [Messiah] is proclaimed*, and in that I rejoice. Yes, and I will rejoice.

Col. 1.27-29 (ESV) - To them God chose to make known how great among the Gentiles are the riches of the glory of this mystery, which is *Christ [Messiah] in you, the hope of glory*. [28] Him we proclaim, warning everyone and teaching everyone with all wisdom, that we may *present everyone mature in Christ [Messiah]*. [29] *For this I toil, struggling with all his energy* that he powerfully works within me.

APPENDIX 25
Summary of Messianic Interpretations in the Old Testament
Rev. Dr. Don L. Davis, adapted from James Smith, The Promised Messiah

Legend

EJ - Early Jewish Interpretation
NTA - New Testament Allusion
NTE - New Testament Exegesis
CF - Church Fathers

	Bible Reference	Summary of the Messianic Prophecy	EJ	NTA	NTE	CF
1	Gen. 3.15	One from the ranks of the seed of the woman will crush the head of the serpent	X	X		X
2	Gen. 9.25-27	God will come and dwell in the tents of Shem	X	X		X
3	Gen. 12.3; 18.18; 22.18; 26.4; 28.14	All nations of the earth will be blessed through the seed of Abraham, Isaac, and Jacob	X	X	X	X
4	Gen. 49.10-11	The scepter won't depart from Judah until Shiloh comes, and all the nations will be obedient to him	X	X		X
5	Num. 24.16-24	A powerful ruler from Israel will come and crush the enemies of God's people	X	X		X
6	Deut. 18.15-18	A prophet like Moses will come and all the righteous will listen to him		X	X	X
7	Deut. 32.43	The angels of God commanded to rejoice as the Firstborn of God comes into the world		X		
8	1 Sam. 2.10	God will judge the ends of the earth but will give strength to his anointed	X			X
9	1 Sam. 2.35-36	A faithful Priest will come and dispense blessing upon the people				
10	2 Sam. 7.12-16	The Seed of David will sit upon an eternal throne and will build the house of God		X		X
11	Ps. 89	God's covenant to send Messiah through David cannot be revoked	X			
12	Ps. 132	God has chosen David and Zion		X		
13	Ps. 8	The Son of Man is made a little lower than the angels, and is exalted as ruler over all creation		X	X	X
14	Ps. 40	Messiah volunteers to enter the world, to suffer, and is delivered			X	X

Summary of Messianic Interpretations in the Old Testament (continued)

	Bible Reference	Summary of the Messianic Prophecy	EJ	NTA	NTE	CF
15	Ps. 118	Messiah survives the power of death to become the chief Cornerstone, the Capstone of God's building			X	X
16	Ps. 78.1-2	Messiah will speak to the people in parables			X	
17	Ps. 69	Messiah's zeal for the house of God will bring hatred and abuse, but his enemies will receive their just dues			X	X
18	Ps. 109	The one who betrays Messiah will suffer a terrible fate			X	X
19	Ps. 22	After unparalleled suffering, Messiah conquers death and rejoices with his brethren			X	X
20	Ps. 2	Messiah is enthroned in Zion, defeats his opposition, and rules over creation	X		X	X
21	Ps. 16	Yahweh will not allow Messiah to see corruption in Sheol			X	X
22	Ps. 102	Messiah the Creator is eternal, though suffering severe persecution				X
23	Ps. 45	Messiah is God, and has been anointed by God to sit upon an eternal throne; his people are his lovely bride	X			X
24	Ps. 110	Messiah is a priest-king after the order of Melchizedek, and he sits at the right hand of God, ruling over all humankind	X		X	X
25	Ps. 72	Messiah reigns over a universal and righteous Kingdom of blessing	X			X
26	Ps. 68	Messiah wins a great victory, then ascends back on high	X		X	X
27	Job 9.33; 16.19-21; 17.3; 33.23-28	A Mediator, Interpreter, Advocate, and Witness will walk in the latter days upon the earth				
28	Job 19.23-27	A Redeemer will stand upon the earth in the latter days and the righteous will see him				X
29	Joel 2.23	A Wonderful Teacher will arise and usher in an age of great abundance	X			X
30	Hos. 1.10-2.1	A Second Moses will lead God's people out of bondage into a glorious new era			X	
31	Hos. 3.5	After the exile, God's people will serve Yahweh their God, and David their king	X			
32	Hos. 11.1	God calls his Son, the Second Israel, out of Egypt			X	

Summary of Messianic Interpretations in the Old Testament (continued)

	Bible Reference	Summary of the Messianic Prophecy	EJ	NTA	NTE	CF
33	Isa. 4.2-6	The beautiful and glorious Shoot of Yahweh will be the pride of the remnant of Israel	X			
34	Isa. 7.14-15	A virgin will conceive and bear a son whose name will be called Immanuel			X	X
35	Isa. 8.17-18	Messiah waits for the time of his coming, and he and his children are signs and wonders in Israel		X	X	
36	Isa. 9.1-7	Messiah will bring light to Galilee and one will sit on the throne of David to usher in the reign of God in righteousness and justice	X	X		X
37	Isa. 11.1-16	A Shoot from the stem of Jesse will be filled with the Spirit of Yahweh, and will usher into the earth a Kingdom of righteousness and peace	X	X	X	X
38	Isa. 16.5	Downtrodden peoples will look to the house of David for justice and lovingkindness				
39	Isa. 28.16	God is going to lay in Zion a tried and tested Stone, a precious Cornerstone	X	X	X	X
40	Isa. 30.19-26	The people of God will see their divine Teacher and will enjoy his abundant blessing as a result of listening to him	X			
41	Isa. 32.1-2	A Leader of the future will be a shelter from the storm, like water in a dry place				
42	Isa. 33.17	The eyes of the people of God will see the King in his beauty				
43	Isa. 42.17	Yahweh's Servant will bring forth justice to the nations, and will be a Covenant to the people, a Light to the nations	X		X	X
44	Isa. 49.1-13	Yahweh's Servant is divinely appointed to teach, to raise up the tribes of Jacob, and to be a Light to the Gentiles	X			X
45	Isa. 50.4-11	Yahweh's Servant is an obedient disciple who endures suffering and indignity				X
46	Isa. 52.13-53.12	God's Servant is rejected, suffers horribly for the sins of others, dies, but then sees his seed and is satisfied	X	X	X	X
47	Isa. 55.3-5	A son of David will be made a Witness, Leader, and Commander for the peoples				X
48	Isa. 59.20-21	A Redeemer will come to penitent Zion	X		X	

Summary of Messianic Interpretations in the Old Testament (continued)

	Bible Reference	Summary of the Messianic Prophecy	EJ	NTA	NTE	CF
49	Isa. 61.1-11	Messiah has been anointed by the Spirit of Yahweh to proclaim the Good News to the poor, and liberty and deliverance to the captives	X		X	X
50	Mic. 2.12-13	The divine Breaker will lead the people of God out of bondage	X			
51	Mic. 5.1-5	A glorious Ruler will arise from Bethlehem to shepherd the people of God and give them victory over their enemies	X	X	X	X
52	Hab. 3.12-15	Yahweh comes forth from the salvation of his Anointed, and will strike through the head of the house of evil				
53	Jer. 23.5-6	God will raise up a Righteous Branch who will act wisely and execute justice and righteousness in the land	X			
54	Jer. 30.9, 21	Upon return from exile, God's people will serve David their King who will serve as Mediator and draw near to God for them	X			
55	Jer. 31.21-22	God will create a new thing in the land	X			X
56	Jer. 33.14-26	Yahweh will raise up his righteous Servant in the land, and will not fail to fulfill his promise to David and to Levi	X			
57	Ezek. 17.22-24	A tender Twig from the house of David will become a stately Cedar with birds of every kind nesting under it	X			X
58	Ezek. 21.25-27	The crown is removed from the last king of Judah until he comes whose right it is				
59	Ezek. 34.23-31	God will set over those who return from Babylon one Shepherd, his servant, David		X		
60	Ezek. 37.21-28	God's people will be united and will have one King, "My Servant David"		X		
61	Ezek. 44.48	A Prince in the future age will be accorded honor, and through him sacrifices will be offered to God	X			
62	Dan. 7.13-14	One like a Son of Man will come before the Ancient of Days to receive an everlasting Kingdom and Dominion	X	X	X	X
63	Dan. 9.24-27	After 69 "weeks" of years, Messiah will appear, he will be cut off, and will cause sacrifice and oblation to cease	X			X
64	Hag. 2.6-9	After the shaking of the nations, the Desire of all Nations will come and fill the Temple of God with glory	X		X	

Summary of Messianic Interpretations in the Old Testament (continued)

	Bible Reference	Summary of the Messianic Prophecy	EJ	NTA	NTE	CF
65	Hag. 2.21-23	Zerubbabel will be made God's signet Ring in the day when the thrones of kingdoms and the Gentiles are overthrown by Yahweh				
66	Zech. 3.8-10	The Servant of Yahweh, his Shoot, is symbolized by Joshua the High Priest and by an engraved stone	X			X
67	Zech. 6.12-13	A man whose name is Shoot shall build the Temple of the Lord, and he will be a Priest and a King	X			X
68	Zech. 9.9-11	The King of Zion comes riding upon the foal of a donkey	X		X	X
69	Zech. 10.3-4	God will send one who is the Cornerstone, the Tent Peg, the Battle Bow, the one who possesses all sovereignty	X			
70	Zech. 11.4-14	Thirty pieces of silver thrown to the potter in the house of God			X	X
71	Zech. 13.7	The sword of divine justice smites the Shepherd and the sheep are scattered			X	X
72	Mal. 3.1	The Lord's messenger will clear the way before him, and the Lord will suddenly come to his Temple	X	X	X	X
73	Mal. 4.2	The Sun of Righteousness will arise with healing in his wings	X	X		

APPENDIX 26
Suffering: The Cost of Discipleship and Servant-Leadership

Don L. Davis

To be a disciple is to bear the stigma and reproach of the One who called you into service (2 Tim. 3.12). Practically, this may mean the loss of comfort, convenience, and even life itself (John 12.24-25).

All of Christ's Apostles endured insults, rebukes, lashes, and rejections by the enemies of their Master. Each of them sealed their doctrines with their blood in exile, torture, and martyrdom. Listed below are the fates of the Apostles according to traditional accounts.

- Matthew suffered martyrdom by being slain with a sword at a distant city of Ethiopia.

- Mark expired at Alexandria, after being cruelly dragged through the streets of that city.

- Luke was hanged upon an olive tree in the classic land of Greece.

- John was put in a caldron of boiling oil, but escaped death in a miraculous manner, and was afterward branded at Patmos.

- Peter was crucified at Rome with his head downward.

- James, the Greater, was beheaded at Jerusalem.

- James, the Less, was thrown from a lofty pinnacle of the temple, and then beaten to death with a fuller's club.

- Bartholomew was flayed alive.

- Andrew was bound to a cross, whence he preached to his persecutors until he died.

- Thomas was run through the body with a lance at Coromandel in the East Indies.

- Jude was shot to death with arrows.

- Matthias was first stoned and then beheaded.

- Barnabas of the Gentiles was stoned to death at Salonica.

- Paul, after various tortures and persecutions, was at length beheaded at Rome by the Emperor Nero.

APPENDIX 27
Old Testament Names, Titles, and Epithets for the Messiah
Adapted from Norman L. Geisler, A Popular Survey of the Old Testament

1. Advocate, Job 16.19
2. Angel (messenger), Job 33.23
3. Anointed, 1 Sam. 2.19; Ps. 2.2
4. Battle-bow, Zech. 10.4
5. Bethlehem's Ruler, Mic. 5.2
6. Breaker, Mic. 2.13
7. Commander, Isa. 55.4
8. Cornerstone (Capstone), Ps. 118.22; Isa. 28.16
9. Covenant of the People, Isa. 42.6
10. Crusher, Gen. 3.15
11. David, Hos. 3.5; Jer. 30.9
12. Desire of all Nations, Hag. 2.7
13. Eternal One, Ps. 102.25-27
14. Eternal Priest, Ps. 110.4
15. Everlasting Father, Isa. 9.6
16. Faithful Priest, 1 Sam. 2.35
17. Firstborn, Ps. 89.27
18. Forsaken Sufferer, Ps. 22
19. Foundation, Isa. 28.16; Zech. 10.4
20. God, Ps. 45.6-7
21. Head, Hos. 1.11; Mic. 2.13
22. Healer, Isa. 42.7
23. He who Comes, Ps. 118.26
24. Horn of David, Ps. 132.17
25. Immanuel, Isa. 7.14
26. Interpreter, Job 33.23
27. Israel, Hos. 11.1; Isa. 49.3
28. King, Ps. 2.5; Hos. 3.5
29. Lamp for David, Ps. 132.17
30. Last, Job 19.25
31. Launderer, Mal. 3.2
32. Leader, Isa. 55.4
33. Liberator, Isa. 42.7
34. Light, Isa. 9.2
35. Light of the Gentiles, Isa. 42.6; 49.6
36. Lord, Mal. 3.1
37. Man, Zech. 6.12; 13.7
38. Man of Sorrows, Isa. 53.3
39. Mediator, Job 33.23
40. Messenger of the Covenant, Mal. 3.1
41. Messiah-Prince, Dan. 9.25
42. Mighty God, Isa. 9.6
43. Mighty Hero, Ps. 45.3
44. My Equal, Zech. 13.7
45. Nail (peg), Zech. 10.4
46. Our Peace, Mic. 5.5
47. Parable Teller, Ps. 78.1-2
48. Pierced One, Zech. 12.10

Old Testament Names, Titles, and Epithets for the Messiah (continued)

49. Poor and Afflicted, Ps. 69.29
50. Priestly Ruler, Jer. 30.21; Zech. 6.13
51. Prince, Ezek. 37.25; 44-48
52. Prince of Peace, Isa. 9.6
53. Proclaimer of Good Tidings to the Poor, Isa. 61.2
54. Prophet like Moses, Deut. 18.15,18
55. Redeemer, Job 19.25; Isa. 59.20
56. Refiner, Mal. 3.2
57. Refuge, Isa. 32.1
58. Rejected Shepherd, Zech. 11
59. Rejected Stone, Ps. 118.22
60. Righteous Shoot, Jer. 23.5; 33.15
61. Root out of Dry Ground, Isa. 53.2
62. Ruler of all Nature, Ps. 8.5-8
63. Ruler of the Earth, Isa. 16.5
64. Scepter, Num. 24.17
65. Second Moses, Hos. 11.1
66. Seed of Abraham, Gen. 12.3; 18.18
67. Seed of David, 2 Sam. 2.12
68. Seed of the Woman, Gen. 3.15
69. Servant, Isa. 42.1; 49.3, 6
70. Shade, Isa. 32.2
71. Shelter, Isa. 32.1
72. Shepherd, Ezek. 34.23; 37.24
73. Shiloh, Gen. 49.10
74. Shoot, Zech. 3.8; 6.12
75. Shoot from the Stump of Jesse, Isa. 11.1
76. Shoot of Yahweh, Isa. 4.2
77. Sign and Wonder, Isa. 8.18
78. Signet Ring, Hag. 2.23
79. Son of God, 2 Sam. 7.14; Ps. 2.7
80. Son of Man, Ps. 8.4; Dan. 7.13
81. Star, Num. 24.17
82. Stone, Zech. 3.9
83. Substitutionary Sufferer, Isa. 53
84. Sun of Righteousness, Mal. 4.5
85. Teacher, Isa. 30.20
86. Teacher for Righteousness, Joel 2.23
87. Tender Shoot, Isa. 53.2
88. Tender Twig, Ezek. 17.22
89. Temple Builder, Zech. 6.12
90. Tent Dweller, Gen. 9.26-27
91. Tested Stone, Isa. 28.16
92. Trailblazer, Ps. 16.11
93. Victor, Ps. 68.18
94. Volunteer, Ps. 40.7
95. Water of Life, Isa. 32.2
96. Witness, Job 16.19
97. Witness to the Peoples, Isa. 55.4
98. Wonderful Counselor, Isa. 9.6
99. Yahweh, Our Righteousness, Jer. 23.6
100. Zerubbabel, Hag. 2.23

APPENDIX 28

Messiah Jesus: Fulfillment of the Old Testament Types

Adapted from Norman Geisler, *To Understand the Bible, Look for Jesus*, pp. 38-41.

Messiah Jesus Fulfills the Tabernacle Types

Tabernacle Types	Jesus of Nazareth as the Antitype
The One Door	I am the Door John 10.9
The Brazen Altar	Gives his life as a ransom for many Mark 10.45
The Laver	If I do not wash you, you have no part with me John 13.8, 10; 1 John 1.7
The Lampstand	I am the Light of the Word John 8.12
The Shewbread	I am the Bread of Life John 6.48
The Altar of Incense	I am praying for them John 17.9
The Veil	This is my body Matt. 26.26
The Mercy Seat	I lay down my life for the sheep John 10.15

Messiah Jesus: Fulfillment of the Old Testament Types (continued)

Contrast Between Aaron's and Melchizedek's Priesthood

Nature of the Order	The Order of Aaron's Levitical Priesthood	The Order of Messiah Jesus' Priesthood (Melchizedek's Priesthood)
Consecration	Temporal and fading	Eternal priesthood Heb. 7.21-23
Priest	Fallible, vulnerable to sin	Sinless and perfect Heb. 7.26
Priesthood	Changeable	Unchangeable priesthood Heb. 7.24
Ministry	Continual offering of sacrifice	Secured an eternal redemption once for all Heb. 9.12, 26
Mediation	Imperfect representation	Perfect representation between God and humankind Heb. 2.14-18
Sacrifice	Unable and insufficient to take the sin of the offenders away	Offered a single sacrifice for sin for all time Heb. 10.11-12
Intercession	Was interrupted by weakness and death	Always lives to make intercession for us Heb. 7.25

Messiah Jesus: Fulfillment of the Old Testament Types (continued)

Messiah Jesus Fulfills the Levitical Sacrifices and Offerings

The Levitical Offering	How Offering is Fulfilled in Jesus of Nazareth
The Burnt Offering	The perfection of his life Heb. 9.14
The Meal Offering	The dedication and presentation of his life Heb. 5.7; John 4.34
The Peace Offering	He is the peace of our relationships and souls Heb. 4.1-2; Eph. 2.14
The Sin Offering	He bore the penalty for our offense Heb. 10.12; 1 John 2.2
The Trespass Offering	Provision for the offender Heb. 10.20-21; 1 John 1.7

Messiah Jesus: Fulfillment of the Old Testament Types (continued)

Messiah Jesus Fulfills the Levitical Feasts and Festivals

Levitical Feast (Lev. 23)	The Fulfillment in Jesus of Nazareth
The Passover (April)	The death of Jesus Christ 2 Cor. 5.17
Unleavened Bread (April)	Holy and humble walk for Jesus 1 Cor. 5.8
First Fruits (April)	The resurrection of Messiah Jesus 1 Cor. 15.23
The Feast of Pentecost (June)	Outpouring of the Spirit by the Father and the Son Acts 1.5; 2.4
Trumpets (September)	Messiah Jesus' regathering of the Nation Israel Matt. 24.31
The Day of Atonement (September)	Propitiation and cleansing through Jesus Rom. 11.26
Tabernacles (September)	Rest and reunion with Messiah Jesus Zech. 14.16-18

APPENDIX 29
Portrayals of Jesus in the New Testament Books
Adapted from John Stott, **The Incomparable Christ**

The Thirteen Letters of Paul				
Approximate Date of Writing	Period	Group	Letters	How Messiah is Presented
48-49	End of 1st missionary journey	A polemical letter	Galatians	Christ the Liberator
50-52	During 2nd missionary journey	The early letters	1 and 2 Thessalonians	Christ the Coming Judge
53-57	During 3rd missionary journey	The major letters	Romans, 1 and 2 Corinthians	Christ the Savior
60-62	During 1st imprisonment in Rome	The prison letters	Colossians, Philemon, Ephesians, and Philippians	Christ the Supreme Lord
62-67	During release and 2nd imprisonment	The pastoral letters	1 and 2 Timothy and Titus	Christ the Head of the Church
General Epistles and Revelation				
Before 70	During the Pauline and Petrine ministry	Epistle to believing Jews	Hebrews	Christ our Great High Priest
45-50	First book of the NT to be written	General epistles	James	Christ our Teacher
64-67	Early period of persecution	General epistles	1 and 2 Peter	Christ our Exemplary Sufferer
90-100	Toward end of Apostle's ministry	General epistles	1, 2, and 3 John	Christ our Life
66-69	Threat and rise of early apostasy	General epistles	Jude	Christ our Advocate
95	Written while in exile	Prophecy	Revelation	King of kings and Lord of lords

APPENDIX 30

A Harmony of the Ministry of Jesus

Adapted from Walter M. Dunnett, Exploring the New Testament, p. 14.

Gospel	The Period of Preparation	The Period of Public Ministry		The Period of Suffering	The Period of Triumph
		Opening	Closing		
Matthew	1.1-4.16	4.17-16.20	16.21-26.2	26.3-27.66	28.1-20
Mark	1.1-1.13	1.14-8.30	8.31-13.37	14.1-15.47	16.1-20
Luke	1.1-4.13	4.14-9.21	9.22-21.38	22.1-23.56	24.1-53
John	1.1-34	1.35-6.71	7.1-12.50	13.1-19.42	20.1-21.25

APPENDIX 31
Communicating Messiah: The Relationship of the Gospels
Adapted from N. R. Ericson and L. M. Perry. **John: A New Look at the Fourth Gospel**

	Matthew	Mark	Luke	John
Date	c. 65	c. 59	c 61	c. 90
Chapters	28	16	24	21
Verses	1,071	666	1.151	879
Period	36 years	4 years	37 years	4 years
Audience	The Jews	The Romans	The Greeks	The World
Christ As	The King	The Servant	The Man	The Son of God
Emphasis	Sovereignty	Humility	Humanity	Deity
Sign	The Lion	The Ox	The Man	The Eagle
Ending	Resurrection	Empty Tomb	Promise of the Spirit	Promise of his Second Coming
Written In	Antioch?	Rome	Rome	Ephesus
Key Verse	27.37	10.45	19.10	20.30-31
Key Word	Kingdom	Service	Salvation	Believe
Purpose	Presentation of Jesus Christ		Interpretation of Jesus the Messiah	
Time to Read	2 hours	1 ¼ hours	2 ¼ hours	1 ½ hours

APPENDIX 32
Appearances of the Resurrected Messiah
Dr. Don L. Davis

	Appearance	Scripture
1	Appearance to Mary Magdalene	John 20.11-17; Mark 16.9-11
2	Appearance to the women	Matt. 28.9-10
3	Appearance to Peter	Luke 24.34; 1 Cor. 15.5
4	Appearance to the disciples on the road to Emmaus	Mark 16.12-13; Luke 24.13-35
5	Appearance to the ten disciples, referred to as the "Eleven" (with Thomas absent)	Mark 16.14; Luke 24.36-43; John 20.19-24
6	Appearance to the Eleven with Thomas present one week later	John 20.26-29
7	Appearance to seven disciples by the Sea of Galilee	John 21.1-23
8	Appearance to five hundred	1 Cor. 15.6
9	Appearance to James, the Lord's brother	1 Cor. 15.7
10	Appearance to the eleven disciples on the mountain in Galilee*	Matt. 28.16-20
11	Appearance to his disciples at his ascension on the Mount of Olives*	Luke 24.44-53; Acts 1.3-9
12	Appearance to Stephen prior to his death as the Church's first martyr (witness)	Acts 7.55-56
13	Appearance to Paul on the road to Damascus	Acts 9.3-6; cf. 22.6-11; 26.13-18; 1 Cor. 15.8
14	Appearance to Paul in Arabia	Acts 20.24; 26.17; Gal. 1.12,17
15	Appearance to Paul in the Temple	Acts 22.17-21; cf. 9.26-30; Gal. 1.18
16	Appearance to Paul in prison in Caesarea	Acts 23.11
17	Appearance to John during his exile in Patmos	Rev. 1.12-20

* Items 10 and 11 describe the events commonly referred to as "The Great Commission" and "The Ascension," respectively.

APPENDIX 33

The Shadow and the Substance
Understanding the Old Testament as God's Witness to Jesus Christ

Rev. Dr. Don L. Davis

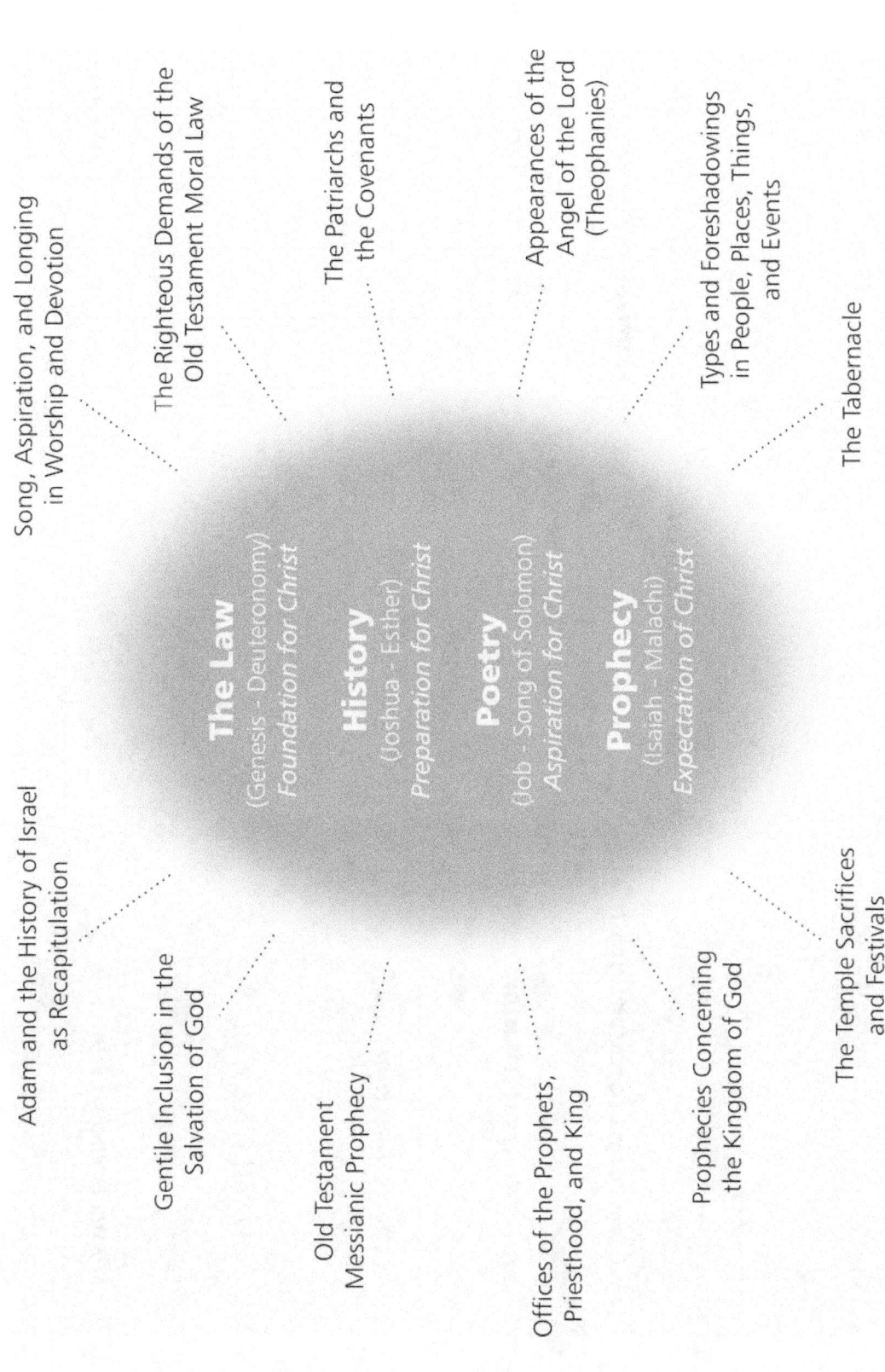

- Song, Aspiration, and Longing in Worship and Devotion
- The Righteous Demands of the Old Testament Moral Law
- The Patriarchs and the Covenants
- Appearances of the Angel of the Lord (Theophanies)
- Types and Foreshadowings in People, Places, Things, and Events
- The Tabernacle

The Law (Genesis – Deuteronomy) *Foundation for Christ*
History (Joshua – Esther) *Preparation for Christ*
Poetry (Job – Song of Solomon) *Aspiration for Christ*
Prophecy (Isaiah – Malachi) *Expectation of Christ*

- Adam and the History of Israel as Recapitulation
- Gentile Inclusion in the Salvation of God
- Old Testament Messianic Prophecy
- Offices of the Prophets, Priesthood, and King
- Prophecies Concerning the Kingdom of God
- The Temple Sacrifices and Festivals

Appendix 34
In Christ
Rev. Dr. Don L. Davis

"In Christ"
The Mystery of Our Total Identification with Christ
John 15.4-5

We are **"made one in Christ,"**
1 Cor. 6.15-17

We were **baptized into him,**
1 Cor. 12.13

We were **crucified with him,**
Gal. 2.20

We **died with him,**
Rom. 6.3-4; Col. 3.3

We were **buried with him,**
Rom. 6.3-4

We were **raised with him,**
Eph. 2.4-7; Col. 3.1

We **ascended with him,**
Eph. 2.6

We **sit with him** in heavenly places,
Eph. 2.6

We will be **caught up together with him,**
1 Thess. 4.13-18

We **suffer with him,**
Rom. 8.17-18

We will be **resurrected in him,**
1 Cor. 15.48-49

We will be **glorified with him,**
Rom. 8.17

We will be **made like him,**
1 John 3.2

We will be **joint-heirs with him,**
Rom. 8.17

We will **reign forever with him,**
Rev. 3.21

APPENDIX 35
The Miracles of Jesus
*adapted from **The Bible Made Easy**. Peabody: Hendrickson Publishers, 1997.*

1	Water changed to wine	John 2.1-11		19	Jairus' daughter raised	Luke 8.41-56
2	Nobleman's son healed	John 4.46-54		20	Woman with hemorrhage healed	Luke 8.43-48
3	Lame man by the Bethesda pool	John 5.1-9		21	Demon-possessed boy delivered	Luke 8.43-48
4	Man born blind	John 9.1-41		22	Mute, demon-possessed man healed	Luke 9.38-43
5	Lazarus raised from the dead	John 11.1-44		23	Crippled woman straightened	Luke 13.11-13
6	153 fish captured	John 21.1-11		24	Ten lepers cleansed	Luke 17.11-19
7	Jesus walks on water	John 6.19-21		25	Blind Bartimeus made well	Luke 18.35-43
8	5,000 people fed	John 6.5-13		26	Malchus' ear restored	Luke 22.50-51
9	Demon-possessed man loosed	Luke 4.33-35		27	Two blind men healed	Matt. 9.27-31
10	Peter's mother-in-law healed	Luke 4.38-39		28	Demon-possessed mute healed	Matt. 9.32-33
11	Large catch of fish	Luke 5.1-11		29	Coin in the fish's mouth	Matt. 17.24-27
12	Leper cleansed	Luke 5.12-13		30	Woman's daughter made whole	Matt. 15.21-28
13	Paralyzed man restored	Luke 5.18-25		31	4,000 people fed	Matt. 15.32-38
14	Shriveled hand made whole	Luke 5.5-10		32	Fig tree cursed	Matt. 21.18-22
15	Centurion's steward healed	Luke 7.1-10		33	Deaf and mute man healed	Mark 7.31-37
16	Widow's dead son raised	Luke 7.11-15		34	Blind man restored	Mark 8.22-26
17	The storm calmed	Luke 8.22-25		35	Man with dropsy healed	Luke 14.1-4
18	The man with Legion exorcized	Luke 27-35				

APPENDIX 36
The Parables of Jesus
adapted from **The Bible Made Easy**. *Peabody: Hendrickson Publishers, 1997.*

1	The Good Samaritan	Luke 10.30-37
2	The Lost Sheep	Luke 15.4-6
3	The Lost Coin	Luke 15.8-10
4	The Prodigal Son	Luke 15.11-32
5	The Dishonest Manager	Luke 16.1-8
6	The Rich Man and Lazarus	Luke 16.1-8
7	The Servants	Luke 17.7-10
8	The Persistent Widow	Luke 18.2-5
9	The Talents	Luke 19.12-27
10	The Wicked Tenants	Luke 20.9-16
11	New Cloth	Luke 5.36
12	New Wine	Luke 5.37-38
13	The House on the Rock	Luke 6.47-49
14	Two Debtors	Luke 7.41-43
15	The Sower	Luke 8.5-8
16	The Lamp	Luke 16.1-12
17	The Watching Servants	Luke 12.35-40
18	The Persistent Friend	Luke 11.5-8
19	The Rich Fool	Luke 12.16-21
20	The Faithful Steward	Luke 12.42-48
21	The Fruitless Fig Tree	Luke 13.6-9
22	The Leafless Fig Tree	Luke 21.29-31
23	The Mustard Seed	Luke 13.18-19
24	The Leaven	Luke 13.20-21
25	The Wedding Guests	Luke 14.7-14
26	The Great Banquet	Luke 14.16-24
27	Tower Building and Warfare	Luke 14.28-33
28	The Pharisee and the Publican	Luke 18.10-14
29	The Returning House Owner	Mark 12.1-9
30	The Growing Seed	Mark 4.26-29
31	The Weeds	Matt. 13.24-30
32	The Hidden Treasure	Matt. 13.44
33	The Pearl of Great Price	Matt. 13.45-46
34	The Net	Matt. 13.47-48
35	The Unforgiving Servant	Matt. 18.23-24
36	The Workers in the Vineyard	Matt. 20.1-16
37	The Two Sons	Matt. 21.28-31
38	The Ten Virgins	Matt. 25.1-13
39	The Sheep and the Goats	Matt. 25.31-36
40	The Wedding Banquet	Matt. 22.2-14

APPENDIX 37
Union with Christ: The Christocentric Paradigm
Christianity as Union with, Allegiance to, and Devotion to Jesus of Nazareth
Representative Texts

Rom. 6.4-5 (ESV) - We were buried therefore with him by baptism into death, in order that, just as Christ was raised from the dead by the glory of the Father, we too might walk in newness of life. [5] For if we have been united with him in a death like his, we shall certainly be united with him in a resurrection like his.

Col. 2.6-7 (ESV) - Therefore, as you received Christ Jesus the Lord, so walk in him, [7] rooted and built up in him and established in the faith, just as you were taught, abounding in thanksgiving.

John 14.6 (ESV) - Jesus said to him, "I am the way, and the truth, and the life. No one comes to the Father except through me."

Gal. 2.20 (ESV) - It is no longer I who live, but Christ who lives in me. And the life I now live in the flesh I live by faith in the Son of God, who loved me and gave himself for me.

Eph. 2.4-7 (ESV) - But God, being rich in mercy, because of the great love with which he loved us, [5] even when we were dead in our trespasses, made us alive together with Christ - by grace you have been saved - [6] and raised us up with him and seated us with him in the heavenly places in Christ Jesus, [7] so that in the coming ages he might show the immeasurable riches of his grace in kindness toward us in Christ Jesus.

Rom. 8.16-17 (ESV) - The Spirit himself bears witness with our spirit that we are children of God, [17] and if children, then heirs - heirs of God and fellow heirs with Christ, provided we suffer with him in order that we may also be glorified with him.

Eph. 5.2 (ESV) - And walk in love, as Christ loved us and gave himself up for us, a fragrant offering and sacrifice to God.

John 15.4-5 (ESV) - Abide in me, and I in you. As the branch cannot bear fruit by itself, unless it abides in the vine, neither can you, unless you abide in me. [5] I

Union with Christ: The Christocentric Paradigm (continued)

am the vine; you are the branches. Whoever abides in me and I in him, he it is that bears much fruit, for apart from me you can do nothing.

Col. 3.17 (ESV) - And whatever you do, in word or deed, do everything in the name of the Lord Jesus, giving thanks to God the Father through him.

1 John 2.6 (ESV) - whoever says he abides in him ought to walk in the same way in which he walked.

Gal. 5.24 (ESV) - And those who belong to Christ Jesus have crucified the flesh with its passions and desires.

Rom. 8.29 (ESV) - For those whom he foreknew he also predestined to be conformed to the image of his Son, in order that he might be the firstborn among many brothers.

Rom. 13.14 (ESV) - But put on the Lord Jesus Christ, and make no provision for the flesh, to gratify its desires.

1 Cor. 15.49 (ESV) - Just as we have borne the image of the man of dust, we shall also bear the image of the man of heaven.

2 Cor. 3.18 (ESV) - And we all, with unveiled face, beholding the glory of the Lord, are being transformed into the same image from one degree of glory to another. For this comes from the Lord who is the Spirit.

Phil. 3.7-8 (ESV) - But whatever gain I had, I counted as loss for the sake of Christ. [8] Indeed, I count everything as loss because of the surpassing worth of knowing Christ Jesus my Lord. For his sake I have suffered the loss of all things and count them as rubbish, in order that I may gain Christ.

Phil. 3.20-21 (ESV) - But our citizenship is in heaven, and from it we await a Savior, the Lord Jesus Christ, [21] who will transform our lowly body to be like his glorious body, by the power that enables him even to subject all things to himself.

1 John 3.2 (ESV) - Beloved, we are God's children now, and what we will be has not yet appeared; but we know that when he appears we shall be like him, because we shall see him as he is.

John 17.16 (ESV) - They are not of the world, just as I am not of the world.

Union with Christ: The Christocentric Paradigm (continued)

Col. 1.15-18 (ESV) - He is the image of the invisible God, the firstborn of all creation. [16] For by him all things were created, in heaven and on earth, visible and invisible, whether thrones or dominions or rulers or authorities - all things were created through him and for him. [17] And he is before all things, and in him all things hold together. [18] And he is the head of the body, the church. He is the beginning, the firstborn from the dead, that in everything he might be preeminent.

Heb. 2.14-15 (ESV) - Since therefore the children share in flesh and blood, he himself likewise partook of the same things, that through death he might destroy the one who has the power of death, that is, the devil, [15] and deliver all those who through fear of death were subject to lifelong slavery.

Rev. 1.5-6 (ESV) - and from Jesus Christ the faithful witness, the firstborn of the dead, and the ruler of kings on earth. To him who loves us and has freed us from our sins by his blood [6] and made us a kingdom, priests to his God and Father, to him be glory and dominion forever and ever. Amen.

2 Tim. 2.11-13 (ESV) - The saying is trustworthy, for: If we have died with him, we will also live with him; [12] if we endure, we will also reign with him; if we deny him, he also will deny us; [13] if we are faithless, he remains faithful—for he cannot deny himself.

Rev. 3.21 (ESV) - The one who conquers, I will grant him to sit with me on my throne, as I also conquered and sat down with my Father on his throne.

APPENDIX 38
The Life of Christ according to Seasons and Years
Adapted from Ray E. Baughman, The Life of Christ Visualized

Key Events - Spring	M	M	L	J	Key Events - Summer	M	M	L	J	Key Events - Fall	M	M	L	J
- Birth at Bethlehem, shepherds, angels			2:1-20							- Baptism of Jesus (Jordan River)	3:13-17		3:21-23	
- Adoration of Simeon, Anna, wise men	2:1-12		2:31-38							- Temptation (Wilderness of Judea)	4:1-11	1:9-11	4:1-13	
- Bethlehem babies killed	2:16-18						1:12-13			- Testimony of John the Baptist				1:15-34
- Into Egypt (Flight of Joseph, Mary, and Jesus)	2:13-15			1:14						- Jesus' first five disciples (Jordan)				1:35-51
- Egyptian exile ended, settled in Nazareth	2:19-23		2:39-40											
- Search for Jesus (12 years old, visit to Jerusalem)			2:41-52											
- Cana, changing water into wine (first miracle)				2:1-11	- First Passover during ministry (Jerusalem)				2:13	- Woman at the well (Sychar)				4:5-42
- Capernaum (first sojourn at future home)				2:12	- First cleansing of the Temple (Jerusalem)				2:14ff.	- Noble man's son made well (Jesus at Cana and son at Capernaum)				4:43-54
					- Nicodemus' interview (Jerusalem)				3:1-21	- Jesus preaches in synagogues of Galilee, is well received (first Galilean tour)		1:14-15	4:14ff.	
					- Judean ministry of John and Jesus				3:22-26					
					- Jesus leaves Judea as John is imprisoned (Machearus)	4:12	1:14	3:19-20	4:1-4					
- Belligerent rejection (1st), at Nazareth			4:16-31		- Impotent man at the pool (Jerusalem)				5:1-47	- Kingdom of heaven parables by the sea (Capernaum)	13:1-53		8:4-18	
- Large catch of fish, call of disciples (Galilee)	4:18-22	1:16-17	5:1-11		- Disciples pluck grain (Galilee)	12:1-8	2:23ff.	6:1-5		- Stilling the sea and the wind	8:18ff.	4:1-34	8:22-25	
- Demoniac healed (Capernaum)		1:21-22	4:31-37		- Man with withered hand (Capernaum)	12:9ff.	3:1-12	6:6-11		- Demoniac in graveyard, swine into the sea (Gadarenes)	8:28-34	4:35-41		
- Peter's mother-in-law healed	4:23-25	1:29-30; 1:35-36	4:38-44		- Jesus chooses twelve apostles (Galilee)		3:13ff.	6:12ff.				5:1-20		
- Galilean Tour (2nd) with four disciples					- Sermon on the Mount (horns of Hattin)	5:1-8:1		6:17ff.		- Crossing back over the sea to Capernaum and four miracles: Jairus' daughter raised, woman touches Messiah's garment	9:18-26	5:21-43	8:40-56	
- Leper healed (sent to Jerusalem)	8:2-4	1:40-41	5:12-16		- Centurion's servant healed	8:5-13		7:1-10		- Two blind men and dumb demoniac healed	9:27-34			
- Roof opened for sick man (Capernaum)	9:1-8	2:1-2	5:17-26		- Widow's son raised (Nain)			7:11ff.						
- Call of Matthew, his party (Capernaum)	9:9-17	2:13-14	5:27-39		- John's disciples inquire of Jesus (Galilee)	11:2ff.		7:18ff.						
					- First anointing of Jesus' feet (Capernaum)			7:36ff.						
					- Galilean tour (3rd) with disciples			8:1-3						
					- Demon possessed, blind-dumb man healed (Capernaum?)		3:20ff.							
					- Beelzebub charged against Jesus	12:22-23	3:21; 32-35							
					- Friends and family believe he is insane	12:46-47		8:18-21						

The Life of Christ according to Seasons and Years (continued)

Key Events - Spring	M	M	L	J	Key Events - Summer	M	M	L	J	Key Events - Fall	M	M	L	J
- Second rejection at Nazareth	13.54-58	6.1-6			- Feeding of the 5,000 (Sea of Galilee)	14.13ff.	6.30-31	9.10-11	6.1-2	- Tabernacle Feast (Jerusalem)				7.1-8.1
- Twelve sent forth (4th Galilean Tour)	9.35-11.1	6.6-13	9.1-6		- Walking on water, Bread of Life discourse				6.16ff.	- Adulterous woman				8.2-11
										- Light of the world				8.12-59
- John the Baptist's death (Machearus)	14.1-12	6.14ff.	9.7-9		- Eating with unwashed hands (Capernaum)	15.1-2	7.1ff.			- Man born blind healed			9.1-41	9.1-41
					- Daughter of Syrophonecian healed (Phonecia)	15.21ff.	7.24-25			- Good shepherd discourse				10.1-21
					- Deaf and dumb man healed		7.31-32			- Seventy sent out (Judea)	10.1-42		10.1-24	
					- Feeding of the 4,000 (Decapolis)	15.29-30	8.1-9			- Good Samaritan			10.25-37	
					- Pharisees and Sadducees seek a sign	15.39-40	8.10-11			- Supper at Mary and Martha's (Bethany)			10.38-42	
					- Warning against false teaching	16.5-6	8.13-14			- Disciples taught to pray			11.1-13	
					- Blind man healed at Bethsaida		8.22ff.			- Accused of tie with Beelzebub, demoniac healed			11.14-36	
					- Peter's good confession (Caesarea Philippi)	16.13-14	8.27-28	9.18ff.		- Eating with Pharisee			11.37-54	
					- Foretelling death, resurrection, second coming	16.21-22	8.31-32	9.22ff.		- Hypocrisy denounced (Judea)			12.1-13.9	
					- Transfiguration (Mount Hermon)	17.1ff.	9.2-13	9.28ff.		- Parables on service				
					- Demon possessed boy healed	17.14-15	9.14ff.	9.37ff.		- Healing of a crippled woman			13.10-21	
					- Foretells death and resurrection (to Galilee)	17.22-23	9.30ff.	9.43-44		- Feast of Dedication (Jerusalem)				10.22-23
					- Coin in fish's mouth (Capernaum)	17.24-25								
					- Instructions to disciples	18.1ff.	9.33-34	9.46-47						
- Teaching in Perea, warned about Herod			13.22-23	10.40-42	- Sunday - Triumphal Entry	21.1-11	11.1-11	19.29-44	12.12-19	- Earthquake as angel rolls away the stone	28.1-4			
- Healing of man on Sabbath			14.1-2		- Monday - Second cleansing of the Temple	21.12-22	11.12-26	19.45-48	12.20-50	- Women visit tomb	28.5-8	16.1-8	24.1-8	20.1-2
- Parables on humility, rewards, excuses, discipleship			14.7ff.							- Peter and John visit tomb			24.9-12	20.3-3
- Lost sheep, coin, son			15.1ff.		- Tuesday - Jesus challenged, Olivet Discourse	21.23-26.16	11.27-14.11	20.1-22.6		- Jesus appears to Mary Magdalene (Jerusalem)		16.9-11		20.11-18
- Rich man and Lazarus			16.19-20							- Jesus appears to other women	28.9-10			
- Raising of Lazarus (Bethany)				11.1-2	- Wednesday					- Guards report to rulers	28.11-15			
- Conspiring to kill Jesus				11.45-54						- Jesus appears to disciples on road to Emmaus (& Simon)		16.12-13	24.13-35	
- Ten lepers healed (Samaria)			17.11-12		- Thursday - Passover supper	26.17-56	14.12-52	22.7-53	13.1-18.12	- Jesus appears to 10 disciples		16.14	24.36-43	20.19-25
- Answered prayer, divorce, little children, rich young ruler	19.1-15 19.16ff.	10.1-2 10.17-31	18.1-17 18.18-19		Upper Room Discourse					- Jesus appears to all, w/Thomas				20.26-31
- Foretold death and resurrection	20.17-18	10.32-45	18.31-32		Gethsemane					- Jesus appears to 7 disciples by the sea of Galilee				21.1-25
- Blind men of Jericho	20.29-30	10.46-52	18.35-36		Arrest					(second miracle of the fish)				
- Zacchaeus's transformation			19.1ff.		- Friday - Trial, crucifixion, burial	26.57-27.66	14.53-15.47	22.54-23.56	18.12-19.42	- Jesus appears to 500 disciples (cf. 1 Cor. 15.5-7)	28.16-20	16.15-18	24.44-53	
- Last stop, 2nd anointing	20.6-7	14.3-9		11.55-12.8	- Saturday - in the tomb					- The Ascension (Acts 1.9-12)		16.19-20		

APPENDIX 39
Faithfully Re-Presenting Jesus of Nazareth
Don L. Davis

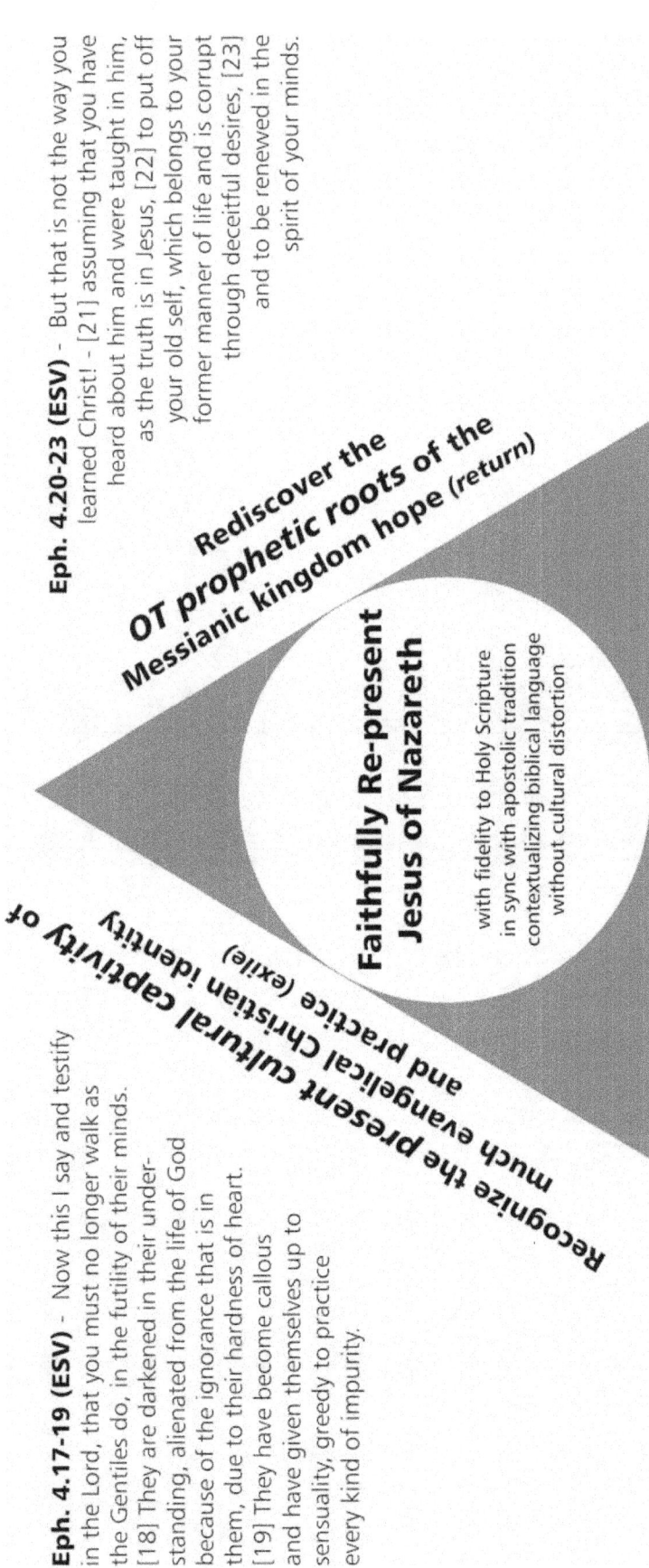

Eph. 4.17-19 (ESV) - Now this I say and testify in the Lord, that you must no longer walk as the Gentiles do, in the futility of their minds. [18] They are darkened in their understanding, alienated from the life of God because of the ignorance that is in them, due to their hardness of heart. [19] They have become callous and have given themselves up to sensuality, greedy to practice every kind of impurity.

Eph. 4.20-23 (ESV) - But that is not the way you learned Christ! - [21] assuming that you have heard about him and were taught in him, as the truth is in Jesus, [22] to put off your old self, which belongs to your former manner of life and is corrupt through deceitful desires, [23] and to be renewed in the spirit of your minds.

Eph. 4.24-25 (ESV) - and to put on the new self, created after the likeness of God in true righteousness and holiness. [25] Therefore, having put away falsehood, let each one of you speak the truth with his neighbor, for we are members one of another.

Rediscover the OT prophetic roots of the Messianic kingdom hope *(return)*

Faithfully Re-present Jesus of Nazareth
with fidelity to Holy Scripture in sync with apostolic tradition contextualizing biblical language without cultural distortion

Re-experience and embrace the power of the NT apostolic vision and drama [myth] *(possession)*

Recognize the present cultural captivity of much evangelical Christian identity and practice *(exile)*

APPENDIX 40
Apostolicity
The Unique Place of the Apostles in Christian Faith and Practice
Rev. Dr. Don L. Davis

Gal. 1.8-9 (ESV) - But even if we or an angel from heaven should preach to you a gospel contrary to the one we preached to you, let him be accursed. **[9]** As we have said before, so now I say again: If anyone is preaching to you a gospel contrary to the one you received, let him be accursed.

2 Thess. 3.6 (ESV) - Now we command you, brothers, in the name of our Lord Jesus Christ, that you keep away from any brother who is walking in idleness and not in accord with the tradition that you received from us.

Luke 1.1-4 (ESV) - Inasmuch as many have undertaken to compile a narrative of the things that have been accomplished among us, **[2]** just as those who from the beginning were eyewitnesses and ministers of the word have delivered them to us, **[3]** it seemed good to me also, having followed all things closely for some time past, to write an orderly account for you, most excellent Theophilus, **[4]** that you may have certainty concerning the things you have been taught.

John 15.27 (ESV) - And you also will bear witness, because you have been with me from the beginning.

Acts 1.3 (ESV) - To them he presented himself alive after his suffering by many proofs, appearing to them during forty days and speaking about the kingdom of God.

Acts 1.21-22 (ESV) - So one of the men who have accompanied us during all the time that the Lord Jesus went in and out among us, **[22]** beginning from the baptism of John until the day when he was taken up from us—one of these men must become with us a witness to his resurrection.

1 John 1.1-3 (ESV) - That which was from the beginning, which we have heard, which we have seen with our eyes, which we looked upon and have touched with our hands, concerning the word of life— **[2]** the life was made manifest, and we have seen it, and testify to it and proclaim to you the eternal life, which was with the Father and was made manifest to us— **[3]** that which we have seen and heard we proclaim also to you, so that you too may have fellowship with us; and indeed our fellowship is with the Father and with his Son Jesus Christ.

"Apostolicity"

- **Focused on Messiah Jesus**
- **Infallible (Authoritative)**
- **Universally acknowledged among the churches**
- **Clear standard for credentialing ordained leaders**
- **Standard for NT canon**

APPENDIX 41
The Self-Consciousness of Jesus Christ
Rev. Dr. Don L. Davis

Prophetic Orientation

John 17.25-26 (ESV) - O righteous Father, even though the world does not know you, I know you, and these know that you have sent me. [26] I made known to them your name, and I will continue to make it known, that the love with which you have loved me may be in them, and I in them.

John 5.34 (ESV) - Not that the testimony that I receive is from man, but I say these things so that you may be saved.

John 3.11 (ESV) - Truly, truly, I say to you, we speak of what we know, and bear witness to what we have seen, but you do not receive our testimony.

John 5.30 (ESV) - I can do nothing on my own. As I hear, I judge, and my judgment is just, because I seek not my own will but the will of him who sent me.

John 8.26 (ESV) - I have much to say about you and much to judge, but he who sent me is true, and I declare to the world what I have heard from him.

John 12.47-49 (ESV) - If anyone hears my words and does not keep them, I do not judge him; for I did not come to judge the world but to save the world. [48] The one who rejects me and does not receive my words has a judge; the word that I have spoken will judge him on the last day. [49] For I have not spoken on my own authority, but the Father who sent me has himself given me a commandment—what to say and what to speak.

God-Consciousness

John 5.17 (ESV) - But Jesus answered them, "My Father is working until now, and I am working."

John 5.19-20 (ESV) - So Jesus said to them, "Truly, truly, I say to you, the Son can do nothing of his own accord, but only what he sees the Father doing. For whatever the Father does, that the Son does likewise. [20] For the Father loves the Son and shows him all that he himself is doing. And greater works than these will he show him, so that you may marvel."

John 8.26 (ESV) - I have much to say about you and much to judge, but he who sent me is true, and I declare to the world what I have heard from him.

John 8.42 (ESV) - Jesus said to them, "If God were your Father, you would love me, for I came from God and I am here. I came not of my own accord, but he sent me."

John 14.10 (ESV) - Do you not believe that I am in the Father and the Father is in me? The words that I say to you I do not speak on my own authority, but the Father who dwells in me does his works.

The Self-Consciousness of Jesus Christ

Divine Representation

John 5.30 (ESV) - "I can do nothing on my own. As I hear, I judge, and my judgment is just, because I seek not my own will but the will of him who sent me.

John 6.38 (ESV) - For I have come down from heaven, not to do my own will but the will of him who sent me.

John 14.10 (ESV) - Do you not believe that I am in the Father and the Father is in me? The words that I say to you I do not speak on my own authority, but the Father who dwells in me does his works.

John 17.8 (ESV) - For I have given them the words that you gave me, and they have received them and have come to know in truth that I came from you; and they have believed that you sent me.

Apocalyptic Imagination

John 5.21-22 (ESV) - For as the Father raises the dead and gives them life, so also the Son gives life to whom he will. [22] The Father judges no one, but has given all judgment to the Son.

John 11.23-26 (ESV) - Jesus said to her, "Your brother will rise again." [24] Martha said to him, "I know that he will rise again in the resurrection on the last day." [25] Jesus said to her, "I am the resurrection and the life. Whoever believes in me, though he die, yet shall he live, [26] and everyone who lives and believes in me shall never die. Do you believe this?"

John 4.25-26 (ESV) - The woman said to him, "I know that Messiah is coming (he who is called Christ). When he comes, he will tell us all things." [26] Jesus said to her, "I who speak to you am he."

Mark 14.61-62 (ESV) - But he remained silent and made no answer. Again the high priest asked him, "Are you the Christ, the Son of the Blessed?" [62] And Jesus said, "I am, and you will see the Son of Man seated at the right hand of Power, and coming with the clouds of heaven."

APPENDIX 42
I Find My Lord in the Book
Author unknown

I find my Lord in the Bible, wherever I chance to look,

He is the theme of the Bible, the center and heart of the Book;

He is the Rose of Sharon, He is the Lily fair,

Where ever I open my Bible, the Lord of the Book is there.

He, at the Book's beginning, gave to the earth its form,

He is the Ark of shelter, bearing the brunt of the storm

The Burning Bush of the desert, the budding of Aaron's Rod,

Where ever I look in the Bible, I see the Son of God.

The Ram upon Mount Moriah, the Ladder from earth to sky,

The Scarlet Cord in the window, and the Serpent lifted high,

The smitten Rock in the desert, the Shepherd with staff and crook,

The face of the Lord I discover, where ever I open the Book.

He is the Seed of the Woman, the Savior Virgin-born

He is the Son of David, whom men rejected with scorn,

His garments of grace and of beauty the stately Aaron deck,

Yet He is a priest forever, for He is Melchizedek.

Lord of eternal glory Whom John, the Apostle, saw;

Light of the golden city, Lamb without spot or flaw,

Bridegroom coming at midnight, for whom the Virgins look.

Where ever I open my Bible, I find my Lord in the Book.

APPENDIX 43
The Center and Circumference: Christianity Is Jesus Christ

Don L. Davis

Introduction: The world that we live in is not the one which appears to be the real one, but typically is the one that we or another has composed for us to live in.

Callin' Something Somethin'

Three umpires at an umpires convention boasting to each other about their prowess as major league umps:

I. Umpire One: Some call 'em balls and others call 'em strikes, but *I call 'em how I see 'em!*

II. Umpire Two: Some call 'em balls and others call 'em strikes, but *I call 'em what they truly is!*

III. Umpire Three: Some call 'em balls and others call 'em strikes, but *they ain't nothin' till I call 'em somethin'!*

What is the essence of the Christian faith journey, the nature of Christian theology and doctrine, the heart of Christian ethics, the core of Christian hope?

It is the person of Jesus Christ. He is the center and the circumference of the Christian's faith and practice.

All that we are, all that we believe, and all that we understand God is doing in the world is related to this unique and yet humble person:

- Of whom we know little regarding his appearance and personage
- Who didn't travel 200 miles from his place of birth
- Of whom we have only a few birth narratives and a story regarding his adolescence
- Whose years of life from twelve to thirty are silent, even from those who adored him the most

The Center and Circumference: Christianity Is Jesus Christ (continued)

- Who ministered only three years, and was rejected by his peers, countrymen, and the religious establishment

- Who died in shame, was executed publicly between two thieves, and placed in a borrowed tomb

Yet all of the persons, books, philosophies, systems, governments, artists, educators, religious leaders, military conquerors, persons of influence and power put together have not had the impact of this one itinerant Jewish preacher has had on the structure and fate of the world.

Christianity is Jesus Christ. The story is about his person and influence and calling and vision and work and future. To understand all that God wants us to know and be and do, all one must do is master the life and person of Christ, which his followers confess to be alive today.

The Text for Today

Col. 1.15-20 (ESV) - He is the image of the invisible God, the firstborn of all creation. [16] For by him all things were created, in heaven and on earth, visible and invisible, whether thrones or dominions or rulers or authorities—all things were created through him and for him. [17] And he is before all things, and in him all things hold together. [18] And he is the head of the body, the church. He is the beginning, the firstborn from the dead, that in everything he might be preeminent. [19] For in him all the fullness of God was pleased to dwell, [20] and through him to reconcile to himself all things, whether on earth or in heaven, making peace by the blood of his cross.

I. **Jesus the Final and Full Revelation of God. In Order to Understand the Father, We Must Come to Know the Person of Jesus Christ, Who Is Both the Means and End of Creation Itself.**

   A. Jesus is the express image of God's person through whom God made the entire created spheres. Col. 1.15-16 (ESV) - He is the image of the invisible God, the firstborn of all creation. [16] For by him all things were created, in

The Center and Circumference: Christianity Is Jesus Christ (continued)

      heaven and on earth, visible and invisible, whether thrones or dominions or rulers or authorities—all things were created through him and for him.

  B. Jesus is the exact representation (exact imprint of his nature) of God in human form, Heb. 1.1-4 (ESV) - Long ago, at many times and in many ways, God spoke to our fathers by the prophets, [2] but in these last days he has spoken to us by his Son, whom he appointed the heir of all things, through whom also he created the world. [3] He is the radiance of the glory of God and the exact imprint of his nature, and he upholds the universe by the word of his power. After making purification for sins, he sat down at the right hand of the Majesty on high, [4] having become as much superior to angels as the name he has inherited is more excellent than theirs.

  C. Jesus is the Word made flesh, the revelator of the splendor and beauty of God.

      John 1.14 (ESV) - And the Word became flesh and dwelt among us, and we have seen his glory, glory as of the only Son from the Father, full of grace and truth.

      John 1.18 (ESV) - No one has ever seen God; the only God, who is at the Father's side, he has made him known.

  D. The person of Jesus is the full and unadulterated picture of the character and beauty of the Father God whom we love and worship. We know God through him.

Many are content to possess a shallow and familiar knowledge of the person of Jesus, neither recognizing nor reveling in the mystery of the meaning of "Christ in you, the hope of Glory."

      During the children's sermon the Assistant Pastor asked the kids, "What is gray, has a bushy tail and gathers nuts in the fall?" One five year old raised his hand. "I know the answer should be Jesus," he began, "but it sounds like a squirrel to me" (*Reader's Digest*).

The Center and Circumference: Christianity Is Jesus Christ (continued)

- For Christians, there exists no saving knowledge of God that is not mediated through the person of Jesus Christ, John 14.6.

- For us who believe, the very glory of God shines in the face of Jesus, 2 Cor. 4.6.

- The fullness of the Godhead, the glorious beauty of God is seen most clearly in the person and work of Jesus Christ, Col. 2.9 (ESV) - For in him the whole fullness of deity dwells bodily.

E. Christianity is the person of Christ, relating to God in the person of Jesus Christ, who we believe lived, died, and rose again in order to bring us into a right relationship with God

- It is not ethics and do-gooding (we live right after we meet Christ)

- It is not merely family life (we become what God wants us to become after we come to know Christ)

- It is not religious studies and liturgies (other religions have fine ethics, great worship programs, devoted teaching, and many holy books)

Jesus Is the Only Way to God

A traveler engaged a guide to take him across a desert area. When the two men arrived at the edge of the desert, the traveler, looking ahead, saw before him trackless sands without a single footprint, path, or marker of any kind. Turning to his guide, he asked in a tone of surprise, "Where is the road?" With a reproving glance, the guide replied, "I am the road."

The Scriptures Point to Christ

Five times in the NT the Scriptures refer to Jesus as the express purpose of the writing of the Holy Scriptures. He is the reason for the story, divided into two unequal halves (Gen. 1.1-3.15, and Gen. 3.16 - Rev. 21). If you look at any part of the Bible, you will see him there. There is a bronze copy of the Declaration of Independence carved right into a bronze slate, done in meticulous accuracy and

The Center and Circumference: Christianity Is Jesus Christ (continued)

splendid detail. If you back away from the rendering of the Declaration, however, you can see the image of George Washington emerge from the writing. It was done with the proper shading and sculpting to reveal the person of Mr. Washington from the rendering of the Declaration. In my mind, the Bible has a single dominating purpose–to reveal the glory of the person of Jesus Christ, so that, through faith in him, we might become one of the Father's children!

All that we do at TUMI is to find ways to declare the majesty and might of the Person and Work of Christ, and how it relates to being an urban disciple and doing urban ministry through urban churches among the poor.

Hundreds of names, types, images, and metaphors refer to Christ in Scripture:

- He is the *Bread of life* - the One of total nourishment and strength
- He is the *Second Adam* - the head of an entire new race of humanity
- He is the *Resurrection and the Life* - the One whose name alone can conquer death and corruption
- He is the *Lord of all* - the chosen ruler of God to restore God's reign
- He is *Prince of Peace* - the One whose power alone will restore peace to our troubled world

Jesus is the key to understanding the person and work of Almighty God.

II. Next, We See that this Text Reveals that Jesus Is the Finished Redemption of God. Jesus Alone Is God's Anointed Prophet and Priest to Bring Us Back into Relationship to God.

A. Jesus is the only way to be reconciled with God; no other person or name exists that can bring us into new and redeemed relation with God. Look again at Colossians 1.17-20 (ESV) - And he is before all things, and in him all things hold together. [18] And he is the head of the body, the church. He is the beginning, the firstborn from the dead, that in everything he might be preeminent. [19] For in him all the fullness of God was pleased to dwell,

The Center and Circumference: Christianity Is Jesus Christ (continued)

[20] and through him to reconcile to himself all things, whether on earth or in heaven, making peace by the blood of his cross.

B. According to the Scriptures, God was in the person of Jesus Christ reconciling the world unto himself. 2 Cor. 5.18-21 (ESV) - All this is from God, who through Christ reconciled us to himself and gave us the ministry of reconciliation; [19] that is, in Christ God was reconciling the world to himself, not counting their trespasses against them, and entrusting to us the message of reconciliation. [20] Therefore, we are ambassadors for Christ, God making his appeal through us. We implore you on behalf of Christ, be reconciled to God. [21] For our sake he made him to be sin who knew no sin, so that in him we might become the righteousness of God.

C. Jesus alone is the sole deliverer, redeemer, and reconciler of humankind back to God.

- He is the just One who died for us unjust ones, in order to bring us to God, 1 Pet.3.18.

- His is the only name under heaven given to us in order that we must be saved, Acts 4.12 (ESV) - And there is salvation in no one else, for there is no other name under heaven given among men by which we must be saved."

- He alone is the One who became God's *Christus Victum* in order to raise and become our *Christus Victor*, Col. 2.13-15 (ESV) - And you, who were dead in your trespasses and the uncircumcision of your flesh, God made alive together with him, having forgiven us all our trespasses, [14] by canceling the record of debt that stood against us with its legal demands. This he set aside, nailing it to the cross. [15] He disarmed the rulers and authorities and put them to open shame, by triumphing over them in him.

The Center and Circumference: Christianity Is Jesus Christ (continued)

The Father sacrificed his very own Son in order to redeem the world, to reconcile the breach between us on account of our disobedience to God, and give us new birth as adopted children into God's family.

> A man had the duty to raise a drawbridge to allow the steamers to pass on the river below and to lower it again for trains to cross over on land. One day, this man's son visited him, desiring to watch his father at work. Quite curious, as most boys are, he peeked into a trap door that was always left open so his father could keep an eye on the great machinery which raised and lowered the bridge. Suddenly, the boy lost his footing and tumbled into the gears. As the father tried to reach down and pull him out, he heard the whistle of an approaching train. He knew the cars would be full of people and that it would be impossible to stop the fast-moving locomotive, therefore, the bridge must be lowered! A terrible dilemma confronted him; for if he saved the people, his son would be crushed in the cogs. Frantically, he tried to free the boy, but to no avail. Finally, the father put his hand to the lever that would start the machinery. He paused and then, with tears he pulled it. The giant gears began to work and the bridge clamped down just in time to save the train. The passengers, not knowing what the father had done, were laughing and making merry; yet the bridge keeper had chosen to save their lives at the cost of his son's.

No one and nothing can detail the expense of the price the Father provided in order to bring us back to himself to Christ. This reveals the awesome majesty of the love of God for each of us, that he would give his only Son up for our redemption.

III. Finally, Not Only Is Jesus God's Full Revelation and Finished Redemption, He Is Also the Final Rule and Standard of True Humanity.

A. Jesus is God's pattern, his ruler, his final standard for all that we are and soon will become. Look again at Colossians 1.18-19 (ESV) - *And he is the head of the body, the church. He is the beginning, the firstborn from the dead, that in everything he might be preeminent. [19] For in him all the fullness of God was pleased to dwell.*

The Center and Circumference: Christianity Is Jesus Christ (continued)

B. God's design is that Jesus be the first, the head, the center, the heart of all that he communicates and does. To know God is to know Christ, to please God is to become like Christ, to obey God is to follow Christ's example: he is our example.

John 13.13-16 (ESV) - You call me Teacher and Lord, and you are right, for so I am. [14] If I then, your Lord and Teacher, have washed your feet, you also ought to wash one another's feet. [15] For I have given you an example, that you also should do just as I have done to you. [16] Truly, truly, I say to you, a servant is not greater than his master, nor is a messenger greater than the one who sent him.

C. A number of texts in the NT clearly reveal that God's purpose is to conform us to the very image of Jesus Christ, to join us to him, and then to make us like him. God intends to make Jesus the head of a new human family which will be conformed to his person and his destiny.

- Rom. 8.28-29 (ESV) - And we know that for those who love God all things work together for good, for those who are called according to his purpose. [29] For those whom he foreknew he also predestined to be conformed to the image of his Son, in order that he might be the firstborn among many brothers.

- 1 Cor. 15.49 (ESV) - Just as we have borne the image of the man of dust, we shall also bear the image of the man of heaven.

- 2 Cor. 3.18 (ESV) - And we all, with unveiled face, beholding the glory of the Lord, are being transformed into the same image from one degree of glory to another. For this comes from the Lord who is the Spirit.

- Paul commands in Philippians 2.5 (ESV) "Have this mind among yourselves, which is yours in Christ Jesus."

- In Philippians 3.20, Paul says that our citizenship is in the heavens where we look for the person of our Lord, Christ Jesus who, according to Philippians 3.21 (ESV) "will transform our lowly body to be like his glorious body, by the power that enables him even to subject all things to himself."

The Center and Circumference: Christianity Is Jesus Christ (continued)

- Peter says in his second epistle in 2 Peter 3.18 (ESV) that we are to "grow in the grace and knowledge of our Lord and Savior Jesus Christ. To him be the glory both now and to the day of eternity. Amen."

- His is the only name under heaven given to us in order that we must be saved, Acts 4.12 (ESV) - And there is salvation in no one else, for there is no other name under heaven given among men by which we must be saved.

- John the Apostle says in his first epistle 1 John 3.1-3 (ESV) - See what kind of love the Father has given to us, that we should be called children of God; and so we are. The reason why the world does not know us is that it did not know him. [2] Beloved, we are God's children now, and what we will be has not yet appeared; but we know that when he appears we will be like him, because we shall see him as he is. [3] And everyone who thus hopes in him purifies himself as he is pure.

D. According to God's will, we have been baptized (placed into and surrounded by) Christ himself, who is our hope of glory, we are now said to be "in Christ." We who believe have been identified with Christ Jesus, and made a part of the Church of God, which is the "Mystery" revealed: the open secret of God

- Romans 16.25-27, the "revelation of the mystery"

- Ephesians 3.7-10, God's wisdom displayed through the Church

- Colossians 1.25-27, Christ in us, the hope of glory

E. Jesus is God's ruler, God's pattern, God's principle of intimacy and identification for the redeemed. God's intention is to conform each of us who believe to the very life and perfection of Christ himself. Listen to what the NT teaches about our connection to our Lord.

- We are "made one in Christ," 1 Cor. 6.15-17.

- We were baptized into him, 1 Cor. 12.13.

- We died with him, Rom. 6.3-4.

The Center and Circumference: Christianity Is Jesus Christ (continued)

- We were buried with him, Rom. 6.3-4.

- We were raised with him, Eph. 2.4-7.

- We are ascended with him, Eph. 2.6.

- We sit in the heavenly places with him, Eph. 2.6.

- In this world, we take his yoke upon us and carry the burden and cross that he has assigned to us, Matt. 11.28-30.

- In this world, we are called to suffer with him, Rom. 8.17-18; Phil. 1.29-30.

- Whether we live or die, we belong completely to the Lord Jesus, Rom. 14.7-9 (ESV) - For none of us lives to himself, and none of us dies to himself. [8] If we live, we live to the Lord, and if we die, we die to the Lord. So then, whether we live or whether we die, we are the Lord's. [9] For to this end Christ died and lived again, that he might be Lord both of the dead and of the living.

- We will be glorified with him, Rom. 8.17.

- We will be resurrected in him, 1 Cor. 15.48-49.

- We will be made like him, 1 John 3.2.

- We are joint-heirs with him, Rom. 8.17.

- We will reign forever with him, Rev. 3.

The Center and Circumference: Christianity Is Jesus Christ (continued)

Hast thou no scar?

No hidden scar on foot, or side, or hand?

I hear thee sung as mighty in the land.

I hear them hail thy bright ascendant star.

Has thou no scar?

Hast thou no wound?

Yet I was wounded by the archers, spent,

Leaned Me against a tree to die; and rent

By ravening beasts that compassed Me, I swooned;

Has thou no wound?

No wound, no scar?

Yet, as the Master shall the servant be,

And, pierced are the feet that follow Me;

But thine are whole; can he have followed far

Who has no wound or scar?

~ Amy Carmichael

I. Jesus the Final and Full Revelation of God: In order to understand the Father, we must come to know the person of Jesus Christ.

II. Jesus the Finished Redemption of God: Jesus alone is God's anointed prophet and priest to bring us back into relationship to God.

III. Finally, not only is Jesus God's Full Revelation and finished Redemption, he is also the Final Rule and standard of true humanity.

APPENDIX 44
Jesus and the Poor
Don L. Davis

Thesis: The heart of Jesus' ministry of the Kingdom was the transformation and renewal of the those on the underside of life, the poor. He demonstrated his personal heart vision in how he inaugurated his ministry, authenticated his ministry, defined the heart and soul of ministry, identifying himself directly with the poor.

I. Jesus Inaugurated His Ministry with an Outreach to the Poor.

    A. The inaugural sermon at Nazareth, Luke 4.16-21

    Luke 4.16-21 (ESV) - And he came to Nazareth, where he had been brought up. And as was his custom, he went to the synagogue on the Sabbath day, and he stood up to read. [17] And the scroll of the prophet Isaiah was given to him. He unrolled the scroll and found the place where it was written, [18] "The Spirit of the Lord is upon me, because he has anointed me to proclaim good news to the poor. He has sent me to proclaim liberty to the captives and recovering of sight to the blind, to set at liberty those who are oppressed, [19] to proclaim the year of the Lord's favor." [20] And he rolled up the scroll and gave it back to the attendant and sat down. And the eyes of all in the synagogue were fixed on him. [21] And he began to say to them, "Today this Scripture has been fulfilled in your hearing."

    B. The meaning of this inauguration

        1. The object of his attention: his choice of texts

        2. The object of his calling: his Spirit anointing

Jesus and the Poor (continued)

      3. The objects of his love:

          a. Good news to the poor

          b. Release to the captives

          c. Recovery of sight to the blind

          d. Letting the oppressed go free

      4. The object of his ministry: the Year of the Lord's favor

    C. *Ministry to the poor as the cornerstone of his inaugural ministry*

II. Jesus Authenticated His Ministry by His Actions toward the Poor.

    A. John's query regarding Jesus' authenticity, Luke 7.18-23

    Luke 7.18-23 (ESV) - The disciples of John reported all these things to him. And John, [19] calling two of his disciples to him, sent them to the Lord, saying, "Are you the one who is to come, or shall we look for another?" [20] And when the men had come to him, they said, "John the Baptist has sent us to you, saying, 'Are you the one who is to come, or shall we look for another?'" [21] In that hour he healed many people of diseases and plagues and evil spirits, and on many who were blind he bestowed sight. [22] And he answered them, "Go and tell John what you have seen and heard: the BLIND RECEIVE THEIR SIGHT, the lame walk, lepers are cleansed, and the deaf hear, the dead are raised up, the POOR HAVE GOOD NEWS PREACHED TO THEM. [23] And blessed is the one who is not offended by me."

    B. Will the real Messiah please stand up?

      1. The question of John, 19-20

      2. The actions of Jesus, 21 (the show-side of "show-and-tell")

Jesus and the Poor (continued)

   3. The explanation of his identity, 22-23

      a. Go and tell John what you have seen and heard.

      b. Blind seeing, lame walking, lepers cleansed, deaf hearing, dead being raising, the poor hearing the Gospel

   C. *Ministry to the poor is undeniable proof of the Messiah's identity.*

III. Jesus Verified Salvation in Relation to One's Treatment of the Poor.

   A. The story of Zaccheus, Luke 19.1-9

   Luke 19.1-9 (ESV) - He entered Jericho and was passing through. [2] And there was a man named Zacchaeus. He was a chief tax collector and was rich. [3] And he was seeking to see who Jesus was, but on account of the crowd he could not, because he was small of stature. [4] So he ran on ahead and climbed up into a sycamore tree to see him, for he was about to pass that way. [5] And when Jesus came to the place, he looked up and said to him, "Zacchaeus, hurry and come down, for I must stay at your house today." [6] So he hurried and came down and received him joyfully. [7] And when they saw it, they all grumbled, "He has gone in to be the guest of a man who is a sinner." [8] And Zacchaeus stood and said to the Lord, "Behold, Lord, the half of my goods I give to the poor. And if I have defrauded anyone of anything, I restore it fourfold." [9] And Jesus said to him, "Today salvation has come to this house, since he also is a son of Abraham."

   1. The palpitations of Zaccheus

   2. The salutation of Zaccheus (to Jesus)

   3. The declaration of Zaccheus

      a. Half of all I own I give to the poor.

      b. I restore those wrongly treated by me four-fold.

Jesus and the Poor (continued)

    4. The salvation of Zaccheus, vv.9-10

  B. Plucking Grain on the Sabbath, Matt.12.1-8

  Matt. 12.1-8 (ESV) - At that time Jesus went through the grainfields on the Sabbath. His disciples were hungry, and they began to pluck heads of grain and to eat. [2] But when the Pharisees saw it, they said to him, "Look, your disciples are doing what is not lawful to do on the Sabbath." [3] He said to them, "Have you not read what David did when he was hungry, and those who were with him: [4] how he entered the house of God and ate the bread of the Presence, which it was not lawful for him to eat nor for those who were with him, but only for the priests? [5] Or have you not read in the Law how on the Sabbath the priests in the temple profane the Sabbath and are guiltless? [6] I tell you, something greater than the temple is here. [7] And if you had known what this means, 'I DESIRE MERCY, AND NOT SACRIFICE,' you would not have condemned the guiltless. [8] For the Son of Man is lord of the Sabbath."

    1. Disciples snacking on corn on the Sabbath

    2. The Pharisees disputation: "Look, your disciples are doing what is not lawful to do on the sabbath."

    3. Jesus' retort: "I desire mercy and not sacrifice."

        a. Mercy to the poor and broken, not ritual faithfulness

        b. Compassion for the broken, not religious discipline

  C. *Ministry to the poor is the litmus test of authentic salvation.*

IV. Jesus Identifies Himself Unreservedly with the Poor.

  A. Those who cannot repay you, Luke 14.11-15

Jesus and the Poor (continued)

Luke 14.11-14 (ESV) - "For everyone who exalts himself will be humbled, and he who humbles himself will be exalted." [12] He said also to the man who had invited him, "When you give a dinner or a banquet, do not invite your friends or your brothers or your relatives or rich neighbors, lest they also invite you in return and you be repaid. [13] But when you give a feast, invite the poor, the crippled, the lame, the blind, [14] and you will be blessed, because they cannot repay you. You will be repaid at the resurrection of the just."

B. The Judgment Seat of the King, Matt. 25.31-45

Matt. 25.34-40 (ESV) - Then the King will say to those on his right, "Come, you who are blessed by my Father, inherit the kingdom prepared for you from the foundation of the world. [35] For I was hungry and you gave me food, I was thirsty and you gave me drink, I was a stranger and you welcomed me, [36] I was naked and you clothed me, I was sick and you visited me, I was in prison and you came to me." [37] Then the righteous will answer him, saying, "Lord, when did we see you hungry and feed you, or thirsty and give you drink? [38] And when did we see you a stranger and welcome you, or naked and clothe you? [39] And when did we see you sick or in prison and visit you?" [40] And the King will answer them, "Truly, I say to you, as you did it to one of the least of these my brothers, you did it to me."

1. Two sets of people: sheep and goats

2. Two responses: one blessed and embraced, one judged and rejected

3. Two destinies: the sheep in the Kingdom inherited, prepared from the foundation of the world, the goats in the eternal fire prepared for the devil and his angels

4. Two reactions: one was hospitable, charitable, generous; the other apathetic, heartless, negligent

5. The same group of people: the hungry, the thirsty, the stranger, the naked, the sick, the prisoner

Jesus and the Poor (continued)

      6. *The same standard: in the way you treated or mistreated these people, those on the underside of life, so you responded to me.*

  C. Jesus made it appear as those who were least deserving but repentant would become heirs of the Kingdom.

      Matt. 21.31 (ESV) - "Which of the two did the will of his father?" They said, "The first." Jesus said to them, "Truly, I say to you, the tax collectors and the prostitutes go into the kingdom of God before you."

      Mark 2.15-17 (ESV) - And as he reclined at table in his house, many tax collectors and sinners were reclining with Jesus and his disciples, for there were many who followed him. [16] And the scribes of the Pharisees, when they saw that he was eating with sinners and tax collectors, said to his disciples, "Why does he eat with tax collectors and sinners?" [17] And when Jesus heard it, he said to them, "Those who are well have no need of a physician, but those who are sick. I came not to call the righteous, but sinners."

  D. Ministry to the poor is ministry to the Lord Jesus - his identification with them is complete.

Conclusion: The heart and soul of Jesus' ministry was directed toward the transformation and liberation of those who were most vulnerable, most forgotten, most neglected. As disciples, may we demonstrate the same.

APPENDIX 45

Documenting Your Work
A Guide to Help You Give Credit Where Credit Is Due
The Urban Ministry Institute

Avoiding Plagiarism

Plagiarism is using another person's ideas as if they belonged to you without giving them proper credit. In academic work it is just as wrong to steal a person's ideas as it is to steal a person's property. These ideas may come from the author of a book, an article you have read, or from a fellow student. The way to avoid plagiarism is to carefully use "notes" (textnotes, footnotes, endnotes, etc.) and a "Works Cited" section to help people who read your work know when an idea is one you thought of, and when you are borrowing an idea from another person.

Using Citation References

A citation reference is required in a paper whenever you use ideas or information that came from another person's work.

All citation references involve two parts:

- Notes in the body of your paper placed next to each quotation which came from an outside source.

- A "Works Cited" page at the end of your paper or project which gives information about the sources you have used

Using Notes in Your Paper

There are three basic kinds of notes: parenthetical notes, footnotes, and endnotes. At The Urban Ministry Institute, we recommend that students use parenthetical notes. These notes give the author's last name(s), the date the book was published, and the page number(s) on which you found the information. Example:

> In trying to understand the meaning of Genesis 14.1-24, it is important to recognize that in biblical stories "the place where dialogue is first introduced will be an important moment in revealing the character of the speaker . . ." (Kaiser and Silva 1994, 73). This is certainly true of the character of Melchizedek who speaks words of blessing. This identification of Melchizedek as a positive spiritual influence is reinforced by the fact that he is the King of Salem, since Salem means "safe, at peace" (Wiseman 1996, 1045).

Documenting Your Work (continued)

A "Works Cited" page should be placed at the end of your paper. This page:

- lists every source you quoted in your paper
- is in alphabetical order by author's last name
- includes the date of publication and information about the publisher

The following formatting rules should be followed:

1. Title

The title "Works Cited" should be used and centered on the first line of the page following the top margin.

2. Content

Each reference should list:

- the author's full name (last name first)
- the date of publication
- the title and any special information (Revised edition, 2nd edition, reprint) taken from the cover or title page should be noted
- the city where the publisher is headquartered followed by a colon and the name of the publisher

3. Basic form

- Each piece of information should be separated by a period.
- The second line of a reference (and all following lines) should be indented.
- Book titles should be underlined (or italicized).
- Article titles should be placed in quotes.

Example:

> Fee, Gordon D. 1991. *Gospel and Spirit: Issues in New Testament Hermeneutics.* Peabody, MA: Hendrickson Publishers.

Creating a Works Cited Page

Documenting Your Work (continued)

4. Special Forms

A book with multiple authors:

Kaiser, Walter C., and Moisés Silva. 1994. *An Introduction to Biblical Hermeneutics: The Search for Meaning.* Grand Rapids: Zondervan Publishing House.

An edited book:

Greenway, Roger S., ed. 1992. *Discipling the City: A Comprehensive Approach to Urban Mission.* 2nd ed. Grand Rapids: Baker Book House.

A book that is part of a series:

Morris, Leon. 1971. *The Gospel According to John.* Grand Rapids: Wm. B. Eerdmans Publishing Co. The New International Commentary on the New Testament. Gen. ed. F. F. Bruce.

An article in a reference book:

Wiseman, D. J. "Salem." 1982. In *New Bible Dictionary.* Leicester, England - Downers Grove, IL: InterVarsity Press. Eds. I. H. Marshall and others.

(An example of a "Works Cited" page is located on the next page.)

For Further Research

Standard guides to documenting academic work in the areas of philosophy, religion, theology, and ethics include:

Atchert, Walter S., and Joseph Gibaldi. 1985. *The MLA Style Manual.* New York: Modern Language Association.

The Chicago Manual of Style. 1993. 14th ed. Chicago: The University of Chicago Press.

Turabian, Kate L. 1987. *A Manual for Writers of Term Papers, Theses, and Dissertations.* 5th edition. Bonnie Bertwistle Honigsblum, ed. Chicago: The University of Chicago Press.

Documenting Your Work (continued)

Works Cited

Fee, Gordon D. 1991. *Gospel and Spirit: Issues in New Testament Hermeneutics*. Peabody, MA: Hendrickson Publishers.

Greenway, Roger S., ed. 1992. *Discipling the City: A Comprehensive Approach to Urban Mission*. 2nd ed. Grand Rapids: Baker Book House.

Kaiser, Walter C., and Moisés Silva. 1994. *An Introduction to Biblical Hermeneutics: The Search for Meaning*. Grand Rapids: Zondervan Publishing House.

Morris, Leon. 1971. *The Gospel According to John*. Grand Rapids: Wm. B. Eerdmans Publishing Co. *The New International Commentary on the New Testament*. Gen. ed. F. F. Bruce.

Wiseman, D. J. "Salem." 1982. In *New Bible Dictionary*. Leicester, England-Downers Grove, IL: InterVarsity Press. Eds. I. H. Marshall and others.

www.ingramcontent.com/pod-product-compliance
Lightning Source LLC
Chambersburg PA
CBHW060234240426
43663CB00040B/2742